Growth and value creation
in asset management

**Growth and value creation
in asset management**

First edition 2010

ISBN 978-87-993151-2-3

Printed in Denmark by Mark Production

Other books in this series

Understanding the financial crisis: investment, risk and governance (July 2009)
ISBN 978-87-993151-0-9

Operational control in asset management: processes and costs (January 2010)
ISBN 978-87-993151-1-6

SimCorp StrategyLab™

This volume is a result of a research programme of SimCorp StrategyLab, an independent research institution founded and managed by SimCorp®.

The research work of SimCorp StrategyLab focusses on identifying, understanding and suggesting solutions to issues pertaining to mitigating risk, reducing cost and enabling growth in the investment management industry.

SimCorp StrategyLab
c/o SimCorp A/S
Weidekampsgade 16
2300 Copenhagen S
Denmark

www.simcorpstrategylab.com

Paul Verdin (ed.)

Growth and value creation in asset management

Contents

List of figures and tables

Foreword

SimCorp StrategyLab regards risk, cost and growth as the most fundamental strategic drivers of the financial industry. Thus it is the mission of SimCorp StrategyLab to identify ways to mitigate risk, reduce cost and enable growth in the global investment management industry. As a research institution, SimCorp StrategyLab has already published two essential volumes; one on risk and one on cost, respectively – both with contributions from some of the most renowned scholars, consultants and industry executives in the global financial industry. With this third and final volume in the trilogy on risk, cost and growth, SimCorp StrategyLab has taken a step towards completing the mission of the institution. 'Growth and value creation in asset management' is like the two previous volumes characterised by contributions from true experts and thought leaders from various parts of the industry. I would like to thank them all for sharing our interest in these for the industry important, strategic matters. A special thanks should go to Professor Paul Verdin for leading the work of editing the works of the contributors.

Lars Falkenberg
Assistant Director of SimCorp StrategyLab

Acknowledgements

I would like to sincerely thank Lars Falkenberg (Assistant Director of SimCorp Strategy-Lab) and my distinguished colleague and friend Professor Ingo Walter (Stern School of Business at NYU and INSEAD, as well as Director of the SimCorp StrategyLab) for envisioning, championing – and including me in – this ambitious project. Last but not least, a warm word of thanks to Dr. Patrick Verghote for his swift and skilful assistance in editing and streamlining various chapters, and in particular to Office Manager Mette Trier at the SimCorp StrategyLab Secretariat for her relentless, effective and ever-gentle way of ushering the herd of contributors and in particular a sometimes distracted or over-committed editor into meeting the tight deadlines of this great project. Thank you very much!

Paul Verdin

INTRODUCTION

1 Growth and value creation in asset management: context and overview

by Paul Verdin (editor)

Paul Verdin (Ph.D., Harvard) holds the Chair of Strategy and Organisation at Solvay Business School (ULB, Brussels) and is Professor of Strategy and International Management at KULeuven in Belgium. He is a former Distinguished Visiting Professor at IN-SEAD, where he has been on the faculty for over 15 years, and other international business schools, and has taught and consulted widely on strategic issues and processes in the financial sector (banking, insurance, asset management). Dr. Verdin's extensively cited research, focusses on the critical role of innovative company strategy and organisation in long-term value creation. His work has been covered in the professional and general business press across Europe and the US, including *CFO Europe,* the Economist Intelligence Unit, *Treasury Management International, Accountancy, Optimize, Wirtschaftswoche, Handelsblatt, Manageris, Expansion Management Review,* the *Wall Street Journal Europe* and the *Financial Times.*
Contact: paul.verdin@ulb.ac.be or paul.verdin@econ.kuleuven.be.

These are interesting times. That would be the understatement of the decade; let us hope not of the century. There have been market failures, management failures and above all organisational and leadership failures in the very institutions that were driving unprecedented growth and those whose very mission was to prevent such crises from happening both in the private and public sectors. Then came the growing concern about public and policy failures around the skyrocketing sovereign debt and the lingering question of proper stimulus vs. exit strategies in the wake of protracted economic weaknesses and imbalances. Growth is not just around the corner – or is it?

Risk

Managing *risk* was first to take centre stage. While the extreme systemic risks seem to have dissipated, the question remains whether this is merely due to a renewed – if somewhat amnesic – risk appetite of investors or the market drugged or pushed by near- or below-zero 'risk-free' returns, or whether the underlying risks have actually succumbed and the system has returned to robustness and solidity.

At the very least, there has been a shift of risk from the private sector to the public, a de-leveraging of households, businesses and financial institutions substituted by re-leveraging of central banks and governments, and, barring the so-much-needed structural changes and regulatory reforms, merely a temporary solution to more fundamental and structural issues. Reduction in the volatility of prices does not necessarily equal absence of mis-pricing nor control or containment of underlying risks. This debate and its many viewpoints and ramifications was the first and the most urgent one to be dealt with in the first volume in this series of publications by SimCorp StrategyLab: 'Understanding the financial crisis: investment, risk and governance' (Thomsen et al., 2009).

Cost

The second major point of attention in this crisis has been the focus on *cost* – in an immediate reaction to secure survival and avoid or at least minimise the risk of corporate failure. It translated into an immediate and renewed attention to operations, processes and control treated in their different aspects in the second volume of this series: 'Operational control in asset management: processes and costs' (Pinedo, 2009). With the dead accounted for and the near-dead gradually coming off life support, the survivors could start thinking again about strategy. As early as August of last year, some analysts observed: "People feel that the worst is now past us. With the clouds parting and a bit of sunshine, groups are starting to again think more strategically" (Jefferies Putnam Lovell, 2009). The most recent events, e.g. around the Greek debt crisis, certainly should keep us on our toes.

Growth

Some have already gone even a bit further. "No matter what business you are in, no matter what you've done till now, there is still time to change your attitude from that of fighting for survival to seeking opportunities for growth," proclaimed *Fortune* magazine (*Fortune*, 2009). And soon it seemed to have become the new buzz-word. In the meantime, the plan for this third volume on *growth* and value creation had already long been forged – only we decided to take a bit more time for reflection and delivery to the benefit from gaining perspective and hopefully some more depth. And thus now has arrived.

We can also benefit from a first look at the currently incoming results from the SimCorp StrategyLab 'Global Investment Management Growth Survey 2010', showing growth shifting up (again?) to a top priority for most asset managers (up to 60% of respondents across different categories) who are also claiming to have a 'clear growth strategy'. Yet, the same survey also shows that it is not so clear what that really means, especially when looking at the admission of most respondents (also up to 60%) that they do not have a clear methodology or growth framework to accompany and support their proclaimed strategies.[1]

The ambition of that volume is not to close the gap or fill the apparent void between growth ambition and specific growth strategies or frameworks, even less to provide a comprehensive coverage of all the strategic issues facing the asset management industry worldwide. It is, however, our ambition to offer some relevant, possibly new approaches, insights and conclusions from recent and ongoing research and developments in the industry from a variety of vantage points, as these are emerging from the recent work of academics, think-tanks, consultants and industry experts.

While each of the contributions has been selected for its originality and thought-provoking qualities, we believe the collection represents a diversity and richness of perspectives which are intended more as pointers to engage in further analysis and strategic reflection rather than as ready-made answers to the various strategic questions and opportunities that are arising out of the current environment.

True to the nature of any strategic probing and strategy-making, we believe that ready-made answers and general prescriptions can never be offered in general discussions or publications anyhow, whatever their nature or objective. Those answers can only be achieved in the specific context of any particular business and organisation and can only be successfully implemented by their own managers and executives.

Outline of the book

We start with a discussion of the industrial organisation and institutional development of the global asset management industry by Ingo Walter of the Stern School of Business at NYU and Director of SimCorp StrategyLab (Chapter 2). He argues that the asset management industry is likely to be one of the largest and most dynamic parts of the global financial services sector and explains why it is likely to resume its long-term growth after the impact of the recent crisis. At the same time, the chapter provides an overview of the major players on the buy side of the business (from pension, insurance and mutual funds and UCITS to private equity and hedge funds) and the main factors affecting them as a basis for the competitive dynamics observed in the industry and as a basis for future strategy development.

Given the growing importance of the European UCITS regime, not only on the European market, the largest regional asset management market so far, but increasingly also on the global scene, Karel Lannoo, executive director of the European Center for Policy Studies (CEPS), elaborates in Chapter 4 on pressures and opportunities coming from the regulatory side, particularly in view of the new UCITS IV European Directive and the continuing trends towards more or different regulations in the field, such as the controversial plans for new hedge fund regulation.

---

1   Results from the 'Global Investment Management Growth Survey 2010' performed by SimCorp StrategyLab.

Conclusions from this discussion are (i) that one should not underestimate the importance and the complexity of the regulatory context, wherever we are operating, and (ii) the regulatory context will continue to change and adapt in the current environment.

In addition, the regulatory context can and will be used by some players and some governments to push their own preferred formats and formulas. The push for uniformity and to 'level the playing field', as it is often called at the European level, may therefore, if one is not careful, produce exactly the opposite result within the European market (providing a definite competitive advantage to certain formulas over others), and worse still, hamper the competitiveness of the European industry worldwide.

On the other hand, carefully conceived and well-implemented regulatory reforms can help support the development of the 'UCITS brand' across and even well beyond the European market. The debate will continue fiercely on the political scene as well as behind the closed doors of various interest and lobby groups and political deal-makers.

Leaving the regulatory complexity and technicalities of different types of investment funds or asset management aside, Massimo Massa from INSEAD takes us in Chapter 3 further into the inner sanctuaries of how this industry is really (dys)functioning, separating fact from fiction, and distinguishing between hope (what he calls 'marketing') and reality (read: 'performance'). These insights are based primarily on his own path-breaking academic research and that of his colleagues.

'What do we know about the mutual fund industry?' turns out to be a sobering and probing chapter, providing further support as well as nuance to what has elsewhere been called 'the investor's dilemma',[2] not only because of the many things we do *not* know – as is often the conclusion of serious academic research – but equally so because we (and certainly many operators in the industry) may not like what we find.

This reminds us of the famous course title offered by our distinguished strategy colleague Richard Rumelt (UCLA and INSEAD) *in tempore non suspecto:* 'What's wrong with this industry?' While the worldwide car industry overall is not exactly the example of a most successful or enviable industry from a strategic, shareholder or even customer point of view, Massimo argues that the mutual fund industry in a sense is 'doing worse' than the beleaguered car industry. Or, depending how you look at it, 'much better', as it continues to be able to make plenty of money from 'selling cars without an engine' while the car industry under severe competitive pressure on the whole is struggling to get back to profitability while car buyers continue to benefit from ever better performing and sophisticated cars at razor-thin margins to the manufacturers – perhaps a preview of what might happen to the asset or parts of the fund management industry?

---

2   See e.g. the provocative book 'The Investor's Dilemma' by Lowenstein, L. (2008).

In so doing, Massa's contribution is quite complimentary to Alistair Byrne's Chapter 7 (Investit Consultancy and Edinburgh Business School), which looks not at what players in the industry say, but what in fact they do, and how this is affected by the organisational dynamics and 'organisational behaviour' within asset management businesses. This is a new kind of 'behavioural finance', which we could call 'organisational behaviour finance' – to complement and join the growing ranks of the more traditional 'behavioural finance' contenders.

Byrne, who has published more comprehensive reviews of 'traditional' behavioural finance findings elsewhere (Byrne, 2008), exposes us in his chapter to a more novel and path-breaking study of customer behaviour and its implications for product design and development. Based on his own empirical research and surveys carried out before the crisis in the growing area of defined contribution (DC) pension plans in the UK, he argues that clients in fact may not know very well what they want; they may not do what they want to do; they may not even want to decide what or where to invest in. However, those who should know best are often reluctant because of regulatory constraints, fear of liability or lack of clear mandates or incentives.

In other words, if 'customer focus' is indeed the answer to a long-term success in an increasingly competitive business, it is not clear how that plays out in practice when one takes into account how the business is really structured, regulated and carried out at present. There are many voids or gaps to be filled – and thus plenty of opportunity, keeping in mind the famous words of Henry Ford that if he had listened to his customers: *"All they ever wanted was 'a faster horse'."*

Things often are not what they seem – such, then, is the joint 'meta-conclusion' from Massa's chapter looking at the actual functioning of some important aspects of the industry and from Byrne's findings looking at the actual behaviour and stated preferences of customers and investors. These are highly provocative and thus promising avenues to pursue if one really wants to get ahead in this strategic game.

But the rules of the game have changed. Asset management is no longer the prodigal son allowing for the easy business-as-usual that is at least in part responsible for the inconsistencies, the oddities or the lack of sustainable strategies, which Massa so aptly points out. Profits will not easily return and it will become harder to make a living. Yet there is plenty of hope if one takes a look at 'the new normal' that Johannes Elsner, Martin Huber and Philipp Koch (McKinsey & Co.) believe we have landed in (Chapter 5). 'Fake alpha' will not do anymore – only true alpha entrepreneurs will remain, but as 'boutique players' alongside a few really large-scale beta factories.

Key to survival, revival, and continued success, however, is to regain the trust from clients and investors, and to take the current crisis as an opportunity for strategic (r)evaluation and reorientation. This is the moment of truth, and it is *the* moment for *strategy*. There is no going back to the old world and no return to 'business as usual'.

Rather, as I further argue in my contribution (Chapter 11), it means that one will need more and true innovation in terms of delivering value to the client if one is to win in this new and challenging environment. It is imperative in a more competitive market to re-focus on creating value for customers and the market rather than just capturing as was the easy game in town before the crisis. Ideally, one should keep both a balance, as it is about a healthy dialogue, or better still a virtuous circle between value creation and value capturing.

The more competitive your market gets, the less you should focus on the competition – and the more you should focus on the client and client value as the only and sure way to get ahead of your competition. It appears that many asset managers would clearly agree, as suggested by results from the SimCorp StrategyLab growth survey (2010) mentioned above, which list improved quality and customer service as well as product innovation as key drivers for future growth.

Barring high barriers to entry or weakening competitive forces, providing value to the client and relentlessly improving and delivering that value is the only way to sustained success. Such was at least the conclusion from some of my earlier research analysing competitive dynamics and successful strategies across a wide variety of industries and businesses, including financial services (Hawawini et al., 2006).

Adam Schneider (Deloitte Consulting) elaborates in Chapter 6 on the innovation challenge by translating it into concrete trajectories, each of which can be seen as a strategic response to major trends he identified in the investment management business today. In passing, these trends are generally in line with our claim of increasing competition in the business allowing fewer and fewer opportunities for easy money-making.

The responses he proposes illustrate how creating more value for clients can be achieved by (i) delivering better, more transparent, more reliable and better-performing products (which the Byrne study shows is not always obvious), (ii) focussing on profitable segments and client satisfaction (i.e. by better delivering them the value proposition they are willing to pay for and thus also fine-tuning the offer and the pricing) and (iii) by streamlining your organisation and processes (e.g. eliminating some of the unproductive waste or side-effects of behavioural and organisational dynamics identified in the Massa chapter).

A strategically and business-driven IT architecture and platform that is focussed, flexible and cost-effective will obviously be critical in this information-driven business, as further illustrated by the results of the above-mentioned SimCorp StrategyLab survey. This point is aptly and strategically discussed on by Pascal Wanner (SimCorp A/S) in Chapter 8, who highlights how strategic IT can be and should be about securing and supporting growth going forward.

As we have heard before, but in practice often remains some ways off: effective and efficient IT investment has to be part of the overall business strategy. In today's asset management environment, this requires regaining trust by delivering real value to clients. The resulting approach necessitates a paradigm change in the qualification and quantification of IT investments in general. Focussing exclusively on cost will limit the potential, as clients also expect more and different sources of value added.

Jacob Elsborg (ATP Investment) takes this further, elaborating on the crucial role of defining and implementing an appropriate operational platform strategy – as distinct from an IT strategy, as it is generally known or referred to. When properly managed and conceived, the operational platform can even be considered a strategic asset, and should be managed as such. Depending on the nature of the business activity, the relevant business model and the market in which you operate, this could indeed become a crucial element in differentiating yourself from the next competitor and in particular could act as a platform for growth (Chapter 9).

Pursuing growth for its own sake is a highly dangerous and risky proposition. The recent debacles and broken dreams of megalomania often intertwined with supposed need and elusive benefits of 'globalisation' have once more illustrated that point painfully and plainly. 'Back to the core' business and core markets seems to be the message, including that of the regulators dictating their prescriptions to the most wounded of institutions (e.g. EU Commission's prescriptions to ING, Dexia, etc. and similar pressures in the US to dismantle or split up 'too large' [to fail] institutions).

Mathias Schmit and Lin-Sya Chao (Solvay Business School and Sagora Consulting) elaborate on this point in Chapter 10, on the basis of literature and empirical findings, and propose a pragmatic framework to better manage this 'growth risk' eminently present in any (growth) strategy. If we make big moves, if we chase growth for its own sake, even if we follow the proper path down the value curves and value segments, we should be aware of the risks we are taking.

It is rather surprising that, with all the sophisticated risk models that have been developed and put in place, 'strategic risks' have been often ignored or poorly treated. One could even argue that strategy essentially comes down to 'risk management', especially if we keep the two sides of the risk coin in mind as seems obvious in the Chinese expression for risk equally pointing to opportunity. A good strategy maximises opportunities (minimises opportunities lost) as a basis for growth without unduly running the risk of failure or disaster.

In some ways, Schmit and Chao bring us back to some of the issues treated in the first volume of the series and in so doing elegantly loop back to where we started with this trilogy on risk, cost and growth. Sustainable growth and value creation can only be based on a sound control of costs and risks, as illustrated in Figure 1.

This brings us to *our basic premise* in the concluding chapter: growth will not return by default if it is to be sustainable and profitable. Back to business as usual will not be the answer, and the future will not mean going back to the past. We can learn from the past, but must carefully consider today's challenge so that our strategies are

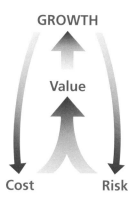

Fig. 1. Sustainable growth and value creation

rooted in the present, as Johan Auters aptly argues with regard to investment strategies (Auters, 2010). In fact, growth in and of itself, in my view, is not really a strategy – it is the *result* of a *good* strategy: a strategy that refocusses on sustained value delivery to clients and appropriate ways to share that value fairly and sustainably with the client for the benefit of management, employees and shareholders. The link between *growth* and *value creation* therefore seems essential.

Is growth an option?

"Growth is not a choice – it's an imperative" (Zook, 2004). The imperative, however, can only be based on and driven by sustained value creation as a result of ever-improving value delivered to clients and/or innovation on processes and systems to reduce costs. "But the risks are substantial" (Zook, 2004), as illustrated by the statistical evidence showing that sustained value creators are rare and only a minority of high-growth companies.[3]

Therefore, integrative risk management ought to be an essential part of any strategy: without it, we risk destroying more value than we create, generating more strategic or long-term costs that we can ever gain with short-term cost-cutting programmes or restructurings. Sustainable profitable growth can only be the result of a good strategy that takes into account the underlying relationships and tensions between these basic dimensions and above all: builds on and leverages on core business, strengths and assets.

It begs the question, 'What is core?' In a sense, this in and of itself is one of the most important strategic questions.[4] Because the answer to this question not only requires a keen understanding of markets, clients and value attributes, it also refers

---

3   Bain&Company Inc. research, also the basis of some of Zook's work at Bain (references in footnote 4 and References).

4   On different aspects of this issue, see for example the seminal publications of G. Hamel and C.K. Prahalad (1990), C. Zook and J. Allen (1990) and C. Zook (2004).

to our ability to deliver through appropriate and leading-edge processes and systems, and ultimately our ability to stay ahead of the game by continuously innovating and improving – in our value proposition and in our processes and business model (*value innovation* or *cost* innovation [Kim and Mauborgne, 1997; Williamson and Zeng, 2009]). In so doing, however we should go for well-understood adjacencies rather than big bold moves – in terms of customers, products, markets and geographies.[5]

We can only hope to excel in what we are good at. Therefore, a simple – if at first sight cynical – answer to the 'what is core' question in my view should be 'everything we can't sell' – *at the right price*, that is – in other words, anything that no one else can make more value out of than we can. To put it popularly, core is 'yes, we can!' Non-core is 'what we cannot do or make the best of'.

In the end, while each of the articles included in this (and the previous) volume are self-standing, independent pieces of work and can easily be read without any need to respect any particular order, they do all fit together in the broader framework and the general stage upon which we have tread in the process. On a strategic level, everything covered in these volumes is connected, and it would be a mistake to stop after the one article (or two) the reader may choose to start with. So: enjoy the journey, connect the dots and bridge the gaps the authors have left for you to fill.

References

Auters, J. (2010), 'Learn from the past but be rooted in the present', *Financial Times*, 6–7 February.

Byrne, A. and M. Brooks (2008), 'Behavioral Finance: Theories and Evidence', *The Research Foundation of CFA Institute Literature Review*.

Fortune, 31 August 2009.

Hawawini, G., V. Subramanian and P. Verdin (2006), 'What Strategic Leaders Do: A New Look at Creating and Capturing Value', *INSEAD-Solvay Business School Working Paper*.

Hamel, G. and C.K. Prahalad (1990), 'The Core Competence of the Corporation', *Harvard Business Review*.

Jefferies Putnam Lovell (2009), 'Winds of Change: First-Half 2009 M&A Activity in the Global Asset Management, Broker/Dealer, and Financial Technology Industries', report, August.

Kim, C. and R. Mauborgne (1997), 'Value Innovation: The Strategic Logic of High Growth', *Harvard Business Review*, pp. 172–180.

Lowenstein, L. (2008), 'The Investor's Dilemma', Wiley.

Pinedo, M. (2009), 'Operational control in asset management: processes and costs', SimCorp StrategyLab.

---

5   See further the work by Zook, C. and Bain&Company as referenced.

Thomsen, S., C. Rose and O. Risager (2009), 'Understanding the financial crisis: investment, risk and governance', SimCorp StrategyLab.

SimCorp StrategyLab (2010), 'Report on Global Investment Management Growth Survey 2010'.

Verdin, P. and N. Van Heck (2001), 'From Local Champions to Global Masters: A Strategic Perspective on Managing Internationalisation', London/New York: Palgave/MacMillan.

Williamson, P. and M. Zeng (2009), 'Value-for-Money Strategies for Recessionary Times', *Harvard Business Review*.

Zook, C. and J. Allen (1990), 'Profit from the Core', Boston: Harvard Business School Press.

Zook, C. (2004), 'Beyond the Core: Expand Your Market Without Abandoning Your Roots', Boston: Harvard Business School Press.

Part I: Growth and value creation in asset management: structure, regulation and business models

About the author

Ingo Walter, Director of SimCorp StrategyLab, is is the Seymour Milstein Professor of Finance, Corporate Governance and Ethics and Vice Dean at the Stern School of Business, New York University. He has been on the faculty at New York University since 1970, and served a number of terms as Associate Dean for Academic Affairs, Chair of International Business, Chair of Finance and, from 1990 to 2003, as Director of the New York University Salomon Center for the Study of Financial Institutions. Since 1985 he has also been affiliated with INSEAD in Fontainebleau, France, and serves as a consultant to various corporations, banks, government agencies and international institutions. Professor Walter's principal areas of academic and consulting activity include international banking and financial institutions, and markets and integrated risk control in financial firms. He has published papers in most of the professional journals in these fields and is the author of 26 books.

Contact: iwalter@stern.nyu.edu.

2

Growth in the global institutional asset management industry: structure, conduct, performance

ABSTRACT This chapter examines the industrial organisation and institutional development of the global asset management industry. It identifies the key components of the 'buy side' of financial markets in terms of its four principal domains: pension funds, mutual funds, discretionary alternative assets and insurance companies. It points out that various kinds of financial firms have emerged to perform asset management functions: commercial banks, savings banks, postal savings institutions, savings cooperatives, credit unions, securities firms (full-service firms and various kinds of specialists), insurance companies, finance companies, finance subsidiaries of industrial companies, mutual fund companies, hedge funds financial advisers and various others. Members of each strategic group compete with each other, as well as with members of other strategic groups. The chapter addresses two key questions. First, what determines competitive advantage in operating distribution gateways to the end investor? Second, what determines competitive advantage in the asset management process itself?

2 Growth in the global institutional asset management industry: structure, conduct, performance

by Ingo Walter

Introduction

This chapter examines the industrial organisation and institutional development of the global asset management industry. Few industries have encountered as much 'strategic turbulence' in recent years as has the financial services sector in general and the asset management – the 'buy-side' of the capital markets – in particular. Indeed, there is ample evidence to suggest that the development of the asset management industry has much to do with intermediation and capital allocation in national and global financial systems. That is, asset gathering and deployment of savings bear on the rate of capital formation and the economic growth process more broadly.

The asset management industry is likely to be one of the largest and most dynamic parts of the global financial services sector, and is likely to resume its long-term growth after the impact of the global financial crisis of 2007–09 based on a number of underlying factors:

- A continued broad-based trend toward professional management of discretionary household assets in the form of mutual funds or unit trusts and other types of collective investment vehicles.

- The growing recognition that most government-sponsored pension systems, many of which were created wholly or partially on a pay-as-you-go (PAYG) basis, have become fundamentally untenable under demographic projections that appear virtually certain to materialise, and must be progressively replaced by asset pools that will throw off the kinds of returns necessary to meet the needs of growing numbers of longer-living retirees.

- Partial displacement of traditional defined benefit (DB) public- and private-sector pension programmes backed by assets contributed by employers and working individuals under the pressure of the evolving demographics, rising administrative costs and shifts in risk allocation by a variety of defined contribution (DC) schemes.

- Substantial increases in individual wealth in a number of developed countries and a range of developing countries, as shown by the changing shares in the growth of assets under management.

- Reallocation of portfolios that have – for regulatory, tax or institutional reasons – been overweight domestic financial instruments (notably fixed-income securities) toward a greater role for equities and non-domestic asset classes, which not only promise higher returns but also may reduce the beneficiaries' exposure to risk due to portfolio diversification across both asset classes and economic and financial environments that are less than perfectly correlated in terms of total investment returns.

The relative size of the main managed asset categories is presented in Figure 1. The growth implied by the first four of the above factors, combined with the asset-allocation shifts implied by the last of the above factors, will tend to drive the dynamics and the competitive structure of the global institutional asset management industry in the years ahead – after taking substantial losses as a result of the global financial crisis of 2007–09 as depicted in Figure 2.

Rank	Fund type	$ billions	Figures as of
1	Private wealth	$ 37,200	2006
2	Pension funds	$ 28,228	2007
3	Mutual funds	$ 26,200	2007
4	Insurance companies	$ 18,836	2007
5	Real estate	$ 10,000	2006
6	Foreign exchange reserves	$ 7,341	2008
7	Sovereign wealth funds	$ 3,300	2007
8	Hedge funds	$ 1,535	2006
9	Private equity funds	$ 1,160	2007
10	REITs	$ 764	2007

Fig. 1. Estimated global assets under management

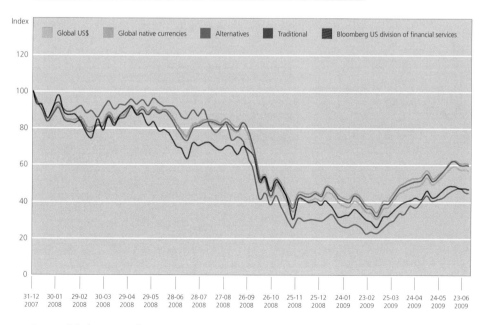

Fig. 2. Global assets under management through the financial crisis. Note: 100 = year-end 2007. Index is weighted by fully diluted market capitalisation. Source: Bloomberg, Jefferies Putnam Lovell.

This chapter reviews the four main components of the asset management industry: pension funds, mutual funds, alternative asset pools such as hedge funds, and private client asset pools. The chapter then discusses key structural and competitive characteristics of the industry and its reconfiguration.

Mapping the global asset management industry

The layout of the global asset management industry can perhaps best be explained in terms of Figure 3. The lower part of the diagram is the institutional side of the market for professional asset management and the upper part is the individual side of the market, although the distinctions are often heavily blurred.

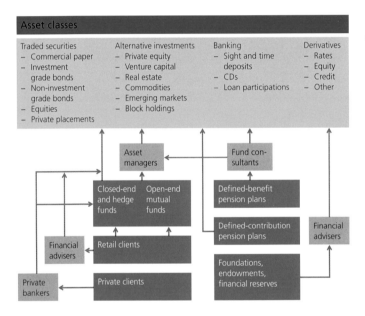

Fig. 3. Mapping the global asset management architecture

First, retail clients have the option of placing funds directly with financial institutions such as banks or by purchasing securities from retail sales forces of broker-dealers, possibly with the help of fee-based financial advisers. Alternatively, retail investors can have their funds professionally managed by buying shares in mutual funds or unit trusts (again possibly with the help of advisers), which in turn buy securities from the institutional sales desks of broker-dealers (and from time to time maintain balances with banks).

Second, private clients are broken out as a separate segment of the asset management market in Figure 3, and are usually served by private bankers who bundle asset management with various other services such as tax planning, estates and trusts, placing assets directly into financial instruments, commingled managed asset pools, or sometimes publicly available mutual funds and unit trusts.

Third, foundations, endowments, and financial reserves held by non-financial companies, institutions and governments can rely on in-house investment expertise to purchase securities directly from the institutional sales desks of banks or securities broker-dealers, use financial advisers to help them build efficient portfolios, or place funds with open-end or closed-end mutual funds.

Fourth, pension funds take two principal forms: those guaranteeing a level of benefits and those aimed at building beneficiary assets from which a pension will be drawn (see below). DB pension funds can buy securities directly in the market or place funds with banks, trust companies or other types of asset managers, often aided by fund consultants who advise pension trustees on performance and asset-allocation styles. DC pension programmes may operate in a similar way if they are managed in house, creating proprietary asset pools, and in addition (or alternatively) provide participants with the option to purchase shares in publicly available mutual funds.

The structure of the asset management industry encompasses significant overlaps between the four types of asset pools to the point where they are sometimes difficult to distinguish. We have noted the linkage between DC pension funds and the mutual fund industry, and the association of the disproportionate growth in the former with the expansion of mutual fund assets under management. There is a similar but perhaps more limited linkage between private client assets and mutual funds on the one hand and pension funds on the other. This is particularly the case for the lower bound of private client business, which is often commingled with mass-marketed mutual funds, and pension benefits awarded to high-income executives, which in effect become part of the recipient's high net-worth portfolio.

Pension funds

The pension fund market for asset management has been one of the most rapidly growing domains of the global financial system and promises to be even more dynamic in the years ahead. Consequently, pension assets have been in the forefront of strategic targeting by all types of financial institutions, including banks, trust companies, broker-dealers, insurance companies, mutual fund companies and independent asset management firms. As noted in Figure 1, dedicated pension assets in 2007 in countries where consistent and comparable data are available were estimated to amount to about $28 trillion, roughly two-thirds of which covered private-sector employees, and the balance covered public-sector employees. The growth rate of pension assets was about 5% per year, what after a decline in asset values during the 2007–09 financial crisis would put the value of pension pools at about $32 trillion at the start of 2010. About 40% of global pension assets under management are in Europe and the

United States, roughly evenly divided, while the rest of the world accounted for the balance – although it shows the most rapid growth, especially in Asia.

The basis for the projected growth of managed pension assets is of course the demographics of gradually aging populations, colliding with existing structures for retirement support, which in many countries carry heavy political baggage. They are politically exceedingly difficult to bring up to the standards required for the future, yet doing so eventually is an inevitability. The near-term foci of this problem will be Europe and Japan, with profound implications for the size and structure of capital markets, the competitive positioning and performance of financial intermediaries in general and asset managers in particular.

The demographics of the pension fund problem are straightforward, since demographic data are among the most reliable. Unless there are major unforeseen changes in birth rates, death dates or migration rates, the dependency ratio (population over 65 divided by the population aged 16–64) will have doubled between 2000 and 2040, with the highest dependency ratios in the case of Europe being attained in Italy, Germany and the Netherlands, and the lowest in Ireland. Japan has dependency ratios even higher than Europe, while the US ratio is somewhat lower – with the lowest generally found in developing countries. All, however, are heading in the same direction.

Alternative pension structures

While the demographics underlying these projections may be quite reliable, dependency ratios remain subject to shifts in working-age start- and end-points. Obviously, the longer people remain out of the active labour force (e.g. for purposes of education), the higher the level of sustained unemployment, and the earlier the average retirement age, the higher the dependency ratio will be. The collision comes between the demographics and the existing structure of pension finance. There are basically three ways to provide support for the post-retirement segment of the population:

–   **PAYG programmes.** Pension benefits under this approach are committed by the state based on various formulas – number of years worked and income subject to social charges, for example – and funded by current mandatory contributions of those employed (taxes and social charges) that may or may not be specifically earmarked to covering current pension payouts. Under PAYG systems, current pension contributions may exceed or fall short of current disbursements. In the former case, a trust fund may be set up which, as in the case of US Social Security, may be invested in government securities. In the latter case, the deficit will tend to be covered out of general tax revenues, government borrowing or the liquidation of previously accumulated trust fund assets.

–   **DB programmes.** Pension benefits under such programmes are committed to public or private-sector employees by their employers, based on actuarial benefit formulas that are part of the employment contract. DB pension payouts may be linked to the cost of living, adjusted for survivorship, etc., and the funds set aside to support future claims may be contributed solely by the employer or with some level of employee contribution. The pool of assets may be invested in a portfolio of debt and equity securities (possibly including the company's own shares) that are managed in house or by external fund managers. Depending on the level of contributions and benefit claims, as well as investment performance, DB plans may be over-funded or under-funded. They may thus be tapped by the employer from time to time for general corporate purposes, or they may have to be topped up from the employer's own resources. DB plans may be insured (e.g. against corporate bankruptcy) either in the private market or by government agencies, and are usually subject to strict regulation – e.g. in the United States under ERISA, which is administered by the Department of Labor.

– **DC programmes.** Pension fund contributions are made by the employer, employee, or both into a fund that will ultimately form the basis for pension benefits under DC pension plans. The employee's share in the fund tends to vest after a number of years of employment, and may be managed by the employer or placed with various asset managers under portfolio constraints intended to serve the best interests of the beneficiaries. The employee's responsibility for asset allocation can vary from none at all to virtually full discretion. Employees may, for example, be allowed to select from among a range of approved investment vehicles, notably mutual funds, based on individual risk-return preferences.

Most countries have several types of pension arrangement operating simultaneously, for example a base-level PAYG system supplemented by state-sponsored or privately sponsored DB plans and DC plans sponsored by employers, mandated by the state or undertaken voluntarily by individuals.

Policy options
The collision of the aforementioned demographics and heavy reliance on the part of many countries on PAYG approaches is at the heart of the pension problem, and forms the basis for the future growth of asset management. The conventional wisdom is that the pension problems that are today centred in Europe and Japan will eventually spread to the rest of the world. They will have to be resolved, and there are only a limited number of options in dealing with the issue:

– Raise mandatory social charges on employees and employers to cover increasing pension obligations under PAYG systems. This is problematic especially in countries that already have high fiscal burdens and increasing pressure for avoidance and evasion. A similar problem confronts major increases in general taxation levels or government borrowing to top up eroding trust funds or finance PAYG benefits on a continuing basis.

- Undertake major reductions in retirement benefits, cutting dramatically into benefit levels. The sensitivity of fiscal reforms to social welfare is illustrated by the fact that just limiting the growth in pension expenditures to the projected rate of economic growth from 2015 onward would reduce income-replacement rates from 45% to 30% over a period of 15 years, leaving those among the elderly without adequate personal resources in relative poverty.
- Apply significant increases in the retirement age at which individuals are eligible for full PAYG-financed pensions, perhaps to age 70 for those not incapacitated by ill health. This is not a palatable solution in many countries that have been subject to pressure for reduced retirement age, compounded by chronically high unemployment especially in Europe, which has been widely used as a justification for earlier retirements.
- Undertake significant pension reforms to progressively move away from PAYG systems toward DC and DB schemes such as those widely used in the US, Chile, Singapore, Malaysia, the UK, the Netherlands and Denmark. These differ in detail, but all involve the creation of large asset pools that are reasonably actuarially sound.

Given the relatively bleak outlook for the first several of these alternatives, it seems inevitable that increasing reliance will be placed on the last of these options. The fact is that future generations can no longer count on the present value of benefits exceeding the present value of contributions and social charges as the demographics inevitably turn against them in the presence of clear fiscal constraints facing governments. This bodes well for the future growth of the asset management industry emanating from the pension sector.

An international mosaic

Whereas there are wide differences among countries in their reliance on PAYG pension systems and in the degree of demographic and financial pressure to build actuarially viable pension asset pools, there are equally wide differences in how those assets have been allocated. The United States (not including the Social Security Trust Fund) and the United Kingdom have relied quite heavily on domestic equities – one result being that pension beneficiaries were seriously impacted during the financial crisis of 2007–09 and had to adjust their levels of living downward or put off retirement. Pension pools in many of the other European countries and Japan have relied more heavily on fixed-income securities and were not as adversely affected, and equity markets in many emerging markets outperformed the developed markets during this period, shielding pension beneficiaries from the worst consequences.

The significant shift from DB to DC pension plans in the United States, as an example, has led to strong linkages between pension funds and mutual funds. Numerous mutual funds – notably in the equities sector – are strongly influenced by 401(k) and other pension inflows. At the end of 2009, about two-thirds of mutual fund assets represented retirement accounts of various types in the United States. Conversely, 50% of total retirement assets were invested in mutual funds, up from about 1% in 1980 – one reason why US pension savers were so badly affected by the financial crisis of 2007–09 and putting an end to talk of replacing Social Security by DC pension arrangements, at least until Social Security itself becomes financially impaired some-time in mid-century.

In the most competitive parts of the pension sector, access to fund trustees often relies on consultants. Company-sponsored retirement plans often seek advice from pension investment consultants before awarding pension mandates, or seek to include particular mutual funds or fund families in the menu they offer to employees in US-type 401(k) plans. Consultants are particularly useful in formal reviews of pension fund managers. Fund management companies may and sometimes do provide fee or expense reimbursement to consultants. In the case of pension funds, the investment manager quotes a single all-in expense to be charged for services which is sufficient to cover expenses and the manager's profit. Pension fund trustees are able to apply the fund's bargaining power to the process.

Drivers of pension fund growth

To summarise, with respect to the pension component of growth in the asset manage-ment industry there is no single 'magic bullet' solution to supporting the retirement of the 'bulge' of baby boomers moving through population structures. Countries that are taking action are using a multi-pronged approach consisting of:

- **Increase working populations.** Immigration and increased labour force partici-pation rates help but cannot solve the problem. Some perverse incentive structures impede improvements in the labour force participation rate.
- **Increase productivity.** Strong productivity growth is the single most important factor in alleviating the burden of global aging. However, productivity growth is difficult if not impossible to predict, and aging countries cannot rely on it.
- **Change the promise.** Although it is politically difficult, countries are changing the minimum retirement age, modifying benefit levels and making it more tax advantageous for the elderly to work. As individuals realise that the benefit reduc-tions already enacted and the future reductions will affect their retirement in-come, they may increase their savings.
- **Change the funding.** Those countries with healthy funded private pension funds are in a better position to support their elderly population than those that rely on unfunded PAYG systems. Some countries are establishing funded pension trusts or using the proceeds of privatisations to establish trust funds for future genera-tions. Others are encouraging personal plans or increasing funding ceilings on existing personal pension plans.

The consensus seems to be that the last option provides the best way forward, both for advanced countries as well as for emerging market countries. And when this is combined with the shift from DB to DC approaches discussed earlier, it should provide ample competitive opportunities for the asset management industry globally. The growth of the DB and DC pension plans worldwide forms the basis for the future growth of asset management, as these programmes involve the creation of large asset pools.

Within this overall context, pension assets and the adequacy of old-age provisioning in the developing countries have, in relative terms, outpaced those in many developed countries. There are several reasons for this. First, they have relatively young populations and gradual aging, so that they have more time to develop pre-funded pension schemes without some of the friction burdens of countries with much older populations. Second, they are much less reliant on PAYG pension systems with high and possibly unsustainable promises to pension beneficiaries. Most systems are DC and therefore pre-funded, although all such systems are prone to investment returns that may not meet expectations – as experienced in the major pension fund markets during the financial crisis of 2007–09. Most developing country pension plans are controlled by the state and offer only limited portfolio discretion for participants, limited reliance on private asset managers, and limited choice of asset classes. Given that DC pension systems represent key pools of investible assets in these countries, increased choice and competition among asset managers – as well as increased choice among asset classes – could make a significant contribution to the development of pension schemes and to capital market development – and of course increase the risks associated with old-age security provisioning.

Mutual funds

The mutual fund industry has enjoyed rapid growth in developed countries in recent decades, although there are wide differences among national financial markets in the pace of development, in the character of the assets under management, and in the nature of mutual fund marketing and distribution. Mutual funds essentially take the form of collective investment vehicles in which the proceeds from share sales to investors are placed in securities of various types. They are usually 'mutual' in the sense that the investors own all of the assets in the fund and are responsible for all of its operating costs. The funds are usually organised by a particular fund management company that undertakes the legal registration of the fund, nominates a board of directors for the fund, and arranges for the distribution and sale of fund shares to the public. The fund's board of directors contracts with an investment advisor (usually the same fund management company) to manage the assets and to handle ongoing operational details such as marketing, administration, reporting and compliance.

Key characteristics

Legally, mutual funds in the US, for example, take the form of 'trusts' representing the undivided sum of assets held on behalf of the investors by the trustees (directors) of the fund. US mutual fund assets never belong to either the fund (trust) itself or to the management company. Rather, they are owned by the fund investors themselves, who can normally redeem their shares instantly at their net asset value (NAV). US mutual funds were created as successors to the investment trusts of the 1920s, which suffered large-scale asset losses during the stock market crash of 1929. The principal legislation governing the modern mutual fund industry is the Investment Company Act of 1940, which covers both the qualifications and registration of management companies of mutual funds sold to the public, as well as the disclosure of pertinent information to investors in the form of selling prospectuses and periodic reporting. A mutual fund's investment advisor must comply with terms of the Investment Advisers Act of 1940 and various state laws.

Mutual funds in Europe, on the other hand, usually take the form of either 'co-property' (co-ownership) or 'company' structures. A typical example is France, where there are two types of mutual funds: *Sociétés d'Investissement à Capital Variable* (SI-CAVs) and *Fonds Communs de Placement* (FCPs). SICAVs invest accumulated capital subscribed by investors in shares, bonds, short-term paper or other financial instruments. They are independent legal entities governed by boards, and the investors are effectively shareholders who vote at annual shareholder meetings. FCPs consist of a 'common property' of assets. They are not separate, independent legal entities, but rather 'co-ownership entities', i.e. unit trusts which invest in different financial instruments – each investor is merely a co-owner of an undivided mass of assets of which he or she owns a percentage.

UCITS

The SICAV model has been adopted under the EU's Undertakings for Collective Investments in Transferable Securities (UCITS) legislation, which governs how a fund can be marketed within the European Union and is designed to allow cross-border fund sales to investors of different nationalities. The objective of the original UCITS directive, adopted in 1985, was to allow for mutual funds investing in publicly issued securities to be subject to the same regulation in every EU member country, so funds authorised for distribution in one EU country could be sold to the public in all others without further authorisation, thereby furthering the goal of a single market for financial services in Europe. However, in practice many EU member nations have imposed additional regulatory requirements that have impeded free operation with the effect of protecting local asset managers; varied marketing rules in each country created persistent obstacles to cross-border marketing of UCITS. In addition, the limited definition of permitted investments for UCITS weakened the single market initiative for mutual funds. So in the early 1990s proposals were developed to amend the 1985 directive and more successfully harmonise laws throughout Europe.

This led to a draft UCITS II directive, which was abandoned as being too ambitious and was followed by a new proposal (UCITS III) which contained (a) a management directive designed to give fund management companies a 'European passport' to operate throughout the EU and widened the activities which they are allowed to undertake; (b) the concept of a simplified prospectus, which was intended to provide more accessible and comprehensive information in a simplified format to assist the cross-border marketing of UCITS throughout Europe; and (c) a product directive intended to remove barriers to the cross-border marketing of units of collective investment funds by allowing funds to invest in a wider range of financial instruments. Under this directive, it is possible to establish money funds, derivatives funds, index-tracking funds, and funds of funds as UCITS.

The latest version of the EU directive, UCITS IV, was proposed in 2009 and was intended to remedy some of the remaining market-access barriers to mutual fund distribution in the market. This includes a Management Company Passport which will allow funds authorised in one member country to be managed remotely by management companies established in another country and be authorised by that country's regulatory body. It also focusses on removal of administrative barriers to cross-border distribution of UCITS funds by improved coordination among national regulators, the creation of a framework for mergers between UCITS funds allowing the use of 'master-feeder' structures to deal with cultural preference towards domestic funds, and the replacement of the previous simplified 'prospectus' with a short two-page 'key investor information' document.

International comparisons

As depicted in Figure 4, in the United States at the end of 2008 there were about 8,000 mutual funds available to the public, compared to over 25,000 funds in Europe and 7,500 funds in Asia. US funds held assets of about $9.5 trillion, compared with $5.5 trillion in Europe and $900 billion in Asia. Consequently, the average US mutual fund held about $1.2 billion in assets under management, compared with $162m in Europe and $108m in Asia, presumably giving US-based funds a substantial cost and marketing advantage.

At the end of 2008 as well, the number of US equity mutual funds was almost three times the number of shares listed on the New York Stock Exchange. Equity mutual funds held 25% of US stock market capitalisation and 10% of bond market capitalisation. Mutual funds accounted for about 21% of US household net financial wealth in the mid-2000s – more than life insurance companies and about equal to the total household deposits in commercial banks.

Competition for asset gathering by mutual funds can be among the most intense

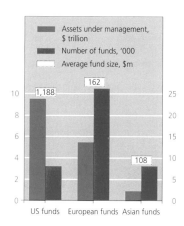

Fig. 4. Number of mutual funds
and assets under management
(December 2008).
Source: Schroders.

within financial systems, marked by advertising and extensive media coverage: they are in effect mass-market investment vehicles involving 'branding' and public performance ratings by independent rating agencies. Mutual fund management companies have aggressively added banking-type services such as checking and cash-management accounts, credit cards and overdraft lines. Despite scale economies associated with the extraordinary growth in the size of mutual funds, costs investors have increased over the years. Mutual fund distribution efforts have targeted individual investors to attract them away from traditional banking and savings institutions: investors who are not particularly sophisticated about the fees, costs, performance metrics and expense reimbursement on the part of the fund management companies.

In Europe, mutual fund distribution through bank branches dominates in countries such as Germany (80%), France (70%) and Spain (61%), with UK distribution concentrated among independent advisers and Italian distribution roughly split between bank branches and independent sales forces. The dominance of universal banks, savings banks and cooperative banks as financial intermediaries in most of the continental European countries explains the high concentration of mutual fund distribution via branch networks. In contrast, 90% of US mutual fund distribution has been concentrated in financial intermediaries – notably on full-service broker-dealers who maintain large retail sales forces capable of penetrating the household sector and which are compensated mainly on the basis of commissions earned and assets under management, as well as discount brokers who have compensated for reduced sales effort and limited investment advice by charging lower fees and expenses. Insurance agents account for 15% of US mutual fund distribution, focussing on mutual funds with an insurance wrapper such as fixed and variable annuities and guaranteed investment contracts (GICs). Bank branches have played a growing role in the US after deregulation in 1999, although they only account for about 15% distribution share, while direct sales by independent fund managers have captured about 10% of sales. As a result of the financial crisis of 2007–09, the acquisition of Merrill Lynch by Bank of

America and Bear Stearns by JP Morgan Chase, the bankruptcy of Lehman Brothers and the conversion of the remaining investment banks (Goldman Sachs and Morgan Stanley) into bank holding companies has correspondingly altered the mutual fund landscape toward somewhat greater concentration.

The product spectrum

Mutual fund managers offer a broad array of money market, fixed-income and equity funds, and invest heavily in technology platforms that enable efficient administration, custody and reporting functions in a customer-friendly manner. Some fund management companies manage dozens of mutual funds. The basis of competition in mutual fund management comprises five elements: perceived performance, fees for performance, expenses, direct and indirect costs of marketing and distribution, and service quality and technology.

- Investors must select from an array of investment types or styles based on asset classes (stocks, bonds, etc.) Fund managers are expected to remain true to their proclaimed investment objectives and attempt to optimise asset allocation in accordance with modern portfolio management concepts.
- Mutual fund managers incur a variety of operating costs and expenses in running their businesses, notably for personnel and facilities, commissions and technology. The fund management company retained by the fund board enters into a contract for services in which it charges a fee for managing the assets, and its expenses, in part, are reimbursed. Combined, these fees are charged against the assets of the fund and comprise the fund's 'expense ratio'. Fund investors may also be subject to a sales charge when they invest (a 'front-end load') or at a later point when they exit (a 'back-end load'), as well as a charge for marketing the fund to its investors. Funds generally subject investors to higher expense ratios when the fund size is smaller, the turnover is higher, or the relative fund performance is better.
- Service quality in fund management involves ease of investment and redemptions, quality and transparency of statements, cash management, tax computation and investment advice.
- Mutual fund management companies tend to invest heavily in IT platforms in order to improve service quality and cut costs, investments that must be paid for in the form of fees and expenses reimbursed by the funds.

One of the key issues relating to the mutual fund industry is assessing performance. Do fund managers, after expenses and fees, outperform available index funds or exchange-traded funds that reflect gains and losses of the market as a whole? Issues that need to be taken into account to address this question include the following:
- time buckets (length, start/end periods) used for performance tracking;
- index benchmark (e.g. S&P 500 vs. Russell 2000) against which performance is measured;

- survivorship bias (upward bias in the performance of surviving managed funds as poor performers fail and no longer appear in the data);
- Sharpe ratio (performance adjusted for risk);
- management fees;
- front loads, back loads, digressive loads in annual return-equivalents;
- fees and other charges – such as US 12b(1) fees – which regulators permit to be loaded onto fund investors;
- performance distribution over market cycles;
- performance distribution relative to sector means;
- the importance of fund names as reflecting investment styles, and the problem of style drift;
- persistence – do firms outperforming in one period continue to outperform in successive periods?

Fiduciary violations

Confidence in mutual funds as transparent, efficient and fair investment vehicles was undermined with the uncovering of major scandals in 2003 and 2004 involving 'late trading' and 'market timing' in the shares of mutual funds with the knowledge and sometimes participation of the fund managers. The disclosures, legal proceedings and settlements led to extensive further investigations of mutual fund practices and governance procedures.

Late trading allows a favoured investor to illegally execute trades at the fund's 4 pm US daily (NAV) sometimes as late as 9 pm the same evening, enabling the investor to 'bet on yesterday's horse race' by profiting from news released domestically after the closing or released overseas in different time zones. Ordinary fund investors are obliged to trade at the 4 pm price until it is reset at 4 pm the following day. The practice, in effect, transfers wealth from ordinary shareholders to sophisticated hedge fund investors who had agreed to invest 'sticky assets' in lucrative (i.e. incorporating high performance fees for the fund manager) hedge funds to be sold to sophisticated buyers. For a fund management group to allow late trading is a major regulatory violation and a serious breach of fiduciary duty owed to the group's investors. One study has suggested that late trading cost investors about $400m per year between 2001 and 2004, or 0.005% in annual returns for international mutual funds and 0.006% for domestic funds.

Market timing trades in mutual fund shares – a practice not in itself illegal – involves rapid-fire trading by favoured investors in shares primarily of international mutual funds across time zones. This practice skims the returns from the mutual fund shareholders, increases mutual fund expenses and requires them to hold large cash balances to meet abrupt withdrawals: costs which have to be borne by all investors, not just the market-timers. Investors permitted to engage in market-timing trades by fund managers again promised to park 'sticky' assets with the fund management companies in their own hedge funds, in effect kicking back some of their questionable market-timing gains to the fund management companies, not to the shareholders of the mutual fund. Market timing trades were estimated to have cost long-term US mutual fund investors about $4 billion of dilution per year in the early 2000s.

By July 2005 prosecutors in the US had extracted over $2.8 billion in fines and penalties from some 24 mutual fund management companies in settlements in which those charged admitted no guilt. The funds managed by the investment groups that were named in the scandals suffered considerably more redemptions than firms that were not charged, including the industry's largest fund managers.

Conflicts of interest

Some observers have argued that profit-making mutual fund managers' earnings are a function of the volume of assets under management, and so there is relentless pressure to grow those assets by offering an increasing variety of fund products to investors who benefit from their performance, liquidity and originality. Such pressure can cause fiduciary violations in all but mutually owned fund managers and index funds, and perhaps should be seen as an unwelcome but tolerable friction to be endured in an industry that has benefited millions of people otherwise unable to invest safely in financial markets. In any event, the late trading and market timing scandals were not seen to cause enough damage to seriously impair mutual funds as investment vehicles, but they did raise serious questions among regulators, policy advocates and prosecutors regarding conflicting interests between mutual fund investors and the fund management companies that invest the assets.

Fund managers want:
- Independent directors who comply with the rules but are cooperative, supportive and not difficult to work with. Investors want directors who will robustly execute their fiduciary duties to the mutual fund shareholders.
- Maximum fees and expense reimbursements. Investors want their fund directors to negotiate minimum total costs and for those costs to be fully disclosed.
- To ensure that they are reappointed. Investors want boards that act vigorously in their interests in selecting managers capable of top-flight risk-adjusted performance.
- To increase assets under management. Investors want optimum investment returns after expenses and taxes.
- To promote their funds through brokers and financial advisers who need to be compensated. Investors do not want to pay these fees if they receive no benefits from them.
- To lower unreimbursed costs through soft dollar commissions from broker-dealers, while investors want best-price execution of trades and lowest commissions.

- To favour their own funds by obtaining 'shelf space' in distribution channels, while investors want access through brokers to the best and most appropriate funds for them.
- To be able to organise funds to assist other business interests of the firm, such as investment banking, and promoting investments in particular stocks, while investors want all investment decisions by the managers to be arm's-length and objective.

These are generic conflicts of interest with which the mutual fund industry will have to come to terms if it expects to be an enduring part of the financial architecture. Containing exploitation of these conflicts will invariably depend on a combination of market discipline and effective regulation. Failure in either domain will drive assets onto the balance sheets of banks and into alternative investment vehicles.

Regulatory issues
Mutual fund regulation in advanced financial markets require strict fit-and-proper criteria for management companies, as well as extensive disclosure of pertinent information. In the US the National Securities Markets Improvement Act of 1996 makes the Securities and Exchange Commission responsible for overseeing investment advisers with over $25m under management, with state regulators alone responsible for investment advisers with smaller amounts under management advisers who had previously been co-regulated together with the SEC. The large investment advisers falling under SEC jurisdiction account for about 95% of US assets under management, although the vast majority of abusive practices and enforcement problems occur among the smaller firms.

A great deal of mutual fund information is in the public domain, which helps market discipline along with the aforementioned high degree of transparency with respect to fund performance and ample media coverage and vigorous competition among funds and fund managers. This means that investors today face a generally fair and efficient market in which to make their asset choices. Overall, the mutual fund business, at least in the more developed markets, is probably a good example of how regulation and competition can come together to serve the retail investor about as well as is possible.

Not unexpectedly, the mutual fund management industry worldwide has seen a host of strategic initiatives among fund managers. These include mergers, acquisitions and alliances among fund managers as well as between fund managers and commercial and universal banks, securities broker-dealers, and insurance companies. In general the effect of competition in the industry has been to make it more customer-friendly, technology-sensitive, adaptive – and more concentrated. However, at least in the United States, there has been little evidence of increasing market concentration in the mutual fund industry over the years. In the mid-2000s, the US mutual funds industry had a five-firm ratio of 39%, a ten-firm ratio of 51% and a 25-firm ratio of 74%; these ratios were roughly constant for the previous 15 years. Factors that seem to argue for greater industry concentration in the future are economies of scale and brand-name recognition. Arguments against further concentration include shifts in performance track records and the role of mutual fund supermarkets in distribution, which increase the relative marketing advantage of smaller funds. One factor that may promote continued fragmentation of the mutual fund industry is that size itself can lead to significant performance problems.

Hedge funds and private equity funds

Hedge funds gained substantial prominence as investment vehicles in the late 1990s and 2000s. At the end of 2007, there were estimated to be about 10,100 active hedge funds in existence worldwide, with assets under management approaching $2 trillion and growing at the time at about 20% per year (see Figure 5).

Hedge funds are lightly regulated investment vehicles – essentially closed-end investment pools with participations sold to wealthy individuals and institutional investors such as foundations, endowments and pension funds. Hedge funds originally sought to 'hedge' the underlying risk of the market using various strategies designed to identify underpriced assets and overpriced assets, taking both long and short posi-

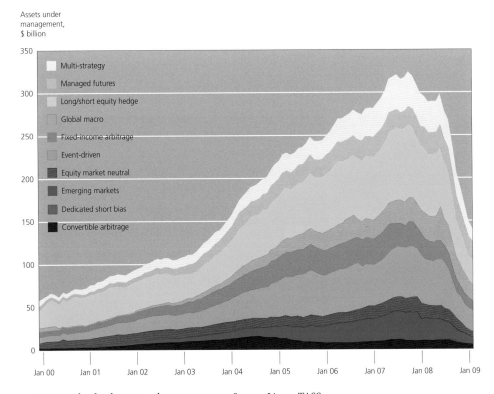

Fig. 5. Hedge fund assets under management. Source: Lipper TASS.

tions in order to remain essentially neutral with respect to overall market risk. Various types of derivatives and leverage were used to neutralise market risk and increase the size of positions in order to benefit from often very small pricing imperfections. Consequently, performance of many hedge fund strategies, particularly relative value strategies, was not dependent on the direction of the bond or equity markets – unlike conventional equities or mutual funds, which are generally 'long only' and fully exposed to market risk.

As the industry developed the classic hedging strategies evolved into a broad array of investment styles, so that hedge funds today are probably best described as 'special-purpose investment vehicles' which may or may not hedge their various exposures. Some strategies which try to be uncorrelated with equity markets are intended to deliver consistent returns with extremely low risk of loss, while others may be as or more volatile than mutual funds. Many, but not all, hedge fund strategies tend to hedge against downturns in the markets being traded. Most are flexible in their investment options and may use short selling, leverage and derivatives such as puts, calls, options and futures.

Hedge fund styles
The following are the principal investment styles that appear in the global hedge fund market today and the investment focus of each:
- **Aggressive growth** invests in equities expected to experience acceleration in growth of earnings per share.
- **Distressed securities** buys equity, debt, or trade claims at deep discounts of companies in or facing bankruptcy or reorganisation.
- **Emerging markets** invests in equity or debt of emerging (less mature) markets which tend to have higher inflation and volatile growth.
- **Income** invests with primary focus on yield or current income rather than solely on capital gains and may utilise leverage to buy bonds and sometimes fixed income derivatives in order to profit from principal appreciation and interest income.
- **Macro** aims to profit from changes in global economies, typically brought about by shifts in government policy which impact interest rates, in turn affecting currency, stock and bond markets.
- **Market-neutral arbitrage** attempts to hedge out most market risk by taking offsetting positions, often in different securities of the same issuer.
- **Market-neutral securities hedging** invests equally in long and short equity portfolios generally in the same sectors of the market.
- **Market timing** allocates assets among different asset classes, depending on the manager's view of the economic or market outlook.
- **Opportunistic** changes from strategy to strategy as opportunities arise to profit from events such as IPOs or sudden price changes.

- **Multi-strategy** is diversified by employing various strategies simultaneously to realise short- and long-term gains.
- **Short selling** sells securities short in anticipation of being able to re-buy them at a future date at a lower price due to the manager's assessment of the overvaluation of the securities, or the market, or in anticipation of earnings disappointments often due to accounting irregularities, new competition, change of management, etc.
- **Special situations** invests in event-driven situations such as mergers, hostile take-overs, reorganisations or leveraged buy-outs.
- **Value** invests in securities perceived to be selling at deep discounts to their intrinsic or potential worth.

In addition, there are funds of funds, which mix and match hedge funds and other pooled investment vehicles. This blending of different strategies and asset classes aims to provide a more stable long-term investment return than any of the individual funds.

Most hedge funds are highly specialised, relying on the specific expertise of the manager or management team. Consequently, hedge fund managers' remuneration is heavily weighted towards performance incentives (20% or more of investment gains) in an effort to attract the best fund management talent. However, hedge fund expense ratios are also high – up to 2% of assets under management – so that hedge fund managers can do very well regardless of performance. Lock-ups usually prevent investors from withdrawing their funds for various periods of time, in order to allow hedge fund managers to execute their strategies. At the same time, since size can be the enemy of hedge fund performance, many successful hedge fund managers limit the amount of capital they will accept.

Hedge funds in the financial crisis

As Figure 5 shows, as a result of the financial crisis of 2007–09, both the number of hedge funds and assets under management declined significantly in 2008 and at the end of 2009 stood at about 8,900 funds with roughly $1.2 trillion under management. It turned out that many hedge funds were not hedged against severe market declines and the disappearance of liquidity, while others were unable to cope with systemic shocks and 'tail events' in the financial system. So many hedge funds have had to rebuild their reputations, cut expenses and renegotiate management fees in order to survive.

Besides declines in asset values and redemptions, hedge funds have been hit by a number of frauds and scandals in recent years. Insider trading scandals are an expected outcome of the hedge fund industry, dependent as it is on capitalising on market imperfections while maintaining a hedged position against the underlying market. Stiff competition can be expected to erode most market imperfections, making it increasingly difficult for hedge funds to earn abnormal returns and justify outsize fees. So there is a strong incentive to access and use non-public information provided by insiders of various types, and in the process violate both civil fraud and criminal insider trading statutes. By the end of the 2000s, at least a dozen hedge funds were alleged to have engaged in such practices. Added to this is outright fraud such as Ponzi schemes, made possible by the secretive and unregulated nature of the industry and its structure of funds of funds and other feeders that extend the reach of fraudulent operators. The $50 billion Bernard Madoff Ponzi scheme, the largest and longest-lasting ever uncovered, is almost a textbook example of aggressive malfeasance in the hedge fund industry and did a great deal to amplify calls for much greater transparency and regulation of the industry.

No doubt hedge funds will remain part of the global asset management architecture, but under much more disciplined conditions and greater scrutiny from regulators concerned about lack of transparency and possible systemic effects of a major hedge fund failure at some point in the future.

Private equity funds

A second alternative class of investment vehicles comprises private equity funds, which probably originated in the late eighteenth century, when entrepreneurs in Europe and the US found wealthy individuals to back their projects on an ad hoc basis. This informal method of financing became an industry in the late 1970s and early 1980s when a number of private equity firms were founded. Private equity at that point became a recognised asset class.

In contrast to hedge funds, private equity is a broad term that refers to any type of equity investment in an asset in which the equity is not freely tradable on a public stock market. Categories of private equity investment include leveraged buyouts, venture capital, growth capital, angel investing, mezzanine capital and others. Private equities are equity securities of companies that have not 'gone public' (companies that have not listed their stock on a public exchange), and are generally illiquid and considered a long-term investment. Private equity usually includes forms of venture capital and management buyout (MBO) financing: i.e. both early-stage (venture) and later-stage (buy-out) investing. In some cases the term 'private equity' is used to refer only to the buy-out and buy-in investment sector. In other cases – for example in Europe but not the US – the term 'venture capital' is used to cover all stages, i.e. synonymous with 'private equity'. In the US, 'venture capital' refers only to investments in early-stage and expanding companies.

Private equity investing reached a peak during the technology bubble of the late 1990s and subsequently focussed more on investment opportunities where the business had proven potential for realistic growth in an expanding market, backed by a well-researched and well-documented business plan and an experienced management team – ideally including individuals who had started and run a successful business before.

Private equity firms have been especially active in restructuring situations, where shifts in technologies, international comparative advantage, overcapacity, bankruptcies and government policy changes have made existing businesses economically non-viable. This includes privatisations and strategic divestitures by major corporations and conglomerates, with substantial activity in this respect in countries like Germany, Japan and China. In this activity, private equity firms – which consider their core competence to be in industrial and financial expertise and relatively long investment periods – have had to compete with hedge funds looking for pure financial plays.

Since private equity firms, notably those specialising in leveraged buyouts, were highly dependent on cheap and abundant debt financing, their growth in the 2000s was heavily fuelled by favourable market conditions. This allowed high returns to private equity investors, due largely to the addition of leverage to target companies, facilitating early withdrawal of equity commitments but leaving the target companies with heavy debt loads and vulnerable to an economic downturn. When the financial markets abruptly turned during the financial crisis of 2007–09, returns to private equity investors plummeted, pending deals were cancelled, and bankruptcies multiplied among firms taken private in LBOs. As in the case of hedge funds, private equity will be a long-term feature of the financial landscape, but at least for a time it will have to be based on superior management as opposed to financial engineering.

Insurance

Alongside pension funds, mutual funds and discretionary alternative asset funds, the fourth major player in asset management worldwide is the insurance industry. This industry manages assets both for its own account (reserves against life and non-life insurance claims) and off the balance sheet in the form of fiduciary assets managed on behalf of retail clients, usually in the form of annuities and other savings and retirement products that incorporate insurance features.

The principal activities of insurance companies consist of non-life insurance, life insurance, and asset management, although the differences between the last two areas have become increasingly blurred. Non-life insurance includes property, casualty and health-related programmes. Reinsurance adds a global activity that provides liability coverage for insurers themselves. Life insurance comprises whole life (life insurance that incorporates a savings or cash-value feature) and term life (pure life insurance) policies, and increasingly savings and pension products that are based on annuities.

The two traditional sources of insurance company income are earnings on policies – known as 'technical profits and losses' – and earnings on invested premiums from policyholders. Technical profits and losses refers to the difference between policy premiums earned and claims or benefits paid. In some countries, insurers are required to invest the majority of their premiums in government bonds, but most countries allow a range of high-quality conservative assets, together with establishing a 'technical reserve' liability on their balance sheet. The technical reserve reflects the estimated cost of claims and benefit payments that the insurer would be ultimately required to make.

Life and non-life insurance

The non-life insurance industry tends to go through substantial underwriting cycles based on excess capital in times of low insured losses and the reverse when claims are high. Normally, substantial capital would be considered a strength in terms of its role as a buffer against future losses, but in terms of industry performance an oversupply of capital can actually be dangerous. Since capital determines underwriting capacity, surplus capital creates overcapacity in the industry. Excess capacity leads to intensified underwriting activity, triggering price wars, which in turn undermines profitability and makes it difficult for weaker companies to survive.

Growth opportunities in life insurance have been more attractive than non-life due to the strong market growth since the early 1990s in retirement savings and pensions. In industrialised countries, the pensions business benefits from an aging population and threatened cutbacks in social security benefits, as discussed earlier. However, life insurance has also been affected by a 'yield pinch' associated with asset allocation to fixed-income securities, mostly government bonds. With these traditional life products, insurers guaranteed their clients a fixed rate of return that was usually set by regulators. However, the spread between the insurer's investment yield and its guarantee to policyholders can be dramatically narrowed in periods of lower interest rates.

From time to time this situation has seriously damaged the profitability of both old and new life insurance business. The life of outstanding liabilities to policyholders often exceeded that of the underlying bond assets, which periodically matured and had to be rolled over at successively lower yields. For new policies, insurers could only invest new premiums at rates that were either close to or below those guaranteed to policyholders. This can be mitigated though profit-sharing agreements with clients and shifts to unit-linked products, where gains and losses are borne largely by policyholders.

Unit-linked products, also known as 'separate asset account' policies, are usually tied to the performance of equity investments. Unlike traditional life products bearing a guaranteed return, the investment risk under a unit-linked product is borne by the policyholder. Under this business model, income is earned from asset-management fees rather than from participating in investment returns. The unit-linked product provides an important benefit by requiring lower capital reserves than traditional policies – sometimes as much as 25% of traditional products' capital requirements – since clients assume the risks directly.

Due in part to unit-linked life insurance, the industry basically reinvented itself into an increasingly asset management-based business. Indeed, some of the larger insurers adopted a strategy of asset management as a 'core' business by leveraging their investment expertise. These companies offered separate asset management products to satisfy demand from both retail and institutional clients and to compete with banks that had made inroads into life insurance with annuity-linked products. As Figure 1 (page 23) shows, the insurance sector in 2007 controlled close to $19 trillion in assets worldwide.

Many life insurers traditionally operated as mutuals, in which ownership was vested in policyholders, not shareholders. Without shareholder pressure, mutual insurance companies are often less efficient than their shareholder-owned competitors. The mutual form of ownership also hinders consolidation through mergers and acquisitions, since a mutual is first required to demutualise after obtaining consent from its policyholders to become a stock company in order to use its shares as acquisition currency. By the late 1990s, the trend toward demutualisation was industry-wide.

The insurance industry had become increasingly consolidated both across and within national markets, and this trend is not likely to fade anytime soon. Because of lower margins from intense competition, insurers feel increasingly pressured to diversify outside of their home markets to spread volatility risks and gain access to new business. Greater size advantage is perceived to provide economies of scale and tighter control of expenses through improved technology. Cost-cutting seems clearly more advantageous at the national level between domestic rivals than between companies based in different countries, or in financial sectors with few overlapping operations.

Structural change and competitive dynamics

Institutional asset management attracts competitors from an extraordinarily broad range of strategic groups. Commercial and universal banks, investment banks, trust companies, insurance companies, private banks, captive and independent pension fund managers, mutual fund companies, financial conglomerates and various types of specialist firms are all active in investment management. This rich array of contenders, coming at the market from several very different starting points, competitive resources and strategic objectives, is likely to render the market for institutional asset management a highly competitive one even under conditions of large size and rapid growth. Securities firms (broker-dealers) have also penetrated the mutual fund market, and so have insurance companies reacting to stiffer competition for their traditional annuities business. Commercial banks, watching some of their deposit clients drift off into mutual funds, have responded by launching mutual fund families of their own or marketing those of other fund managers. Such cross-penetration among strategic groups of financial intermediaries, each approaching the business from a different direction, makes mutual fund markets highly competitive.

Competitors in asset management in many markets include domestic and foreign-based commercial banks and savings institutions, securities firms (full-service investment banks and various kinds of specialists), insurance companies, finance companies (including financial subsidiaries of non-financial companies such as General Electric), investment and financial advisers, private banks, and independent mutual fund management companies. Members of each strategic group compete with each other, as well as with members of other strategic groups. Success or failure depends heavily on portfolio management skills and service quality, as well as economies of scale, capital investment and key technologies.

Figure 6 shows the ownership structure of the asset management industry in Europe and the United States, and illustrates the substantial diversity of firms active in the industry. Several ownership structures are solely on the 'buy side', notably stand-alone and independent asset managers – some of which are either cooperatives or closely held – and those controlled by insurance companies. The remainder is controlled either by banks or by financial conglomerates active in both banking and insurance. Such asset managers arguably suffer from potential conflicts of interest since their parent organisation may well be active on the capital-raising or 'sell side' as well, and in any case may be subject to intense performance pressure which could turn out to be detrimental to the investor clients.

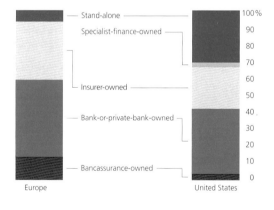

Fig. 6. Owners of asset managers, 2009. Source: Oliver, Wyman & Company.

As shown in Figure 7, there have been a number of very large M&A deals in the asset management sector, symptomatic of the industry's restructuring in recent years. The basic motivation has to do with the search for economies of scale and operating cost efficiencies, as well as the development of marketing platforms to form the basis for future growth.

Date	Target	Ctry	Type	Acquirer	Ctry	AUM($MM)	% acquired
Jun 09	Barclays Global Investors	US	Div	BlackRock, Inc.	US	$ 1,440,000	100%
Dec 06	Mellon Financial Corporation Inc.	US	Div	Bank of New York Company, Inc.	US	947,000	100%
Feb 06	Merrill Lynch Investment Managers	US	Div	BlackRock, Inc.	US	544,000	100%
Jun 05	Citigroup Asset Management	US	Div	Legg Mason	US	437,000	100%
Jan 09	Société Générale Asset Management	FR	Div	Crédit Agricole SA	FR	343,085	75%*
Sep 01	Zurich Scudder Investments	US	Div	Deutsche Bank AG	GY	278,000	100%
Nov 99	PIMCO Advisors L.P.	US	Inst	Allianz AG	GY	256,153	69%
Oct 08	Aberdeen Asset Management plc	UK	Div	Mitsubishi UFJ Financial Group	JN	226,300	10%
Jul 08	Russell Investments	US	Div	Nippon Life Insurance	JN	211,000	5%
Jun 00	United Asset Management (UAM)	US	Inst	Old Mutual PLC	UK	203,150	100%

* The CAAM/SGAM transaction was a contribution deal where Crédit Agricole received 75% and Société Générale received 25% of the equity in the combined entity. Data converted to US currency at time of announcement. Announced transactions only. Bold transactions indicate 1H2009 deals.

Fig. 7. World's largest asset management M&A deals by AUM, 2000–2009. Source: Jefferies Putnam Lovell.

The balance of forces

To summarise, this chapter has identified the key components of the 'buy side' of financial markets – the asset management industry in terms of its four principal domains: pension funds, mutual funds, discretionary alternative assets and insurance companies. There are several other special categories not discussed here, including fiduciary assets managed on behalf of foundations, endowments, central banks, sovereign wealth funds and other large asset holders, as well as assets managed individually on behalf of private clients.

We have noted earlier that various kinds of financial firms have emerged to perform asset management functions: commercial banks, savings banks, postal savings institutions, savings cooperatives, credit unions, securities firms (full-service firms and various kinds of specialists), insurance companies, finance companies, finance subsidiaries of industrial companies, mutual fund companies, hedge funds, financial advisers and various others. Members of each strategic group compete with each other, as well as with members of other strategic groups. There are two questions. First, what determines competitive advantage in operating distribution gateways to the end investor? Second, what determines competitive advantage in the asset management process itself?

One supposition is that distribution of asset management services is both scope-driven and technology-driven. That is, asset management services can be distributed jointly with other types of financial services and thereby benefit from cost economies of scope as well as demand economies of scope (cross-selling). Commercial banks may be able to cross-sell asset management services with banking products. Insurance companies may be able to cross-sell asset management services with insurance by incorporating insurance features in asset management products – like fixed and variable annuities do. Broker-dealers may be able to cross-sell asset management services with brokerage services and use broker networks to distribute funds, benefiting in the process from greater earnings stability and possibly captive buy-side placing power for securities. Non-financial corporations may be able to incorporate asset management services into in-house pension plan management.

Such cross-links would tend to give retail-oriented financial services firms such as commercial and universal banks, life insurance companies and savings institutions a competitive advantage in distribution. At the same time, more specialised firms may establish cost-effective distribution of asset management services using proprietary remote-marketing techniques like the mails, telephone selling or the Internet, or by 'renting' distribution through the established infrastructures of other financial intermediaries like banks, insurance companies or mutual fund supermarkets. They may also gain access through fund management consultants and financial advisers.

Asset management itself, of course, depends heavily on portfolio management skills as well as economies of scale, capital investment and technologies involved in back office functions, some of which can be outsourced. Since fiduciary activities must be kept separate from other financial services operations that involve potential conflicts of interest, either through organisational separation or Chinese walls, there is not much to be gained in the way of economies of scope.

Competitive dynamics

Inter-sectoral competition, alongside already vigorous intra-sectoral competition, is what makes asset management one of the most competitive areas of financial intermediation, even in the presence of rapid growth in the size of the market for asset management services. Certainly the dynamics of competition for the growing pools of DB and DC pension assets in various parts of the world, and its cross-linkage to the mutual fund business, has led to various strategic initiatives among fund managers. These include mergers, acquisitions and strategic alliances among fund managers as well as between fund managers, commercial and universal banks, securities broker-dealers, and insurance companies. Figures 8 and 9 show the existing state of play among the largest and most rapidly growing asset managers in the world.

Manager	Total assets, $ trillion
UBS AG	2.45
Barclays Global Investors (Great Britain)	1.81
State Street Global (United States)	1.75
AXA (France)	1.74
Allianz (Germany)	1.71
Fidelity Investments (United States)	1.64
Capital Group (United States)	1.40
Deutsche Bank Group AG (Germany)	1.27
Vanguard Group (United States)	1.17
BlackRock Group (United States)	1.12
Crédit Suisse (Switzerland)	1.09
JPMorgan Chase (United States)	1.01
Mellon Financial* (United States)	1.00
Legg Mason (United States)	0.96
BNP Paribas (France)	0.82
ING (Netherlands)	0.79
Natixis (France)	0.77
AIG Global Investment (United States)	0.73
Crédit Agricole (France)	0.70
Aviva (Great Britain)	0.70
* Now Bank of NY	

Fig. 8. World's largest asset managers, January 2007. Source: Pensions & investments/Watson Wyatt.

Fig. 9. World's fastest-growing asset managers, 2001–2007. Source: Watson Wyatt.

Market valuations of asset management companies have traditionally been quite high in comparison with other types of firms in the financial services industry, and this has been reflected in prices paid in M&A transactions. Besides gaining access to distribution and fund management expertise, the underlying economics of this deal flow presumably have to do with the realisation of economies of scale and economies of scope, making possible both cost reductions and cross-selling of multiple types of funds, banking and/or insurance services, investment advice, high-quality research, etc. in a one-stop-shopping interface for investors, despite a good deal of evidence that investors are quite happy to shop on their own with low-cost fund managers.

References

Epstein, N. and B.R. Brewington (1997), 'The Investment Management Industry in the United States', New York: Putnam, Lovell & Thornton.

Holzmann, R. (1996), 'Pension Reform, Financial Market Development and Economic Growth: Preliminary Evidence from Chile', *IMF Working Paper*, 96/94, August.

Hurley, M.P., S.I. Meers, B.J. Bornstein and N.R. Strumingher (1995), 'The Coming Evolution of the Investment Management Industry: Opportunities and Strategies', New York: Goldman Sachs & Co.

Neave, E. (1992), 'The Economic Organization of a Financial System', London: Routledge.

Patel, J., R.J. Zeckhauser and D. Hendricks (1994), 'Investment Fund Performance: Evidence from Mutual Funds, Cross-Border Investments, and New Issues' in Ryuzo, S., Levich, R. and Ramachandran, R. (eds.), 'Japan, Europe and International Financial Markets: Analytical and Empirical Perspectives', Cambridge: Cambridge University Press.

Reid, B. and J. Crumrine (1997), 'Retirement Plan Holdings of Mutual Funds', Washington, DC: Investment Company Institute.

Sittampalam, A. (1993), 'Coming Wars in Investment Management', Dublin: Lafferty Publications.

Smith, R.C. and I. Walter (2003), 'Global Banking', New York: Oxford University Press.

Turner, J. and N. Watanabe (1995), 'Private Pension Policies in Industrialized Countries', Kalamazoo: W.E. Upjohn Institute for Employment Research.

Warther, V.A. (1995), 'Aggregate Mutual Fund Flows and Security Returns', *Journal of Financial Economics,* September.

About the author

Massimo Massa is the Rothschild Chair Professor of Banking and Finance at INSEAD, where he teaches international finance, corporate finance, information financial economics and behavioural finance in MBA, Ph.D. and Executive programmes. He has obtained an MBA from the Yale School of Management and an M.A. and Ph.D. in Financial Economics from Yale University. His research interests include portfolio theory, theory of information in financial markets, behavioural finance, market microstructure and mutual funds. His articles have been published in academic journals such as the 'Review of Financial Studies', 'Journal of Finance, Journal of Financial Economics', 'Journal of Business', 'Journal of Financial and Quantitative Analysis', 'Journal of Financial Markets', 'Review of Finance', and 'European Journal of Financial Management'. Massimo Massa has previously worked in the Bank of Italy in its Banking Division (1989–1992) and in the Research Department of its Monetary and Financial Markets Division (1993–1997).
Contact: massimo.massa@insead.edu.

3
What do we know about
the mutual fund industry?

ABSTRACT The analysis of the mutual fund industry is a story that has little to do with finance and a lot to do with marketing. It is one of the most successful cases in history of marketing in which the true quality of the product has been hidden and camouflaged. The starting point in understanding the mutual fund industry is to look at the service the mutual fund is expected to deliver. The same way as buying a car provides a bundle of services – speed, reliability, comfort, etc. – so does the purchase of a fund deliver a set of services: performance, liquidity, checking facilities, etc. However, just as a car would not be a car without a proper engine, a fund would not be a fund if it were not able to deliver a consistently superior performance. This self-explained truth and the structural inability to generate performance have given birth to the brilliant creation of the 'family model'. If performance is illusory, the problem faced by the industry is just like selling cars with inferior engines. How can you do it? You stress the role of other 'characteristics' – the colour, the chassis or the brakes – and rely on product differentiation and market segmentation to make product comparison difficult. And indeed, the mutual fund industry has developed in a way that has stressed product differentiation and market segmentation.

3 What do we know about the mutual fund industry?

by Massimo Massa

Is there an engine in the car?

The Holy Grail in the mutual funds literature has always been the analysis of performance. The literature has searched to answer whether funds generate performance, whether they persist in doing so and whether it is enough to compensate for the fees that are charged. The answers have been mostly negative. Thus, a new question arises: if performance is not sizable and not persistent, what helps justify the existence of the industry? The answer we will give in the following analysis is marketing. We will see how marketing strategies help to disguise poor performance and attract clients by focussing on non-performance-related features.

The myth of measurability of performance

We start as the standard analysis of the asset management industry has always done: by focussing on performance. Mutual funds have always been considered self-standing entities engaged in a competition with each other to deliver higher performance ('alpha'). Performance has been defined as the ability to beat a 'benchmark' – i.e. deliver a return higher than the return of a portfolio which proxies for the investment in assets with similar risk as the fund. Various definitions of benchmarks have been provided. The first was the market portfolio – i.e. the return on a portfolio representing the main stocks in the market weighed according to their market capitalisation. Next, a more sophisticated analysis has included other benchmarks: book to market and size portfolios. These represent the exposure to other classes of risk: the risk of investing in value stocks and the risk of investing in small stocks. Then, a fourth 'factor' has been considered: momentum. This proxies for the degree of autocorrelation of the returns of the assets in the relatively short period – momentum within a 6–12-month horizon and reversal beyond that period. Each new factor added to the benchmark was meant to proxy for new and different types of risk exposure of the fund (e.g. Carhart, 1997). However, as the ability to proxy for the degree of risk exposure improved, the quality of the detected performance deteriorated and quickly tipped to the negative side. More sophisticated models based on the observations of the actual stock holdings of the funds have not made the picture of the industry less bleak. The results in general have been dismal: mutual funds do not seem to outperform the market (e.g. Wermers, 2000). If we also include the fees charged by the fund, the picture gets gloomier: not only do funds not seem good at delivering superior performance, but after-fee they seem to underperform considerably.

Some trace of performance could be found in some funds – extreme tail funds. However, this overperformance is very patchy and haphazard. Moreover, if we look at whether funds that overperform keep on doing it consistently over time, the answer seems to be negative. Mutual fund performance does not seem to persist, except in the case of negative performance. Some evidence of persistence of performance has been uncovered only recently. For example, funds with more incentive-loaded compensation structures for management seem to deliver better performance in a more consistent fashion (Massa and Patgiri, 2009).

Overall, scepticism remains. This is rooted in some of the characteristics of the process that generate performance: constraints on the ability to scale up the investment in profitable investment opportunities, negative size and organisational externalities. The existence of a directly observable link between fund-specific characteristics and performance would induce investors to flock to such funds, abnormally increasing their size and therefore, given these characteristics, limiting the ability of the funds to replicate such performance.

Given these considerations, it is instructive to look at how funds choose to present their performance and the benchmark they use. Funds characterise themselves in terms of investment styles. Performance is evaluated relative to the other competing funds operating in the same style. The idea is that, by using the other funds as a reference, investors can better identify fund managers' skills. For example, fund managers investing in value stocks should be judged relative to other managers investing in value stocks. However, any comparison with funds investing in growth stocks would be misleading, as investors, by choosing a value fund, have already decided to pass on the higher returns of growth stocks to obtain the relatively greater safety of the value ones.

Unfortunately, the use of relative performance evaluation directly affects the behaviour of fund managers, making evaluation of performance illusory. Indeed, benchmarks are conveniently selected by the managers themselves and, when imposed by outside assessors – e.g. Morningstar and Lipper – managers enact timing and window-dressing techniques meant to get around them.

Managers react to the setting of investment-style benchmarks in two ways. On the one hand, they may position themselves close to their peer-group benchmark or just replicate their asset class. Alternatively, managers may focus less on their investment style average and take idiosyncratic bets in order to rank first in their investment style. In either case, the mere setting of a benchmark affects managerial behaviour in a way that nullifies the role of the benchmark.

A nice case study about this is provided by the Lipper reclassification. In September 1999, Lipper Inc., a fund data vendor and a leader in fund ranking services, adopted a new fund classification methodology. Instead of asking the funds about their self-reported style, Lipper decided to reclassify the funds as a function of the style they actually belonged to by directly observing the fundamental characteristics of the securities held by the funds – e.g. value/core/growth and the small/mid/large-cap. This reclassification has changed the way some funds were defined. For example, Fidelity's Magellan, a self-professed 'growth' fund in the old system, was reclassified as a 'large-cap growth' fund. It was joined in that new category by Janus Twenty, which previously was a 'capital appreciation' fund.

Fund managers reacted to the reclassification by increasing their loading on the stocks corresponding to their new Lipper classification and reducing their loading on the remaining stocks. For example, after the Lipper reclassification, 'large-cap growth' fund returns are more sensitive to the return of the stock index that tracks the returns of 'large-cap growth' stocks (i.e. the 'S&P/BARRA 500 Growth' stock index) and less sensitive to the other stocks. At the same time, however, this reclassification has induced funds to change their behaviour vis-à-vis the other competing funds. The increased co-movement with their new peers – defined according to the new Lipper classification – has been accompanied by a lower co-movement with the peers defined according to their self-reported styles (Massa and Matos, 2005). The implication is clear. When the benchmark was self-reported, the funds were declaring they belonged to one style but were effectively investing as if they belonged to another style. The assignment of an exogenously imposed holding-based benchmark has forced them to change their behaviour to more closely track the new style. However, this also induced them to increase idiosyncratic bets that allow them to be within the constraints of the new style but still diverge in terms of idiosyncratic risk taking. This has unintended consequences in terms of risk taking.

Also, the very fact that, after the reclassification, funds load on the size and value/growth factors in a way more similar to that of the corresponding stocks from each S&P/BARRA stock index has made funds less easily distinguishable on the basis of their return characteristics. In a sense, the classification grid has worked somewhat against itself and blurred the real difference between the size and value/growth orientation of funds.

Moreover, even if partially better, the setting of benchmarks based on holdings requires a truthful disclosure of information. However, such disclosure would negatively affect the information collection incentives of the funds by reducing the informational advantage of the good funds. Indeed, fund managers seem to condition their investment decisions on the information contained in the holdings of their peers. 'Copy-cat' funds purchasing the same assets as funds that disclose these asset holdings can earn returns similar to these actively managed funds (Myers et al., 2001). Funds investing in the stocks previously disclosed by other funds seem to display a positive persistence in future returns, while 'word-of-mouth' effects in fund holdings make managers more likely to hold a stock if other managers in the same city are holding that same stock (Hong et al., 2005).

The international dimension provides an answer

Is there some structural reason why funds may be able to overperform? To answer this question we need to look internationally. While most of our knowledge on the mutual fund industry is based on US data, recent evidence on international funds has also opened up new perspectives in determining where the sources of competitive advantage in the industry lie and what limits them. A caveat is required. Unlike traditional US mutual funds, international mutual funds can, in some instances, also invest in derivatives, borrow and go short. This should allow them to deliver higher gross-of-risk performance and higher risk.

International funds provide a way of studying the role of location as a source of comparative advantage. Traditionally, location has been seen as a source of performance, given the identification between proximity and information. If funds located closer to an asset have better information about it, closely related managers may deliver better performance (Coval and Moskowitz, 1999 and 2001). This would suggest that international funds deliver a lower performance than the domestic ones.

However, location provides an even greater source of advantage: a negative correlation between flows in the fund and investment opportunities. One of the biggest problems for mutual funds is their liquidity management (Edelen, 1999; Massa and Phalippou, 2005).

Mutual funds suffer from liquidity problems. Mutual funds investors are entitled to redeem their shares at the market value of the fund at the end of the trading day. Mutual funds that suffer large outflows need to liquidate at ruinous prices, i.e. hold financial fire sales (Coval and Stafford, 2007). This is accentuated if a fund is forced to sell when the prices of the assets are tumbling, i.e. in the presence of a positive correlation between fund flows and returns of the stocks in which it invests. This implies that the higher the uncertainty of the flows, the more the fund should invest in liquid assets and therefore forefeit performance. That is, funds need to hold cash and liquid assets in order to be ready to meet withdrawals and redemption claims.

However, if a fund is located far away from the assets in which it invests, it may enjoy a lower correlation between its flows and the performance of these assets. For example, a fund that invests in Japanese stocks and is sold mostly to European investors will experience withdrawals from European investors, either if it underperforms or if its investors suffer liquidity shocks. European investors are less exposed to liquidity shocks that are correlated with the Japanese market than the Japanese investors. In the ideal case of a negative correlation between its flows and the investment opportunities of the markets in which it invests – i.e. a negative correlation between the Japanese and European markets – the European fund will be able to buy Japanese stocks that are sold by Japanese investment funds when these funds experience outflows and sell at the times they receive inflows. In other words, the fact that the European fund targets European investors allows it to buy when the prices are low and sell when the prices are high.

This allows distantly located funds to outperform the domestic ones. In general, if the flows in the fund are scarcely – or even better negatively – related to the performance of the assets the fund invests in, the fund will be investing in assets at the time in which their price is lower and selling at the time in which the price has increased. This provides a sort of insurance for the fund analogous to a 'natural hedge'. This hedge allows the fund to take more risk and to invest in assets at the right time, improving both timing and selectivity. Funds with a more negative correlation between flows and investment opportunities are able to exploit this strategic advantage by taking more risky positions and delivering higher performance. Indeed, the natural advantage provided by the negative correlation increases the fund's ability/willingness to take more risk. The funds do exploit their advantage by either loading up more on market risk or increasing their idiosyncratic risk by investing in more risky stocks than the market or implementing a dynamic trading strategy and 'active management' (Ferreira et al, 2009).

While this can be seen also in the case of domestic funds, the lack of reliable identification of the location of fund flows makes it difficult to establish this point. However, the analysis of international funds allows a direct study of it. And indeed, it is very strongly the case that the correlation between the flows in the markets in which the fund sells its units and the markets in which it invests its assets (client-stock correlation) – i.e. the distance between the location of the investor in the fund and the location of the assets in which the fund invests – is directly and negatively related to performance.

This is a genuine source of performance that can be supported in equilibrium and that can explain the presence of fund performance both at home and internationally. However, this source of competitive advantage requires a segmentation between the financial markets in which the funds source and the financial markets in which the funds invest. The process of market integration, internationalisation and direct competition from hedge funds will likely alter and destroy this advantage.

Some structural limits to the industry

If mutual funds are able to successfully use the patterns of flows they are endowed with as a source of strategic advantage and to generate performance, other players in the markets may do even better. These investors are the hedge funds.

The fact that hedge funds source from sophisticated institutional investors located across the globe makes the capital sourcing of the hedge funds more stable than that of the mutual funds. Indeed, a hedge fund specialised in Japanese market investments will not face major outflows when the Japanese market collapses, as its investors are more equally distributed around the world. Also, hedge funds have a series of instruments – lock-up clauses, clauses that defer the liquidation of the stake in the fund as well as its payment – that reduce the volatility of flows. Moreover, hedge funds sell mostly to investors – the long-term institutional ones such as endowments – who have naturally fewer short-term liquidity needs. Finally, hedge funds have more freedom: they can borrow, invest in derivatives or sell short. All these elements provide the hedge funds with a strong strategic advantage that allows them to better exploit the investment opportunities available in the market. In doing so, hedge funds limit the ability of the mutual funds to manoeuvre and to take clients away from them. The fact that much of the performance of the hedge funds can be attributed to their ability to exploit the locational stability of their flows confirms it.

Hedge funds can also even directly 'prey on' the mutual funds themselves, exploiting their fire sales. Indeed, hedge funds provide liquidity to the mutual funds when they most need it and reduce their liquidity risk. This risk takes different forms. One form of liquidity risk is simply related to the fact that the funds cannot promptly sell the assets in the market without incurring sizable transaction costs due to the market impact or buy without moving the market. Alternatively, liquidity risk can be related to the co-movement with the market. Funds that suffer more outflows at the times in which liquidity is more expensive suffer more. Who stands to gain? The hedge funds do. They prey on mutual funds by investing in the assets sold by the mutual funds (Chen et al., 2008). While this activity generates returns for the hedge funds, it also provides liquidity to the market. This has two implications. The first implication is that the positive performance of the hedge funds can be seen as remuneration for the service of liquidity provision. That is, hedge funds sell the market put options that are exercised at times of liquidity pressure. This implies that we should expect hedge funds to deliver higher performance in areas/markets in which there are more mutual funds that are willing to pay for their services of liquidity provision. This, however, also implies that hedge funds represent a sort of a limit to the expansion of the mutual funds. Indeed, by providing very expensive liquidity and preying on the mutual funds, they reduce the room to manoeuvre that the mutual funds have in terms of delivering higher performance, subtracting valuable clients. The second implication is more striking: by providing liquidity, hedge funds play a role of stabilisation in the market and even more so in markets characterised by structural liquidity needs, i.e. less developed markets, markets with less financially developed intermediation systems.

How do you sell a car with no engine?

Funds as differentiated products

The mutual fund industry has developed in a way that stressed product differentiation and market segmentation. One of the most striking features of the mutual fund industry is its market structure. This is based on a very high number of funds differentiated into market styles and belonging to relatively few families. In the US alone, the number of mutual funds is now higher than that of the stocks traded on NYSE,

NASDAQ and AMEX added together. Over the period 1990–2000, the number of mutual funds grew from 3,081 to 8,171. At the end of 2008, it reached 16,262 mutual funds, closed-end funds, exchange-traded funds, and unit investment trusts managing $10.3 trillion in assets. The number of families has barely changed (from 361 to 431). At the same time, the degree of segmentation of the industry also grew, reaching roughly 33 different effective styles (Massa, 1998 and 2003).

All these facts can be hardly reconciled with the standard tenets of finance. In fact, the number of existing securities is already offering a sufficient degree of differentiation, and the existence of segmented funds makes it more difficult for the asset managers to generate absolute performance. Indeed, segmentation reduces the scope and range of activity of the manager and forces him to invest only in the assets specific to the fund's style, potentially hampering his market timing skills. For example, a manager with a mandate to invest in Asian stocks may see the arrival of the crisis in Asia, but cannot easily and swiftly reallocate investment to other areas of the world, as his investment mandate prevents him from doing so. This lack of ability to reorient the fund investments cannot be compensated for by superior investment skills of the investors in the funds or by a better ability to hedge investor-specific sources of uncertainty.

Market segmentation and fund proliferation are instead marketing strategies devised to exploit investors' heterogeneity. Funds can be seen as differentiated products sold by multi-product firms – 'families' – engaged in product differentiation and marketing. Funds are differentiated in terms not only of fund-specific characteristics but also in terms of affiliation with families. For example, in the case of Magellan, the investors are likely to be equally affected by fund performance, fees and risk, as well as by its affiliation with a big family called Fidelity. Affiliation with a family provides a branding image in terms of quality as well as family-specific characteristics.

One typical example of these services is the possibility of moving money in and out of funds belonging to the same family at very low cost ('low switching fees'). This can be seen as an option the family provides to its investors that reduces the effective fees they pay. The higher the number of funds in the family, the greater the value of this option, because the effective fees decrease as a function of the number of funds. An investor who is considering investing for a long period of time and is planning to rebalance his portfolio between equity and bond funds will prefer, all else equal, to invest in a big family, as this reduces the switching costs he will incur in the future when he rebalances his portfolio. A 'boutique' family specialised in few equity funds will have to offer a very significant superior performance in order to attract investors. And indeed, investors with a shorter or more volatile investment horizon tend to go for the funds with lower load fees that are parts of big families (Massa, 2003).

In fact, the existence of high load fees and low switching fees creates a sort of barrier to entry that protects big families and stimulates the existence of big families. The greater the value of the free-switching option, the lower the degree of competition between funds and the greater the segmentation of the industry. A family facing high costs in producing a decent level of performance will focus on other ways of attracting investors, such as playing with the fee structure and/or with the number of funds within the family.

A direct implication is that performance maximisation is not necessarily the optimal strategy. In fact, the profit-maximising mix of fees, performance and number of funds may even induce a level of performance that would otherwise be defined as 'inferior' in a standard performance evaluation analysis.

The fact that families are able to differentiate themselves in terms of non-performance-related characteristics makes performance *negatively* related to the degree of product differentiation in the style the fund is in and fund proliferation *positively* related to it. Styles characterised by a higher degree of product differentiation – i.e. a lower degree of competition – systematically provide lower performance and higher fund proliferations: in other words, each family offers more funds and each one of them is on average lower-performing.

The 'family model'

These few considerations have already suggested that a key role in the mutual fund industry is played by the families. Indeed, the mutual fund industry, unlike the hedge fund industry, has evolved adopting a model based on 'families' in charge of managing many funds. Mutual funds tend to organise themselves in big groups ('families'), while hedge funds tend to belong to much smaller groups if they have any affiliation at all. In the US, almost all the non-tiny mutual funds are affiliated with fund complexes, and the top 50 fund families have steadily concentrated over 80% of all the equity assets under management. Families help in terms of defraying fixed and research costs, by spreading them over many managed funds and by offering the potential for economies of scale and scope.

The family model is rooted in some main characteristics of the demand of mutual fund investors (Guedj and Papastaikoudi, 2004). The first characteristic is the convex flow performance relationship: high performance attracts large inflows; bad performance does not deter outflows (Sirri and Tufano, 1998; Chevalier and Ellison, 1997 and 1999). A similar effect is not there in the case of hedge funds: the flow performance relationship is far more linear. The convex flow performance relationship, plus the fact that the profits for the family are a function of the asset under management – given the linear ('fulcrum') fee structure – and are not directly linked to performance, increases the incentives for the families to 'play favourites'. Indeed, the expected assets of a family are higher if the family is able to produce one top-performing and one badly performing fund than it is if they have two funds whose performance is average. This creates the incentive to produce well-performing funds, even if it comes at the direct cost of generating badly performing ones (Gaspar et al., 2006).

The second characteristic of mutual fund investors' demand is the positive spillover externalities generated by having 'star funds'. Investors tend to select first a fund family and then the individual fund to invest in. In doing so, they use information about the family to draw inferences about the quality of the specific fund. This means that the good performance of an individual 'star fund' has disproportionately large effects on all the funds of the family. This effect is amplified by the fact that investors tend to see the positive performance of the best-performing funds of the family without being influenced by the underperforming ones. This makes a 'star' performing fund have a positive spillover effect on the inflows of the other funds in the same family, even if there seems to be no negative effect from poorly performing funds ('dogs') (Nanda et al., 2003). Incubation fund strategies are used by the families to amplify this effect (Evans, 2009).

The convex flow-performance relationship, linear fee structure and positive spillover externalities provide the rationale for the existence of families as well-structured marketing devices. Families generate many funds in order to capitalise on the convex flow-performance sensitivity and the positive sensitivity of profits to risk. Offering many funds is just like creating many options. The same way a portfolio of options is worth more than the option on a portfolio, a family offering many funds is worth more than an individual fund with a similar amount of assets under management. Enhanced risk-taking at the fund level and fund proliferation are related ways of implementing this strategy. Market segmentation and fund proliferation are marketing strategies used by families to exploit investors' heterogeneity, showing the positive spillover that having a 'star' fund provides to all the funds belonging to the same family. New mutual funds are added to the overall family menu as a function of economies of scale and scope, the family's prior performance, and the overall level of funds invested.

Families do also coordinate actions across funds in order to enhance the performance of the funds that are the most valuable to the family, even if this comes at the expense of the performance of other member funds. For example, families can charge different levels of fees on each of its member funds, making different funds contribute unequally to the total family profit. Alternatively, families may enhance the performance of funds likely to become stars or which are already the best-performing ones ('cross-subsidisation') (Gaspar et al., 2006).

Evidence supports the existence of family cross-subsidisation. This takes the form of enhancement of the performance of high-fee funds at the expense of low-fee ones, enhancement of the performance of currently high-performing funds – i.e. funds with high year-to-date performance likely to be well placed in fund rankings – at the expense of low-performing funds, and enhancement of the performance of young funds at the expense of old funds. This behaviour is more prevalent at times when the styles of 'low-value' funds are doing relatively well, but is scaled down when the styles of these funds are underperforming, and this is more common in families that are large, manage many funds and are heterogeneous in terms of the size of the funds they offer.

How does this subsidisation take place? One way is through cross-trades. The family directly coordinates the trades of its member funds so that the 'low-value' funds trade in the market to buffer the price pressure of orders by the 'high-value' fund, or directly cross-buy and -sell orders with the 'high-value' funds without going to the open market ('cross-trading'). Another way is through preferential allocation of the 'best deals' to the favoured funds. For example, fund families allocate relatively more underpriced (hotter) IPOs to high-fee and high-past-performance funds.

Mutual funds are not just affiliated with complexes of mutual funds (families), but they often belong to broader financial conglomerates that exercise other activities, such as banking and insurance. In the US alone, approximately 40% of the mutual funds between 1990 and 2004 belonged to such financial conglomerates. This implies that the manager of a fund (e.g. ABN Amro Equity Plus Fund) is effectively working for a broader organisation (ABN Amro) whose main interests may not be aligned with those of the fund holders. This phenomenon is magnified many times in the case of international funds for which the affiliation with big banking and insurance groups is more prevalent.

Affiliation with a financial conglomerate provides mutual funds with access to a broader set of resources, better research facilities, lower transaction costs, and distribution externalities. For example, the manager of a fund affiliated with a group that also has a commercial bank may use the inside information acquired from the lending activity of the affiliated bank to select stocks. Knowledge of private trading forecasts, confidential reports, and presentations at bankers' meetings could be an invaluable resource that might help these funds in identifying the right stocks to invest in. A firm taking out a loan generally agrees to provide the lender with certain information, sometimes including monthly financial updates. Investors in a public company's stocks or bonds, by contrast, receive only quarterly reports. If a firm is considering whether to refinance debt or secure financing for a merger or acquisition, it could share those intentions with the lenders. Firms with problems threatening to break the terms of a loan must disclose them to the lenders.

While such sharing of information violates the law, and the Securities and Exchange Commission (SEC) has repeatedly tried to enforce it by sanctioning firms doing it, there is now ample evidence that this has not discouraged funds from taking advantage of it. US evidence documents the fact that funds condition their investment activity on the lending decisions of their affiliated banks. Mutual funds affiliated to lending banks, on average, increase their holdings in the stocks of borrowing firms around the initiation of the loan deal. This helps to boost fund net-of-risk performance (Massa and Rehman, 2005). This may just be the result of mutual funds being located in close geographical proximity to their affiliated banks as opposed to a deliberate coordinated activity at the family level. However, this still makes it more convenient to have families.

What are the implications of the family model for the investors? It does not seem that investors benefit from such strategies in terms of subsequent period returns. However, the family model may help to explain the apparent inconsistency between the performance results at the fund level and those at the family level. While there is no or very scarce evidence of fund performance, there seems to be evidence of performance persistence at the family level. One way to reconcile these results is to argue that families purposefully allocate resources across funds in an unequal way.

The fund structure

A common adage in the industry is that 'fund management always involves more than one person and thus team management is primarily about what you tell the outside world.' According to some industry participants, stars are good for marketing, especially with retail investors, but (named) managers are more expensive to pay. The family model requires a coordinated behaviour of the fund managers and a well-defined attribution of credit for performance. Therefore, the disclosure of the name of the fund manager becomes critical.

While almost any mutual fund is managed by the coordinated behaviour of a team of experts, many funds have nonetheless been consistently marketed as sole-managed funds. That is, mutual fund families have traditionally chosen to identify a specific individual as the manager of each fund. For example, Fidelity's Magellan fund has been closely identified with Peter Lynch.

The choice between named and anonymous management is a strategic decision for the family. By linking the fund and its performance to a named manager, the family shares the credit for the fund performance with the manager. The better the performance, the higher the reputation of the manager is and thus also his bargaining power vis-à-vis the family. This makes the cost of the named manager higher and indirectly increases the fixed cost for the family.

Why would a family do it? For marketing reasons. By naming a manager, the family deliberately chooses the way it channels information to the market and exploits investor psychology. Investors tend to empathise with named managers, being more lenient in the case of negative performance and more bullish in case of positive performance. 'Regret' for having invested in a bad fund is attenuated if the fund manager is known. Nothing of this sort happens for team-managed funds.

This 'empathy' is magnified by the families that play the marketing card. Families buy ads in major newspapers and receive 'soft' media coverage as part of the deal. This coverage generates media mentions that are used to make the market aware of the managers as opposed to the fund themselves. Name-managed funds receive significantly more media mentions than comparable team-managed funds. This higher coverage boosts the fund flows by increasing the sensitivity of the flows to good performance and reducing the sensitivity to bad performance.

Moreover, as a part of a coordinated 'game', cross-family subsidisation helps to boost the performance of the name-managed funds at the expense of the team-managed ones. This is due to both the effort to market the fund and the higher bargaining power of the named managers, who can appropriate more family resources. There is evidence of a broad concerted effort of strategic cross-subsidisation of name-managed funds. For example, name-managed domestic equity funds receive more favourable allocations of underpriced initial public offerings, and name-managed international equity funds experience less dilution from market timing or late trading (Massa et al., 2009).

A second important aspect of the overall marketing strategy of the family is the choice of the distribution channel. Mutual funds are distributed through many channels and, when brokers are used, through many different brokers. In the US, an average mutual fund is distributed through 32 different independent brokers. This is over and above the direct distribution network directly managed by the family the fund belongs to as well as the retail network of the branches of the affiliated bank. For example, Fidelity Contrafund is distributed by 34 independent brokers as well as the direct channel run by Fidelity. Unlike other industries, the mutual fund industry is characterised by the lack of exclusivity in the distribution channel.

This glut of brokers does not have cost-reducing goals. Indeed, it does not seem that having more brokers allows the fund to benefit from a lower cost of intermediation obtained by putting the different brokers in competition with one another. Nor does it help to simply increase flows. Indeed, a higher number of brokers, while it helps to attract more flows in the case of a positive performance, drastically increases outflows in the case of negative performance. Therefore, the use of a multiple broker strategy can only be understood in terms of the overall family strategy.

Given that a good performance is amplified by the multiplicity of brokers, the availability of a multiple-broker channel increases the incentives to take risk and deliver higher performance. Funds with more brokers tend to take more risk, hold more illiquid assets and to generate better performance. Also, it induces families to coordinate the multiple-broker strategy with their family 'coordination and cross-subsidisation' strategy. The better performance of some 'subsidised' funds is enhanced by a multiple-broker strategy.

Broker multiplicity also allows the fund to approach different segments and target different segments of the population. For example, some brokers are better at reaching Internet users, while other brokers are better at approaching households and so on. Approaching different clienteles of investors increases the disparity of fund investors' views and priors. Given that funds cannot be sold short, dispersion of opinions among investors increases the value of the fund, but only for the more optimistic investors, while the more pessimistic ones sit on the sidelines. Fund management companies are able to increase the dispersion of opinions by choosing to distribute the funds through many different brokers. Each broker caters to an alternative demand (Massa and Yadav, 2010).

Another key element of the family model is related to its internal organisational form. Consider a typical bond mutual fund. It is organised as a multi-layer hierarchical ('vertical') structure. At the top is the CEO of the fund, below that the head of fixed income and below that again the portfolio manager. How do families choose between a more vertical and a flatter organisational structure? A more vertical structure lends itself to better risk management by helping reduce managerial moral hazard and lowering the incentives to take (un)necessary risk. However, a more vertical structure, by reducing the discretion of the portfolio manager, also lowers his incentive to collect difficult-to-transfer information ('soft information') – i.e. the information based on direct personal interaction with the managers of the firm in question – and to engage in proximity investment.

Given that performance is positively related to the collection of soft information on the firms located close by, more vertical structures, by reducing proximity investment and collection of information, deliver worse performance. Moreover, by forcing 'codification' of the information passed on to a portfolio manager's superiors and by reducing the direct attribution of the fund performance to the portfolio manager, a vertical structure increases the incentives of the manager to herd with the other fund managers and to hold less concentrated portfolios. Both more herding and a more limited collection of soft information result in more hierarchical funds with less concentrated portfolios.

Therefore the family faces a trade-off between better performance and flatter structures and between better risk/managerial control and more vertical structures. And indeed, more risk-conscious families tend to prefer more vertical structures. Overall, the organisational structure imposed by the family directly affects performance and impacts proximity investment, herding and portfolio concentration (Massa and Zhang, 2009).

A view to the future

The last decade has witnessed a growing threat to the family model. A main direct threat has come from the gradual disappearance of the main characteristics of the family model. The need to compete with cheap no-load index funds has reduced the ability of the families to impose high load fees. This has made it more difficult to remunerate a multi-broker distribution channel. New solutions have involved cross-selling: families have started selling each other funds. Big families now actually act like big supermarkets offering funds from other families as well.

However, the gradual reduction and/or disappearance of load fees and the rise of the 'fund supermarket approach' have also eliminated one of the main reasons for existence of the families themselves. Investors do not need to choose to invest in a big-family fund to take advantage of the free switching option. In fact, investors can freely pick and choose the best funds available across the different families. If these funds are then offered on the same platform by a big fund supermarket, the investor 'free-shopping' attitude is reinforced and the barriers to entry that underpinned the family model collapse.

Also, the past decade has witnessed a decline in the number of name-managed funds. The incidence of anonymous management increased from 4% of the total in 1993 to more than 20% in 2004. One of the main reasons to explain this phenomenon is the increased competition for successful fund managers provided by the rising hedge fund industry. The hedge fund boom has multiplied the outside opportunities of successful named mutual fund managers and therefore increased the expected rent-sharing costs to mutual fund firms of naming their managers.

Finally, the recent scandals on market timing and late trading, as well as the contemporaneous investigations on insider trading in investment banks, have made it more difficult to keep pursuing cross-subsidisation strategies or strategies based on the use of information from the other members of the group the fund is affiliated with.

A second and trickier threat has come from the competition. The family model has come under increasing attack by two alternative competitors: the index funds that provide cheap benchmark replication – i.e. beta strategies – and the hedge funds that provide better performance, i.e. alpha strategies. Greater financial sophistication of the investors and a refocussing of the interest of both hedge funds and mutual funds in big institutional clients such as endowments or pension funds have made it more difficult for families to keep playing the same marketing game.

Mutual funds suffer from legal constraints – inability to borrow, short-sell and use derivatives – as well as structural limitations from the shorter and more unstable investment horizons of its investors. These greatly hamper the ability of mutual funds to directly compete with the hedge funds in the alpha generation process. At the same time, however, the rise of index funds and more recently of exchange traded funds (ETFs) has cornered the market in a low-cost game that heavy-structure high-fixed-cost organisations such as mutual fund families cannot successfully play.

The combined effect of these direct and indirect developments has made it doubtful that the industry will proceed in the same way in the immediate future. There are two main alternative outcomes. The first is a blurring of the line between mutual funds and hedge funds. This may come from the mutual funds being allowed to operate in the same way as the hedge funds or from a new regulation forcing the hedge funds to behave like mutual funds. Allowing the mutual funds to operate like hedge funds involves allowing them to short, invest in derivatives and lever up. It may also involve lifting the restrictions on the classes of assets in which mutual funds can invest and on the way managers can be compensated. The alternative is to force upon the hedge funds the same regulations that now apply to every fund targeting retail investors. In terms of overall efficiency, clearly the former solution is the one that would increase the efficiency of the system.

For example, abolition of the imposition of fulcrum fees and a higher reliance on performance fees would not only increase the ability of the mutual funds to deliver better performance, but would also drastically change the incentives beyond the family model. Indeed, family affiliation would become important in terms of resource sharing – e.g. research – but the incentive to pursue marketing strategies based on fund proliferation would be reduced. The studies showing that more incentives reduce herding and therefore lower the incentive to ride the bubble also suggest that this change could be welfare-enhancing, as it would reduce the excesses linked to the existence of a price bubble. However, after the more recent crisis, the second solution – a so-called 'retailisation' of the hedge fund industry – is clearly becoming more likely. While less efficient and more demagogic, this solution seems the only one that is politically feasible.

The second scenario does not involve a blurring of the line between mutual funds and hedge funds. In this case, the better ability of the hedge funds to deliver performance – alpha – and of the index funds to deliver replication of risk factors – beta – would in the long run almost make it impossible for the mutual funds to support the competition. The industry answer would be an even greater stress on the family model and on marketing and branding. Mutual funds would offer additional – non-performance-related – features that would allow them to compete on other parameters, e.g. services and convenience. The application of this model to its extreme consequences would involve the transformation of the mutual fund families into providers of sophisticated advice to the retail investors. These investors would find it costly to invest directly in hedge funds, given the investment limits and given their lack of diffused distribution networks.

There are, however, two other factors that will help the industry and slow down its transformation. The first is the relationship with the banks. Outside the US, the dominant model sees a strict connection between commercial banking and mutual funds. This provides a unique distribution network that will 'push' the bank-affiliated funds through the local bank branches. This effectively segments the market, keeping unwanted competition at bay.

The second element is the role of the government. In most countries investors are forced to invest in poorly performing mutual funds simply because they are the only vehicles that can legally be used to defer capital gains. A typical example is France. A French investor willing to defer capital gains taxes can only invest in vehicles that are listed in France or the EU (the so-called *Plan d'Epargne en Actions,* or PEA).

If the investment is above a certain relatively low threshold (about 132,000 euros), the investment can only take the form of 'life insurance contracts', which are effectively a form of investing in the asset management industry with the possibility of deferring capital gains. However, they only allow investment in mutual funds; index funds and hedge funds are effectively ruled out. This segmentation created at the expense of the taxpayer will allow an underperforming industry to survive for a long time, with negative implications in terms of value destruction.

Policy and normative implications

The family model – and especially fund cross-subsidisation or fund support – has relevant ethical and legal implications. Indeed, this model distorts the incentives of fund managers, possibly inducing them to sacrifice the interests of fund investors if the overall family stands to benefit. Even if the likely aggregate effect of cross-fund subsidisation is zero, the gains accruing to investors in subsidised funds are still borne by subsidising fund investors. This practice can represent a breach of fiduciary duty.

At the same time, however, practices such as the use of inside information accruing from separate parts of the same financial conglomerate are not detrimental to mutual fund investors and may actually be highly advantageous to them.

Finally, practices such as using some funds to smoothen the market impact of other funds with no systematic bias in the direction of specific funds may actually increase performance for all the investors in the funds of the family. And indeed, this is one of the arguments used by the mutual fund industry to argue in favour of lifting the restrictions on within-family cross-trades.

It is therefore difficult to pass judgment on the family model per se without properly accounting for both the pros – sizable economies of scales and scope, potentially better research and information – and the cons – cross-subsidisation and excess wastage in marketing activities.

However, there is one dimension in which the 'social implications' of mutual fund behaviour can be properly assessed: the impact on financial markets. This is rooted in the linkage between fund flows and fund portfolio strategy. The logic is simple. If a US fund holds equity of both Japanese firms and US firms, a shock to the US market may be transmitted to the Japanese market even if no direct shock takes place there. Indeed, the US funds facing redemption calls may sell Japanese stocks in order not to realise a loss by selling US assets whose price has collapsed. This behaviour induces a transmission of the crisis that is not mere contagion, as very often no direct link exists between different assets in different countries or between different classes of assets – e.g. corporate bonds and ABS or MBS – except the joint ownership by financial investors.

A typical example on this transmission role of mutual funds is provided by the recent subprime crisis. As the crisis started, mutual funds were holding a lot of 'toxic' assets, i.e. ABS and MBS. In September 2007, their value collapsed and the market froze. The crisis almost immediately spread from the toxic market to the corporate bonds market. Yields on lower-quality bonds jumped, while high-quality bonds did not seem to be affected. Mutual fund investment behaviour directly contributed to this transmission.

The drop in value of one class of assets – the toxic ones – induced the mutual funds to sell other assets in order to meet potential redemption claims. In particular, funds realised that selling toxic assets would have meant the realisation of sizable capital losses, while selling liquid assets and holding the toxic ones would have allowed postponement of the loss. The ensuing drop in performance would have triggered outflows. They therefore decided to sell their most liquid assets first. In particular, mutual funds with short-term investor horizons did not sell their most liquid assets – above investment grade bonds – first, as a high probability of large future withdrawals induced them to store away liquidity for the future needs (Manconi et al., 2010).

Mutual funds started out by first selling the more liquid assets, but they proceeded first with the assets that were relatively less liquid in order to store the most liquid ones for the future. Thus they sold mostly thinly traded bonds or bonds for which there was a paucity of readily-available counterparties in the market: the low-rated corporate bonds. This induced the crisis to spread from the financial sector – toxic assets – to the corporations, which had a real effect on their ability to raise sub-investment grade bonds. Therefore, the role of mutual funds in directly transmitting the crisis from the sector of toxic assets to the more liquid corporate bond market helps to explain the jump in the spread between low-quality corporate bonds and high-quality bonds.

At the same time, however, and as we argued above, some funds also belong to financial conglomerates containing the banks that participate in the securitised debt markets and perform due diligence on the instruments. Affiliation with a bank provides the institutional investor with inside information acquired from the lending activity of the affiliated bank to select stocks. At the same time, however, affiliation with a conglomerate may constrain the fund manager and reduce his freedom to manoeuvre. The fund manager may be required to pursue the interests of the group at the expense of those of the investors, for example, by loading up on stocks of firms to which the banking arm of the group is lending in order to support the stock price of these firms.

Recent evidence suggests that, in the case of a crisis, institutional investors are constrained by their affiliation with the bank or actually use the inside information. Some fund-affiliated institutions are used in support of the overall policy of the bank of the group of which they are part, while other funds are helped by the use of inside information. Both behaviours affected the transmission mechanism in the crisis. Indeed, while the first set of considerations induced a short-term international institution to sell Japanese stocks even though the crisis originated in the US, banking affiliation reduced this incentive, slowing transmission of the crisis to the stocks of the firm to which the affiliated bank was lending.

Overall, the role of the investor flows in affecting mutual fund behaviour has deep implications in terms of the role of international institutional investors (e.g. mutual funds, insurance companies, hedge funds and pension funds) in propagating financial market instability and on the mediating role of the banking sector. Indeed, turmoil in one class of assets trade in a geographical region propagates to other classes of assets in other regions.

References

Carhart, M.M. (1997), 'On persistence in mutual fund performance', *Journal of Finance*, 52(1): 57–82.

Chen, J., S. Hanson, H. Hong and J. Stein (2008), 'Do hedge funds profit from mutual-fund distress?', working paper.

Chen, J., H. Hong, M. Huang and J. Kubik (2002), 'Does fund size erode performance? Liquidity, organizational diseconomies and active money management', working paper.

Chevalier, J. and G. Ellison (1997), 'Risk taking by mutual funds as a response to incentives', *Journal of Political Economy*, 105: 1167–1200.

Chevalier, J. and G. Ellison (1999), 'Career concerns of mutual fund managers', *Quarterly Journal of Economics*, 114: 389–432.

Coval, J.D. and T.J. Moskowitz (1999), 'Home bias at Home: local equity preference in domestic portfolios', *Journal of Finance*, 54: 2045–2073.

Coval, J.D. and T.J. Moskowitz (2001), 'The geography of investment: Informed trading and asset prices', Journal of Political Economy, 109: 811–841.

Coval, J. and E. Stafford (2007), 'Asset fire sales (and purchases) in equity markets', *Journal of Financial Economics*, 86: 479–512.

Edelen, R.M. (1999), 'Investor flows and the assessed performance of open-end mutual funds', *Journal of Financial Economics*, 53: 439–466.

Evans, R. (2009), 'Mutual funds incubation', working paper.

Gaspar, J., M. Massa and P. Matos (2006), 'Favoritism in mutual fund families? Evidence on strategic cross-fund subsidization', *Journal of Finance*, 73–104.

Ferreira, M., M. Massa and P. Matos (2010), 'Strategic market coverage and mutual fund performance', working paper.

Guedj, I. and J. Papastaikoudi (2004), 'Can mutual fund families affect the performance of their funds?', MIT working paper.

Hong, H., J.D. Kubik and J. Stein (2004), 'Social interaction and stock market participation', *Journal of Finance*, 59(1): 137–163.

Hong, H., J.D. Kubik and J.C. Stein (2005), 'Thy neighbour's portfolio: Word-of-mouth effects in the holdings and trades of money managers', *Journal of Finance*, 60(6): 2801–2824.

Manconi, M., M. Massa and A. Yasuda (2010), 'The behavior of intoxicated investors: the role of institutional investors in propagating the financial crisis of 2007–2008', working paper.

Massa, M. (1998), 'Why so many mutual funds? Mutual fund families, market segmentation and financial performance', INSEAD mimeo.

Massa, M. (2003), 'How do family strategies affect fund performance? When performance maximization is not the only game in town', *Journal of Financial Economics*, 67: 249–304.

Massa, M. and L. Phalippou (2005), 'Mutual funds and the market for liquidity', working paper.

Massa, M. and P. Matos (2005), 'Beyond Grid? How style categorization affects mutual fund performance', working paper.

Massa, M. and Z. Rehman (2005), 'Information flows within financial conglomerates: Evidence from the banks-mutual funds relationship', *Journal of Financial Economics*, forthcoming.

Massa, M. and V. Yadav (2010), 'Mutual fund demand and multiple brokers', working paper.

Massa, M and L. Zhang (2009), 'The effects of organizational structure on asset management', working paper.

Massa, M. and R. Patgiri (2009), 'Incentives and mutual fund performance: Higher performance or just higher risk taking?' *Review of Financial Studies*, forthcoming.

Massa, M., J. Reuter and E. Zitzewitz (2009), 'When should firms share credit with employees? Evidence from anonymously managed mutual funds', *Journal of Financial Economics*, forthcoming.

Myers, M., J.M. Poterba, D. Shackelford and J.B. Shoven (2009), 'Copycat funds: Information disclosure regulation and the returns to active management in the mutual fund industry', working paper.

Nanda, V., J. Wang and L. Zheng (2003), 'Family values and the star phenomenon', University of Michigan working paper.

Sirri, E. and P. Tufano (1998), 'Costly search and mutual fund flows', *Journal of Finance*, 53: 1589–1622.

Wermers, R. (2000), 'Mutual fund performance: An empirical decomposition into stock-picking talent, style, transaction costs, and expenses', *Journal of Finance*, 55(4): 1655–1695.

About the author

Karel Lannoo has been chief executive of the Centre for European Policy Studies (CEPS) since 2000 and senior research fellow since 1997. CEPS is one of the leading independent European think tanks, with a strong reputation in economic and foreign policy research. It has total revenues of €7m (2010) and employs about 50 people. Mr. Lannoo has published books and numerous articles in specialised magazines and journals on general European policy, and specifically financial regulation and supervision matters. He has spoken at several hearings held by the European Parliament, Commission and related institutions and has participated in studies for national and international bodies (EU institutions, OECD, ADB, World Bank). He is a regular speaker at international gatherings and in executive programmes. Before joining CEPS, Mr. Lannoo was employed in the cultural sector and worked for the Italian conglomerate Ferruzzi and a professional federation. He was also active as a freelance writer for several specialised financial sector publications. Karel Lannoo holds a baccalaureate in philosophy, an M.A. in history from the University of Leuven in Belgium (1985) and obtained a post-graduate in European studies (CEE) from the University of Nancy in France (1986). Mr. Lannoo is an independent director of BME (Bolsas Y Mercados Espanoles), the company which runs the Madrid stock exchange. He also directs the European Capital Markets Institute (ECMI) and the European Credit Research Institute (ECRI), both separate legal entities which are managed by CEPS.

Contact: klannoo@ceps.eu

4
Regulatory challenges for the European asset management industry

ABSTRACT The European asset management industry is in a squeeze from different sides in growing prudential, product and conduct regulation. A new directive, UCITS IV, has only recently been enacted, and new challenges are emerging in the regulation of hedge and venture capital funds, the review of the regulatory regime of depositaries, and amendments to the MiFID Directive. In addition, a new European supervisory framework is in the making, which implies much stricter controls on enforcement. This is happening in the context of one of the biggest declines in the industry in the past two decades, something many fund managers have not yet overcome. This article reviews the recent changes in the EU's asset management industry and discusses the regulatory framework for asset management and the challenges ahead. It focusses primarily on the UCITS and emerging non-UCITS investment fund regime, and its interaction with the MiFID regime covering investment services. It also makes a comparison with the US regulatory regime and puts this into the context of the global challenges.

4 Regulatory challenges for the European asset management industry

by Karel Lannoo

Introduction

The European asset management industry is in a squeeze from different sides in growing prudential, product and conduct regulation.[1] A new directive, UCITS (Undertakings in Collective Investments in Transferable Securities) IV, has only recently been enacted, and new challenges are emerging in the regulation of hedge and venture capital funds, the review of the regulatory regime of depositaries, and amendments to the MiFID (Markets in Financial Instruments Directive) directive. In addition, a new European supervisory framework is in the making, which implies much stricter controls on enforcement. This is happening in the context of one of the biggest declines in the industry in the past two decades, something many fund managers have not yet overcome. The era of light regulation is thus definitely over.

In regulatory terms, the asset management industry as such does not exist. Rather, the regulatory regime depends upon the particular licence that the financial institution in question possesses: it could be licensed as an asset management company, a bank, an insurance company, a pension fund, a broker or an investment fund, which immediately raises the question of possible inconsistencies across regulatory regimes, duplication or arbitrage among regimes. For certain segments of the asset management business, the choice of regulatory regime will be non-existent, as they unambiguously fall into one of the aforementioned categories; for others, however, the vertical regulatory framework does not lend itself well to the range of activities they undertake. This is especially true of investment firms that may manufacture and distribute insurance, pensions and investment products, all while conducting regular banking activities such as deposit-taking.

The diversity across the EU of the institutional framework governing the sector is striking. It reflects fundamental differences in consumer preferences, cultural habits and institutional heritage, and it explains the variation from one country to another in the relative importance of these various sectors as conduits of financial intermediation. Although sectoral regulation has been harmonised to a great extent at the European level, implementation of EU rules may vary, with supervisory structures and practices continuing to differ from country to country.

In this chapter,[2] we will, after a brief review of the recent changes in the EU's asset

---

1   A brief comparison with the regulatory challenges facing US investment funds is highlighted in the box insert at the end of this chapter (see box on page 87).

2   This chapter draws upon a 2007–2008 CEPS task force report; see Casey and Lannoo (2008).

management industry, discuss the regulatory framework for asset management and the challenges ahead. We focus primarily on the UCITS and emerging non-UCITS investment fund regime, and its interaction with the MiFID regime covering investment services. We will make reference to the treatment under other regimes, as necessary.

The fund management industry

The crisis fundamentally changed the face of the asset management industry, allowing the insurance industry to re-emerge as the leading player. Of the three traditional groups of institutional investors – investment funds, insurance companies and pension funds – the first had dominated the sector in total asset terms since 2004. By the end of the third quarter of 2009, net assets of the European investment fund industry totalled €6,840bn, an increase of 12.4% as compared to end 2008, but still a decline of 14.5% as compared to the end of 2007, when net assets totalled €7,909bn. In comparison, by the end of 2008, European insurance industry assets totalled €6,910bn, a decline of 5% as compared to end 2007. The pension funds managed assets totalling €3,094bn by the end of 2007, which are expected to have declined by 15–20% by the end of 2008.[3]

The dramatic decline in the European investment fund industry in 2008 was a reflection of the extraordinary events in financial markets around that period, with huge declines in global stock markets and big outflows of money out of the financial system – and out of equity investment funds in particular. The decline in the European investment fund industry was even more dramatic, as equity funds comprise only 35% of funds in Europe (by assets), and a significant part of these assets were invested in funds with a guaranteed minimum equity. By comparison, the European insurance industry, which also manages long-term saving plans in life insurance products and group insurance plans, managed to consolidate its image as a truly long-term institutional investor.

As Figure 1 suggests, the evolution of the European and US fund industry has been fairly comparable in previous years, although the recent decline was more pronounced in the EU, as was the recovery in the USA. Assets managed by the EU and US fund industry amount to 88% of the global fund management industry (according to ICI).

Events in financial markets had a direct bearing on the investment fund industry, and on its future structure. The demise of Lehman Brothers revealed that some funds were blocked in the bankruptcy procedures, as derivative financial instruments were used by the bank in the management of the funds. Some banks had also made use of structured products (CDOs) to support guaranteed equity products. The large-scale fraud by Bernard Madoff, which was revealed at the end of 2008, was a further blow

---

3 The sources for sector data are taken from the European professional organisations: EFAMA for investment funds (ICI for the USA), CEA for insurance companies and EFRP for pension funds. Investment fund data do not include data for private equity and hedge funds, as the latter are mostly domiciled outside the EU.

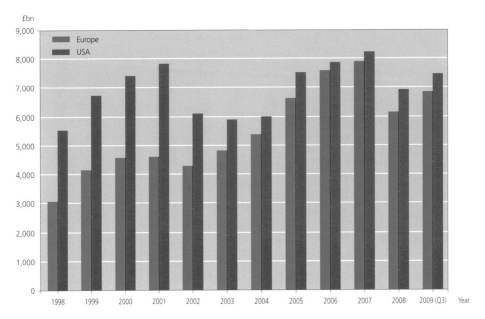

Fig. 1. European and US total net fund assets compared. Sources: EFAMA and ICI. European data include UCITS (about 75%) and special funds (including limited number of hedge funds); US data include primarily mutual funds (about 90%), closed-ended funds, exchange-traded funds and units of investment trusts. Q3 data for the last three were at the moment of writing not yet available.

to the fund industry, but also signalled that regulatory issues should be dealt with at a global level. Many European professional fund managers had invested in Madoff funds (in fund of funds or feeder fund structures) but had not taken proper measures to ensure a complete separation between fund manager and depositary or custodian.

The decline in the European fund industry emphasised even more the need for further consolidation in the fund industry, as the average size per fund declined. The average size of European funds is one-fifth of that of an average US fund. The sub-optimal average UCITS fund size brings about higher operational costs for investment management, a high total expense ratio (TER) and duplication of infrastructure.[4] In this sense, the asset management industry performs below its potential, the cost of which is passed on to the user. The main causes are to be found in the high level of fragmentation, the absence among investors and firms of a European market concept and the remunerative *niche* markets that funds can target, exploiting differences in tax and regulatory regimes across Europe. The UCITS IV amendments, discussed below, address only some of these challenges.

The long-term impact of the financial crisis for the fund industry is not yet entirely clear, but some initial conclusions could be drawn. Firstly, too many funds were too closely run by the deposit-taking banks as alternative savings instruments. Today,

---

4   The average total expense ratio in Europe is easily 25 to 50% higher than in the USA, where it is 0.85% for equity funds and 63% for bond funds (ICI data).

about 75–80% of the funds are distributed by banks in the EU, a situation that can hardly be considered healthy in the aftermath of the financial crisis. Hence, measures should be expanded to support the separation between banks and fund managers and to come to a truer application of the open architecture framework. This calls for, amongst other things, a stricter application of conflict of interest rules, as enshrined in the EU's MiFID Directive.

The UCITS regime

With the latest changes in the course of implementation, the UCITS regime governing the EU's investment fund sector has reached a high degree of maturity, but a high degree of complexity as well. The latest legislative text, which consolidates the different measures in one single document, should open a further phase of truly pan-European consolidation of the sector, but at the cost of a higher degree of specialisation. Compared to the initial 1985 Directive, UCITS IV is five times longer, measured by the wordiness of the text (Directive 2009/65/EC).

EU regulation governing the free provision of financial services in the asset management industry across borders under home country rules started with the UCITS Directive of 1985. The UCITS Directive introduced harmonised *product* regulation for investment funds that were allowed for cross-border sales in the EU (and the countries of the European Economic Area). It was followed in the early 1990s by directives defining the terms under which the banking, insurance and investment services sectors could 'passport' their *services* across the EU on the basis of authorisation from their home state regulator (see the table in Appendix 1).

The UCITS Directive was amended and expanded in 2002 and later in 2009 to become more of a horizontal asset management directive to reflect the increasing convergence of the core sectors of the financial services industry. An agreement was also reached in 2002 on the last outstanding piece of free provision of cross-border services regulation in the financial services sector, the pension funds directive. In the meantime, the new wave of the Financial Services Action Plan (FSAP) had started to come into effect, most importantly with the MiFID Directive.

The 1985 UCITS Directive opened the way for the cross-border sale of investment funds in the EU. Subject to some general criteria regarding authorisation, legal structure, investment policies and disclosure, units of open-ended funds that invested in transferable securities could be sold freely throughout the EU. Marketing and tax rules do not fall within the scope of this directive, which means that they remain regulated by host-country regulators. Prospectuses have to be translated into the official language of the host country, for example, and local consumer protection regulation – often very different from one country to the next – must be respected. The 1985 Directive did not harmonise the prudential requirements of the companies managing investment funds either, e.g. it did not set a minimum capital standard or solvency requirements. This was subsequently modified by the 2002 amendments.

The asset allocation rules of the first UCITS directive were essentially quantitative. UCITS funds could invest in a diversified portfolio of listed equity and debt securities, respecting the 5/10/40% rule: 5% limits apply to stock of a single body (which can be extended to 10% by the home country authorities), and an overall limit of 40% for the total of large single blocks of securities. A limit of 10% applied for non-listed securities. Exceptions applied for government or government-guaranteed paper. The limit applicable for investment in other funds was 5% of the whole portfolio, meaning that funds of funds were not permitted. Real estate and commodity funds were excluded from the directive, as were other alternative investments, including hedge funds and private equity, and money market instruments.

The 2002 UCITS amendments expanded the scope of activities that were possible under the UCITS I Directive. One directive – the UCITS III Product Directive – widens fund investment options to include instruments such as derivatives and allows for new types of funds such as funds of funds, money market funds, cash funds or index tracker funds. A second directive – the UCITS III Management Directive – detailed minimum standards, including the introduction of a minimum level of own funds to be held by a fund management company for prudential purposes, and broadened the permissible activities of the fund management company. It also introduced a simplified prospectus, which requires key factual information about a UCITS to be presented to investors in an accessible and uniform format.

The UCITS III Management Directive grants the 'single license' to fund management companies in the broad sense of the word. It comprises not only the management of investment funds – the core services – but also other activities related to portfolio management, such as pension funds for individuals, investment advice, safekeeping (custody) and administration of investment funds, which are classified as non-core or ancillary services.[5]

In 2007, the European Commission proposed a further set of amendments to the directive. UCITS IV was formally adopted by the EU in April 2009 and must be implemented by July 2011 at the latest. The latest amendments formally allow for a genuine European passport for UCITS management companies, allowing for the separation between the location of the management company and the location where funds are registered. UCITS IV facilitates cross-border mergers of UCITS funds, which will make it possible to increase the average size of European funds. In the same vein, UCITS IV allows for master-feeder structures, which had previously been specifically excluded due to fund diversification rules.[6] All these measures should allow for entity

---

5   Other forms of portfolio management, i.e. management of pension fund portfolios or those of individuals, are presented as a form of derogation from the central objective of the directive, which is management of investment funds as authorised under the directive (Art. 5).

6   A feeder UCITS is a UCITS or an investment compartment thereof that invests at least 85% of its assets in one other UCITS, called the 'master UCITS'.

pooling, generate scale economies and thus contribute to a consolidation of the sector, which should serve the end users of funds. UCITS IV further eases cross-border marketing of UCITS by simplifying administrative procedures: there will be immediate market access once the authorisation has been granted by the country of origin of the UCITS. The host country will be able to monitor the commercial documents but not to block access to the market.

UCITS IV should also improve investor information by creating a standardised summary information document, the 'key investor document (KID)', which should make it easier for consumers to understand the product. The KID will replace the simplified prospectus of the UCITS III. One objective is to improve the supervision of UCITS funds and of the companies that manage them through enhanced cooperation between supervisors: the directive encourages the exchange of information between supervisors, harmonises the powers of supervisors and allows for the possibility of on-the-spot investigations, consultation and mutual-aid mechanisms for the imposition of penalties, in particular.

Notwithstanding the recent decline, UCITS is considered a European regulatory success and a worldwide brand. It started from a limited basis in 1985, covering product rules for equity, bond and money market funds, which are still intact in the latest amendments, although the scope of the directive has been considerably enlarged. The UCITS III Product Directive signalled a first expansion and allowed for funds investing in money market instruments, bank deposits, financial derivatives, index funds, units of other UCITS and non-UCITS funds (funds of funds). The investment limits of the 1985 Directive have been further detailed, depending on the instruments. Overall, the 5/10/40% rule continues to apply. Maximum levels of 10% apply for investments in money market instruments issued by the same entity, and of 20% for investments in one other UCITS fund (for funds of funds and index tracker funds or exchange-traded funds) and for deposits with credit institutions. Investments in non-UCITS funds are limited to 30% of the assets of the UCITS fund.

In 2007, the EU adopted an implementing directive (Directive 2007/16/EC) which details the asset classes eligible for inclusion in UCITS funds: asset-backed securities, listed closed-end funds, Euro commercial paper, index-based derivatives and credit derivatives. This decision makes use of the limited (and only) 'comitology' provisions under UCITS I, which allow for clarifications to the definitions to be made via a simple decision taken in the European Securities Committee (the so-called 'Level 2 Committee').[7] These changes allowed for the use of hedge-fund based techniques in UCITS funds, such as the 130/30 funds.

The European Commission also adopted two recommendations in 2004 explaining its interpretation of the information to be provided in the simplified prospectus

---

7 'Comitology' provisions allow changes to be made to an EU measure without going through the formal EU decision-making process, but by the agreement of a specialised committee. This only applies for those articles of a directive or regulation where this was foreseen in the original text.

and on the use of financial derivative instruments in UCITS funds. The first recommendation establishes common interpretations of the presentation and measurement of fund performance, subscription and redemption fees, soft commissions and fee-sharing arrangements (Commission Recommendation 2004/384/EC). The Commission recommended that a total expense ratio (TER) should be disclosed, as well as the expected cost structure, i.e. an indication of all costs applicable; all subscription and redemption charges and other expenses directly paid by the investor; an indication of all the other costs not included in the TER; and the portfolio turnover rate. Equally, it established that the existence of fee-sharing agreements and soft commissions must be disclosed. The second recommendation proposes a uniform understanding of risk measurement methodologies in the UCITS area with regard to derivative products (Commission Recommendation 2004/383/EC).

In addition, the European Commission adopted an interpretative communication in 2007 on the respective powers of the home and the host member state in the marketing of UCITS, which tried to elaborate on a common understanding of some unclear provisions of the UCITS III Directive discussed above (COM[2007]112). According to the European Commission's interpretation, home member states clearly have exclusive responsibilities under UCITS III on which the host member states should not encroach. The residual host country areas of authority are advertising, marketing and the distribution infrastructure as strictly related to UCITS. Host member state rules falling outside the scope of the directive are, in any event, harmonised at the EU level under MiFID and various marketing and consumer protection directives, according to the European Commission. This interpretative communication was adopted by the European Commission in March 2007, awaiting the results of the White Paper and the consultation process of the UCITS review, which resulted in UCITS IV.

In response to the Madoff scandal, which broke out at the end of 2008, the European Commission started an investigation on the application of the depositary safe-keeping duties. Madoff revealed that European asset managers had not properly applied the segregation of fund management from depositary, which is an obligation in the EU according to UCITS (but not in the USA), but also that the UCITS rule had not been correctly implemented in the EU member states. The problem is, however, that once certain derivative financial instruments are allowed to be used in UCITS funds, a 100% separation between fund manager and depositary is very costly to implement.

Creating an EU regime for non-regular funds

The financial crisis crystallised a consensus that European or global regulation of alternative funds was necessary. Before 2008, the dramatic growth of hedge funds assets was not seen to necessitate a regulatory response. The registration of these funds was considered to be sufficient.

The London G20 summit (April 2009) attendees agreed that "all systemically important financial institutions, markets and instruments should be subject to an appropriate degree of regulation and oversight." Leaders of the world's main economies intended to put an end to regulatory arbitrage, seen to be one of the drivers of the crisis. The G20 said hedge funds should be registered and disclose information about their leverage to supervisors. In addition, they should be subject to effective risk management.

The EU's draft directive follows the G20 commitment. The problem was to find a comprehensive way of regulating the sector, as many of the funds are registered in off-shore jurisdictions. The EU's draft directive applies to *managers* of alternative investment funds – wherever they are registered – not only to the funds. In this sense, and by adding a reciprocity provision, the Commission ensures that all of the non-harmonised funds sector that falls outside the scope of the UCITS Directive is covered, including also private equity, commodity and real estate funds. Managers of funds domiciled in third countries will be able to provide services in the EU provided their domestic regulatory regime is considered to be equivalent.

The Commission proposal follows the provisions of the UCITS Directive and MiFID (see below) on the conduct of business; organisational (including outsourcing), reporting and prudential requirements. The draft added elements that have come up in the crisis, such as the need for appropriate liquidity management, segregation between asset management and the depositary function, and additional reporting requirements for highly leveraged funds.

The draft directive applies some 'generous' thresholds: it will not be applicable to leveraged funds below €100m or to non-leveraged funds below €500m. Such thresholds do not apply to investment advisers or asset managers that fall under the EU's MiFID (brokers) or UCITS rules. The transparency threshold for private equity funds with stakes in non-listed companies is 30%, while it is 3% for listed companies. In addition, 'empty' voting rights (a common tool for alternative funds) will indirectly be included in the threshold set by the proposal.

Although intensely criticised by the industry, which claims it will lead to a flight of fund activities out of the EU, the draft creates a single licence for non-regular funds in the EU, something which does not exist at present. More transparency in the hedge funds and private equity sector will be a benefit for users and regulators, and in the end for the industry as well. The directive is expected to be adopted by mid-2010, to be applicable by 2012.

The interaction with MiFID

Whereas, strictly speaking, UCITS regulates products, MiFID regulates investment services, which also include asset management, except for the insurance sector. MiFID, which was adopted in 2004 (Directive 2009/65/EC), updates and replaces the

1993 Investment Services Directive. It allows for the free provision of investment services all over the EU with a single licence, subject to detailed conduct of business and organisational provisions. The problem for the asset management industry is to deal with the intersection between both.

MiFID is probably one of the most far-reaching and complex financial services directives recently enacted in the EU. MiFID brings more competition to exchanges in equity trading by abolishing their monopoly and through the introduction of alternative trading facilities ('systematic internalisers' and 'MTFs'). In return, it imposes much stricter requirements on banks in securities transactions through best execution, client categorisation (suitability and appropriateness test), conflict of interest and transaction reporting requirements, which have been harmonised to a high degree. These measures should reduce transaction costs and increase transparency to users.

In theory, UCITS funds are collective investment undertakings that are coordinated at Community level; hence the funds, their managers and depositaries do not come under MiFID rules. However, UCITS III allowed for discretionary asset management, investment advice and custody and administration, in which case certain MiFID conduct of business rules apply. In addition, up to 80% of UCITS funds are distributed by banks in Europe, meaning that the MiFID rules apply. For the asset management industry, this concerns above all organisational requirements (Article 13 of MiFID), in particular regarding conflicts of interest, and conduct of business obligations (Article 19), in particular client suitability and best execution.

An important issue for the fund management industry is the regime for inducements under MiFID. Inducements are payments by an investment firm of a fee, commission or non-monetary benefit that could place the firm in a situation where it would not be acting in compliance with the principle in MiFID's Article 19(1) requiring the firm to act honestly, fairly and professionally in accordance with the best interests of its clients. This means that firms will have to demonstrate that commission charges do not reflect any bias and facilitate an enhanced service for clients.

Conflict of interest provisions create difficulties for widely accepted distribution practices in the fund management industry, namely the retrocession of fees from product providers to distributors. In particular, in some instances product providers and intermediaries (which are not in the same immediate parent company) may be contemplating significant up-front payments as a condition for the provider's products being placed on, or even considered for, the intermediary's panel or recommended list. These payments would be unconnected with, and additional to, conventional commissions, which would be paid on the sale of particular products. Such payments would not be consistent with the standards of conduct for firms – irrespective of whether they are 'whole of market' or 'multi-tied'. Such introductory payments are thus incompatible with the fundamental principle that a firm must not conduct business under arrangements that might give rise to a conflict with its duty to its clients.

As a result of the financial crisis, some aspects of the MiFID Directive will be reviewed in 2010. This concerns the extension of the pre-trade price transparency provisions to the non-equity markets, particularly bond and derivative markets, and the clarification of the rules applicable to in-house matching by investment banks ('dark pools'). In addition, action can be expected to reinforce the implementation of the directive, more in particular regarding the best execution, client suitability and conflict of interest requirements. The new supervisory set-up, discussed below, is expected to contribute greatly to this.

The impact of the new supervisory set-up

So far, much EU rulemaking is lost at member state level as a result of differences in implementation and enforcement of rules. Under the new supervisory structure, adopted further to the de Larosière report from March 2009, a much tighter control on enforcement and consistent application of rules can be expected. In addition, a new European body will monitor and warn against systemic risk.

The financial crisis revealed serious shortcomings in the oversight of financial markets, which led to the recommendations contained in the de Larosière report, which called for the creation of a European System of Financial Supervisors (ESFS) – comprising three functional authorities covering banking, insurance and securities markets – and a European Systemic Risk Board administered by the European Central Bank. These new authorities will bring a sea change to financial market regulation and supervision in the EU by having the formal responsibility to enforce EU rules and supervise its application by national supervisors. The end goal is to have a single rulebook, i.e. to have exactly the same rules all over the EU.

In the field of asset management, the new supervisory structure means that discussions among member states over interpretations of technical aspects of directives or disagreements among member states as to what is a host and a home responsibility should soon become things of the past. The new authorities will have the formal responsibility to mediate between supervisory authorities and to delegate supervisory powers in the supervision of fund managers, for example.

Towards a horizontal asset management regime

The major challenge for the years to come is to work out a coherent regime for retail investment products and to regain confidence after the crisis. Households are now faced with increasingly difficult investment choices that have ever more serious consequences in light of an ageing population and the increasingly obvious unsustainability of the pay-as-you-go pensions regime. Households are often ill-prepared to make well-informed choices on a self-directed basis due to a lack of financial literacy.

A comparison of various national regimes within the EU covering retail investment products reveals an immense diversity, with a patchwork of different obligations on distributors regarding disclosure and investor protection, different forms of prudential supervision and a high degree of variation in marketing and advertising rules (see appendix). MiFID, with its far-reaching harmonisation of conduct of business rules, is triggering a horizontal review, which is accelerated by the implementation of UCITS IV.

An additional complexity is added to the exercise by the fact that many constituent elements of the retail investment product regime are areas of authority shared by the EU, the member states and the industry, which militates against the emergence of a coherent framework. This problem was clearly stated in the Delmas-Marsalet report, a study that was commissioned by the French Minister of Finance to examine the issue (Autorité des Marchés Financiers, 2005). It proposed a charter for the commercialisation of financial products, covering rules on client suitability and appropriateness, the impartiality of investment advice, the need to better educate and target consumers, and the creation of a financial ombudsman. Properly addressing these concerns would require an extension of the MiFID regime to cover other investment products (such as unit-linked life insurance), cross-sectoral consistency of national implementation of EU legislation (as opposed to merely at the vertical directive level) and the elaboration of pan-European industry codes of conduct.

It is clear that the current EU framework governing retail investment products remains primarily vertical, which will be strengthened by the coming into force of the AIFM directive (see Figure 2). The level of mandatory fiduciary care afforded to retail investors as well as the level of supervision undertaken by regulatory authorities may vary depending on the distribution channel through which they access investment products, even if, in terms of outcomes or payoff profiles, the products are broadly similar. MiFID provides a detailed framework for ensuring a coherent approach to disclosure and point of sale regulation by investment firms for all financial instruments, including all funds and structured notes.

In addition, it includes rules on inducements which influence the remuneration structures that are permissible in the distribution of financial instruments. Nothing comparable exists today at European level for other products (although it may exist at national level). As regards insurance products, the Insurance Mediation Directive only sets out some very basic requirements for insurance intermediaries to deliver advice, taking into account the demands and needs of the policy-holder. For other listed securities, the Prospectus Directive sets out detailed disclosure rules, but addresses marketing rules only to a very limited extent (for example the language regime). For private placements, the MiFID rules will apply to the extent that the products are sold via banks, brokers or financial advisers licensed under this directive. For professional investors and large undertakings, a lighter regime applies.

Products Regime	UCITS	Non-UCITS (i.e. hedge funds)	Life-insurance products (and UCITS distributed by insurers	Listed security	Un-listed security/ structured products
Marketing rules	UCITS/local rules	(AIFM)/ MiFID	Insurance mediation directive	Prospectus directive (part)	–
		Distance marketing of financial services directive (2002/65/EC)			
Disclosure	UCITS/MiFID	(AIFM)/MiFID	Life insurance and insurance mediation directive	Prospectus directive	MiFID
Asset allocation rules	UCITS	(AIFM)	Life insurance or Solvency II directive/ (UCITS)	–	–
Prudential rules	UCITS/MiFID/CRD	(AIFM)CRD	Life insurance or Solvency II directive/ (UCITS)	–	–

Fig. 2. EU regulatory framework for retail investment products (long-term)

In view of the above, elaborating a more coherent regime will be a complex exercise. Some products would be tightly regulated at EU level, whereas for others, there would only be general service level regulation. The problems raised by the interaction of a product directive (UCITS) with a services directive (MiFID) indicate that many questions have yet to be answered.

Conclusion

A well-developed regulatory framework is in place for the asset management industry in the EU. With the arrival of UCITS IV, further consolidation of the EU fund business is in the cards, which should increase its efficiency. More regulation is also expected for the alternative investment fund sector, which will level the playing field with the traditional fund business. The implementation of the new EU supervisory structure will lead to a stricter enforcement of rules, most notably with regard to the conduct of business rules enshrined in MiFID.

Post-crisis, the challenges for the industry and policy makers are to restore confidence and allow a re-diversification of the savings of households. As a result of the financial crisis, the increase in the protection offered by deposit guarantee schemes and the government bail-out of the banking system, savings have concentrated in the banking sector. This is however an unhealthy situation, both for households and the economy, as a proper transfer of savings to productive investments is hindered.

In the long term, the objective should be to create a more coherent framework for a retail investment product regime across sectors. Too many differences remain in the rules applicable to the fund business and other asset managers. This creates distortions of competition, but leads also to inefficiencies and maintains the vertical structure of the financial industry as we know it today. A more open architecture of the financial industry should be the imperative across the board, in the interest of consumers, regulators, central bankers and the public at large.

References and selected bibliography

Autorité des Marchés Financiers (2005), 'Rapport relatif à la commercialisation des produits financiers' (Rapport Delmas-Marsalet).

Casey, J. & K. Lannoo (2008), 'Pouring old wine in new skins. UCITS and Asset Management in the EU after MiFID', *CEPS-ECMI Task force report.*

Cinquegrana, P. (2008), Summary of the open hearing on 'retail investment products', June. Available from http://www.eurocapitalmarkets.org.

European Commission (2009), 'Communication from the Commission to the European Parliament and the Council on packaged retail investment products', April.

European Commission (2009), 'Update on Commission work on packaged retail investment products', December.

Lannoo, K. (2009), 'The road ahead after de Larosière', *CEPS Policy Brief,* August. Available from http://www.ceps.eu.

Loehr, J. (2009), 'Moving from UCITS III to UCITS IV', *RBC Dexia,* May.

US investment funds

The US investment funds that are comparable to UCITS are known as 'mutual funds'. The mutual funds legal regime was laid down about half a century prior to the European one, and is mainly based on federal statutes, i.e. the Investment Company Act of 1940 ('the 1940 Act') and the Investment Advisers Act of 1940, and on additions to or interpretations of the core securities laws, i.e. the 1933 Securities Act and the 1934 Securities Exchange Act.

According to the 1940 Act, fund managers can register four types of investment companies: open-end investment companies (i.e. mutual funds), closed-end investment companies, exchange-traded funds (ETFs) and unit investment trusts (UITs). The vast majority of funds are mutual funds, both in terms of numbers and assets under management – over 90% of the assets are in mutual funds. In comparison to the 1940 Act, the UCITS Directive applies only to open-ended investment funds, as UCITS funds must allow the redemption of their units by investors at any time.

While the UCITS Directive is identified as a product regime, the 1940 Act is more of a horizontal legal regime that regulates the registration, structure and operations of investment companies through a combination of disclosure requirements and other structural and operational requirements, including capital structures, custody of assets, governance, conflicts of interest, and fiduciary duties. Moreover, the 1940 Act includes provisions related to the enforcement of the Act, including public (by the SEC) and private enforcement (through civil actions).

Another difference between Europe and the USA in the legal regime refers to the purpose set by the lawmakers when enacting the rules. The European regulation, i.e. the UCITS Directive, aims at allowing the cross-border provision of European investment fund services, while the purpose of US regulation, i.e. the 1940 Act, was to protect investors from misrepresentation by fund managers and advisers and to ensure that those managers comply with their fiduciary duties and refrain from misusing their powers.

The differences in approach are reflected in the application of the rules in Europe and the USA. In this regard, UCITS is based on a 'voluntary' registration by the fund promoters/managers that are interested in acquiring the so-called 'European Passport' to allow them to distribute their fund across the EU. In contrast, the US 1940 Act is based on an obligatory registration for every company that falls under the statutory definition, unless exempted by the Act.

Unlike the EU, registration of investment companies in the USA is under both state and federal law. A fund can be licensed as a corporation, business, trust, partnership or limited liability company under state law. It is also registered with the SEC as an investment company pursuant to the 1940 Act and authorised to sell its units to the public pursuant to the Securities Act of 1933. In addition, a fund must make additional filings and pay certain fees in each state (except Florida) in which the fund's shares will be offered to the public. In Europe, no central authority is responsible for licensing and monitoring the activities of investment companies. Instead, licensing of investment funds is handled by the national authorities in each Member State and combined with a notification procedure that applies whenever funds are distributed in a Member State other than the one in which it is registered (defined by the UCITS Directive as the 'Host Member State'). Therefore, the US investment companies' regime is considered to be less flexible than the EU regime: in the EU, national law implementing the UCITS Directive applies, while in the USA there is direct application of the federal rules.

The EU is currently considering bringing all non-regular funds under an EU-wide regulatory umbrella in the so-called 'Alternative Investment Fund Managers Directive'. This would bring the entire fund sector under EU rules, with some exemptions for small funds.

	Capital requirements directive (Basel II)	Insurance directives (and Solvency II)	Pension funds directive
Initial capital	Minimum €5m	Minimum €3m guarantee fund (€2m for some classes of non-life insurance). Solvency II will introduce model-based measures.	Where the institution itself underwrites the liability, the rules of the life insurance directive apply.
Additional capital requirements	Minimum 8% of risk-weighted assets (Basel accord) or VAR for trading book (under review).	Solvency margin must be three times the guarantee fund, and a proportion of technical provisions (in general 4%).	(idem)
Permissible activities (non-exhaustive, only when related to asset management)	Portfolio management, safekeeping and administration of securities, trading in and underwriting of securities.	Life insurance (including group insurance). Non-life insurance (large and mass risk).	Management and investment of funded occupational pension schemes.
Asset allocation	Holdings in non-financial institutions limited to 60% of own funds and 15% of a single holding. Large credit exposures to single clients are limited to 800% of own funds and 25% for a single exposure.	Harmonised minimum rules: < 10% single holding of real estate < 5% non-listed securities < 10% of assets in single security, except for public debt, and < 40% for total large exposures of blocks of 5% < 20% in other currency than liabilities. These quantitative restrictions are abolished by Solvency II.	Prudent Man Rule. Member states may set more stringent rules for institutions active on their territory, but within certain limits. Investment in sponsoring undertaking are limited to 5% of the technical provisions.
Conduct of business	Host country rules on advertising and 'general good'	Host country rules on advertising and 'general good' provisions	Host country social and labour rules
Disclosure	Pillar III	Limited	Disclosure of investment policies, risk and accrued benefits to fund members.
Investor compensation	Deposit guarantee directive	Insurance guarantee fund	
Final date for implementation	2007-2008	New framework (Solvency II) by 2012	2004
Technical adaptations	European Banking Committee (EBC), limited.	European Insurance and Occupational Pensions Committee, limited.	European Insurance and Occupational Pensions Committee, limited.

Appendix: *Basic rules for capital adequacy and asset allocation under the EU financial services directives. Source: Updated from Casey and Lannoo (2008).*

MiFID	Investment funds directives (UCITS III and IV)	Alternative investment fund managers (EU Commission draft)
Minimum €125,000, may be reduced to €50,000 for local firms or €25,000 for investment advisers (Directive 2006/49/EC).	Minimum €125,000 plus 0.02% of total assets (as soon as assets exceed €250m), with maximum of €10m (UCITS III).	Minimum €125,000 plus 0.02% of total assets (as soon as assets exceed €250m).
Function of trading book (Directive 2006/49/EC, under review).	Capital requirement may never be less than required under Art. 21 of Directive 2006/49/EC. Special rules for position and foreign exchange risk (see Annex I Art. 47-56 of Directive 2006/49/EC).	Capital requirement may never be less than required under Art. 21 of Directive 2006/49/EC. Special rules for position and foreign exchange risk (see Annex I Art. 47-56 of Directive 2006/49/EC).
Individual portfolio management, securities brokerage and order execution activities.	Management of investment funds. *Non-core:* Discretionary asset management (including pension funds). Investment advice. Safekeeping (custody) and administration of UCITS.	Management of alternative investment funds (not covered under UCITS) including hedge funds, funds of hedge funds, private equity, real estate and commodity funds. Administration. Marketing.
Rules on large exposures	< 10% of assets in single security, except for public debt, and < 40% for single investments of 5%, < 10% non-listed securities, < 10% of same body for money market instruments, and < 20% for investments in single other funds and deposits with credit institutions. Special rules for master-feeder structures.	Qualitative rules. Liquidity requirements.
Harmonised, but host country in charge of enforcement of rules for branches.	Host country conduct of business rules (unless subject to MiFID rules for non-core). Host country advertising and marketing rules.	Conflict of interest provisions. Risk and portfolio management subject to separate review. Rules on outsourcing. Rules on remuneration (Council). Rules on valuation.
Extensive full price transparency (for equity securities), unbundling of cost of transactions.	Key investor information (KII).	Annual report, disclosure of investment strategy, risk management, depository, fees and charges. Reporting to authorities. Controlling stake notification rules.
Investor compensation schemes directive	Investor compensation schemes (depending upon national implementation)	n.a.
November 2007	August 2003 (UCITS III), July 2011 (UCITS IV).	(2012)
European Securities Committee (ESC), extensive.	European Securities Committee (ESC), limited.	European Securities Committee (ESC), extensive.

Part II: Opportunities and strategies for growth in the new financial environment

About the authors

Johannes Elsner is an engagement manager working in McKinsey's Munich office. Since joining the firm in 2006 he has been working for clients in the European, Asian and Middle-Eastern financial services industry with a focus on asset managers, investors and universal banks. Aside from his client activities, Mr. Elsner is a core member of McKinsey's European asset management practice. He has co-authored several publications, for example 'The Asset Management Chessboard 2012'. Prior to joining McKinsey, he studied law at the University of Munich in Germany (qualifying as state attorney) and economics at the London School of Economics. Contract: johannes_elsner@mckinsey.com.

Martin Huber is a senior partner working in McKinsey's Cologne office. Since joining the firm in 1996, he has been working for several international clients in the European and Middle-Eastern financial services industry. Mr. Huber serves asset managers, investors, insurance companies and private banks on a broad range of topics. Furthermore, he is the co-leader of McKinsey's global asset management practice and responsible for the annual pan-European survey on the economics of asset managers. Mr. Huber also leads McKinsey's recruiting efforts in Germany. He received an MBA and holds master's and doctorate degrees in law from the University of Vienna, as well as an LL.M. from the University of Chicago. He is also a member of the New York bar. Contact: martin_huber@mckinsey.com.

Philipp Koch is a partner working in McKinsey's Hamburg office. Since joining the firm in 2001, he has been working for clients in the banking and insurance industry, with a special focus on asset management. He is a core member of the European asset management practice. He served numerous asset managers and institutional investors worldwide on questions on strategy, PMM, distribution strategy, product development, alternative assets – in particular real estate – and organisational set-up. Prior to joining McKinsey, Dr. Koch received a M.Sc. from the London School of Economics in Political Science. He holds a Ph.D. from the Helmut-Schmidt University Hamburg and his doctoral dissertation was entitled 'Optimizing Distribution Systems in the Asset Management sector – institutional arrangements as key factor of success'. Contact: philipp_koch@mckinsey.com.

5
Keys to growth in the new normal

ABSTRACT The asset management industry has gone through interesting times. It has both witnessed and acted in the deepest financial crisis since the 1930s, and must now prepare itself for 'a new normal' in which profits most likely will not return to their 2007 peak by 2012 and in which it will no longer be everyone's darling. This 'new normal' will bring about discontinuities in the broader economy, the regulatory environment, the distribution landscape, product demand, and the international competitive intensity. The asset management industry will look significantly different, and asset managers will have to find new ways to ensure excellence in execution as well as to successfully search for new 'kingdoms' to conquer. Besides a brief outline of the status of today's asset management industry, this chapter focusses on potential discontinuities, possible scenarios and the outlook for the industry landscape.

5 Keys to growth in the new normal

by Johannes Elsner, Martin Huber and Philipp Koch

Introduction

The asset management industry is currently experiencing interesting times. It has witnessed and acted in the deepest financial crisis since the 1930s, and the industry is still under intense pressure. Determining the path ahead is far from straightforward: the crisis has altered traditional growth drivers and accelerated trends that were present before the downturn.

Nevertheless, even in a world where client trust has been badly damaged and the industry is under close scrutiny from regulators, shareholders and corporate parents, it is still possible for asset managers to identify and position themselves on trajectories for growth.

After briefly outlining where the industry stands today, this chapter will look at some potential discontinuities, possible scenarios and the outlook for the industry landscape.

The new normal

The economic crisis ripped through the financial services sector in North America, Europe and beyond, and one of the first casualties was client trust. Scrutiny and scepticism rose to new heights as confidence in asset managers plunged.

Retail investors began to question the advice they were receiving from distributing intermediaries and asset managers. The notion spread that financial services firms were acting more in their own interest and not that of their clients. Even the less cynical investors are confused and have begun to question the value for money they are getting from investment advice and asset management products.

On the institutional side, the crisis shed light on vulnerabilities within investors' own asset allocation and control processes. Risk budgets have been significantly constrained, and pressure on asset managers is mounting as risk management solutions are gaining much greater prominence. Moreover, lock-up periods are about to be reduced, and mandates are in the process of being switched to new asset managers.

To rebuild broken trust, asset managers need to return to a focus on their core business. The way forward is a value proposition built around robust and reliable investment processes combined with superior risk management capabilities.

Economic impact

The vertigo-inducing drops in stock market prices and the headline collapses of illustrious institutions are well-known. What is perhaps less understood is that the underlying economics of the asset management industry have been dealt a body blow from which it may never fully recover. The stock market revitalised itself in 2009, but even the more optimistic scenarios predict that it will take until 2012 or longer for the asset management industry to return to its 2008 profit level, dismal as it was.

Since 2007, net revenues have shrunk to unprecedentedly low levels, while costs continue to be sticky despite intensified efforts by asset managers to pare back on spending. Looking ahead to 2012, little is expected to change (see Figure 1). Operating profits will exceed 2008 levels, but let's not forget that 2008 was one of the industry's worst years ever. Nor is this a purely European phenomenon: developments in the US and Asia are very similar.

The profit levels that the industry has become used to may be gone forever. This is what can be considered as 'the new normal'.

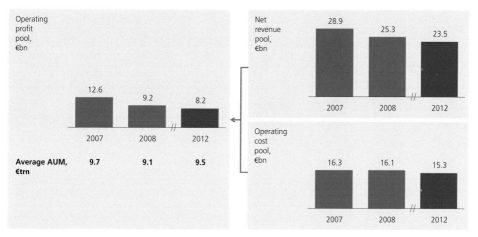

Fig. 1. Economics have been hit: profits will most likely not return to their 2007 peak by 2012.

Another element of this new normal is that it will be increasingly challenging to make a living in asset management (see Figure 2). In 2004, 16 per cent of institutional asset managers posted a loss in the wake of the dot-com crisis. Two years later, the situation had improved: only eight per cent of institutional firms were still unprofitable. By 2008, however, the share of loss-makers in institutional asset management had jumped to an astonishing 30 per cent.

Yet even in this dire industry landscape, the most profitable players in 2008 outperformed the best players of 2004. But the worst performers in 2008 fared worse than their peers four years earlier. In other words, the new normal is not only a tougher environment; it also separates the winners from the also-rans more sharply.

No longer everyone's darling

Asset managers' corporate parents, typically banks or insurance companies, used to

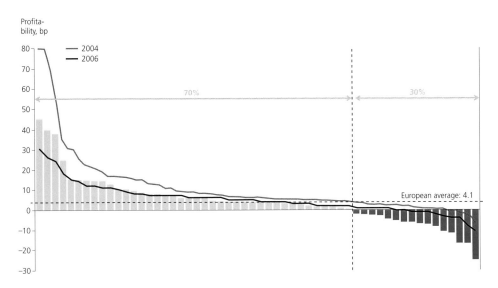

Fig. 2. Institutional segment, 2008: It's becoming increasingly difficult to make a living.

be able to gaze proudly at their well-behaved offspring. Reliable profits, low risk and a clear strategic fit made asset management a popular business within financial services groups. Independent asset managers enjoyed a similar relationship with their shareholders. Those days are gone (see Figure 3).

Profits are volatile; capital requirements have increased significantly; and risks have shot up – not only investment risks, but also reputational risks. Perhaps most worryingly, where the strategic fit used to be obvious, corporate parents are now questioning whether an asset management unit is such a perfect match after all, and they are challenging its culture, modus operandi and business mix.

In a nutshell, the asset management business is no longer a source of stability but just another piece in the shareholder's strategic portfolio jigsaw.

Glimmers of hope

While the story thus far has been gloomy, it is very important to recognise that the industry's underlying fundamentals continue to drive generally in the right direction, even if recent events have blown players onto a slightly different course.

So, although the new normal involves coming to terms with some hard realities, it also offers some encouraging signals for the future. There will, after all, always be assets to be managed.

There are, for example, at least six global mega-trends that will reinforce the long-term relevance of asset managers.

–   **Deleveraging in mature economies.** In most economies, debt grew rapidly to unprecedented levels before the crisis. Now, following the crisis, a period of significant deleveraging is expected. As has been observed in the past, decreasing

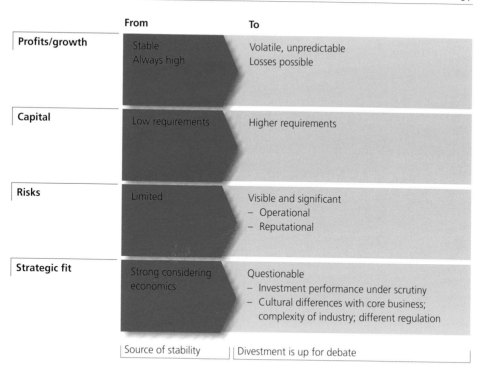

	From	To
Profits/growth	Stable Always high	Volatile, unpredictable Losses possible
Capital	Low requirements	Higher requirements
Risks	Limited	Visible and significant – Operational – Reputational
Strategic fit	Strong considering economics	Questionable – Investment performance under scrutiny – Cultural differences with core business; complexity of industry; different regulation

Source of stability   Divestment is up for debate

Fig. 3. Asset management is no longer everyone's darling. Source: McKinsey & Company.

debt will be a drag on GDP growth. For example, US households are reducing consumer spending to an extent not seen before. This contraction will most likely have major implications not only for spending levels and the speed of the economic recovery, but also for financial planning as retail customers rebuild and restructure their 'balance sheets'.

– **Ageing populations.** The population in mature economies is ageing rapidly. By 2025, nearly 30 per cent of the population will be over 60 years old. Even before the crisis, two-thirds of US baby boomers had not saved enough for retirement. The meltdown of capital markets and real estate values has been severely detrimental to boomers' already insufficient retirement nest eggs. As a result, US baby boomers are planning to work longer to meet their financial needs, and this is expected to affect retirement saving patterns.

– **Natural resource scarcity.** The global energy demand is accelerating, driven almost entirely by demand from developing economies. Without higher prices, energy demand is projected to exceed supply as early as 2010 to 2012. With higher energy prices, however, renewable energy sources will become economically viable. The shift in investment towards 'clean energy' is already beginning and raises an important question for the asset management industry: how large will the alternative energy and clean tech sectors be for investors?

- **Innovation.** Innovation will play a prominent role in the new normal, and is expected not only to take place within sectors such as the automotive or chemical industries, but also to accelerate significantly at the intersections between sectors. This shift of innovation patterns could set in motion many changes in how the asset management industry typically designs its investment strategies.
- **New models of globalisation.** International trade as a share of GDP is expected to keep growing after the crisis is over. Increasing globalisation will, in turn, highlight how interdependent companies, capital markets and nations are, which will bring sustained change to the dynamics of the world economy. New opportunities and risks from growing trade/capital flows will emerge and increase the need for greater diversification and effective risk policies in asset management.
- **The rise of emerging markets.** This trend offers substantial growth potential for asset management in particular. To get a sense of the potential in some of the world's largest countries, consider private consumption. In China, the private consumption of the middle class will *grow* by $2.5trn by 2025. In India, the figure is $0.6trn. This growth alone equals the *total* 2008 private consumption levels of Japan and Spain respectively. In Brazil, meanwhile, it is not even necessary to look into the future. The size of the asset management market today in terms of AUM is just shy of the total Italian market, and AUM in domiciled mutual funds in the first half of 2009 actually exceeded the level in the UK (€441bn vs. €430bn).

The new normal, then, is not just about the end of easy money and adapting to a harsher landscape. It is also shaped by these positive trends. Capturing the potential from these trends, while mitigating and minimising the negative impact of weaker economics, will determine the winners in the next evolutionary phase of the industry.

Discontinuities and scenarios

Having laid out the context for change, it is time to turn to what that change might look like. How will the industry evolve in terms of players, products and regions? What discontinuities can we expect; what scenarios could play out; and how will the landscape be affected?

We assume that the shape of the industry will be driven by:
- **The economy** – the pace of growth (GDP, employment and inflation), the stability and health of financial markets, and the macroeconomic and geopolitical balance;
- **Regulation** – especially the pressure on the level and structure of fees, inducements, disclosure requirements, etc.;
- **Distribution** – the shifting balance of power between producers and distributors and the degree of intermediation from an asset manager's perspective;

- **Production** – the evolution of passive/exchange-traded fund products and the survival of active asset management in response to increasing scrutiny and demands by investors;
- **Competition** – specifically the widening gap between winners and losers and the internationalisation of the playing field.

The evolution of all these drivers is creating a number of changes that will have a profound effect on the industry landscape. We would like to focus on three particular discontinuities that could be the most critical shapers of the new normal.

The regulator steps in

In recent years, the industry has focussed more on the costs associated with regulation than on the regulation itself. Given the current climate of client distrust, regulation is becoming more than just a cost. Regulators are actors capable of reshaping the landscape.

Regulators in all mature retail markets are seeking to enforce more stringent disclosure and fiduciary requirements. In the United States, the Investor Protection Act is expected to influence the distribution environment, as it aims to establish consistent standards for those who provide investment advice. Broker dealers and investment advisers are expected to review all of their internal procedures, documentation, standard agreements and business practices. In Europe, UCITS IV will bring significant new requirements for transparency and disclosure by asset managers. In the UK, the Retail Distribution Review aims to encourage a shift towards fee-based advisory models as well as issue more rigorous professional and disclosure guidelines on advisory services.

The effect of the Review is likely to be a consolidation of distributors. The resulting increased concentration of client access could help them to gain even more power. Producers will need to respond by creating or strengthening their own access to clients and their relationships with third-party distributors. The impact could be substantial: one estimate is that consolidation could halve the number of IFAs in the UK. It remains unclear who will fill this gap, or indeed whether it will be filled at all.

The implications in the UK are still up for discussion, and the effects of the Retail Distribution Review will not be felt for two years. But, in another part of the world, a very similar shift is occurring with more immediate impact.

In India's strong economic climate, the regulators acted in August 2009 to increase investor protection and modernise the asset management industry. The move was so bold – abandoning entry fees and capping exit fees – that it caught asset managers off guard. The impact was dramatic. Distributors lost as much as 60 per cent of their profitability and producers as much as 40 per cent. The loss of these revenue components put severe pressure on the distribution channel for asset management products and resulted in outflows of unprecedented magnitude.

If such developments occur in the UK, the EU or the US, and players are similarly unprepared, the revenue losses for the industry could be as high as $3–4bn.

Production: the end of 'fake' alpha?

The terms of the long-standing debate over the merits of active and passive asset management are also changing. The numbers suggest that passive/exchange-traded fund (ETF) products are growing fast, which may all but eradicate the low end of active management. In 2008, $120bn poured into ETFs in the US and $77bn in Europe.

The characteristics of the ETF market vary between regions. In the US, they are primarily retail products. Retail customers accounted for 72 per cent of net inflows between 2003 and 2007, compared to just 15 per cent in Europe, where these products have found favour with institutional investors. While there is still heterogeneity in client coverage, the industry at least recognises that the market is expanding in the direction of passive management, despite some lingering reluctance to accept that it is an irreversible landslide. Still, the most frequent question now is whether it makes sense to enter the game as an asset manager.

It is certainly possible to carve out a meaningful share of the market. Back in 2006, db x-trackers had less than one per cent of the market, but by Q3 2009 this share had grown to 17 per cent, approaching that of Lyxor, which held 25 per cent of the market in 2005.

For asset managers that have large stakes in active management but fail to deliver high alpha, the rise of passive management could have a very large downside. But it is not too late to take action, and more and more players have been announcing ETF launches.

Barbarians at the gate

One more substantial discontinuity facing the industry is the collapse of the barriers to international competition. This could happen under the pressure of increased demand by institutional players for international assets and the ambition of asset managers themselves to expand their positions through organic or external growth.

Prominent institutional investors already expect to internationalise their asset allocation, especially in equities. A glance at some of the largest US institutional investors reveals a desire to reduce their dependency on domestic equity, fuelled by a wish to diversify exposures and risk.

The practical questions are: where exactly are investors going to place their money, and who will help them? Can any one adviser make sense of the heterogeneous emerging markets from Brazil to China and from Korea to India? Investors must determine whether global or pan-European players with local presence have more credibility than local players with increasingly broad distribution coverage. Whatever the answers, it is clear that this will be global competition, and it is certainly not competition in which only the largest players will participate.

The changing game

In 2007, McKinsey developed its chessboard metaphor for the evolution of the asset management industry (see Figure 4). Very simply, it explained that the shape of the board would change and the boundaries between asset management and other services would blur, as represented by different types of pieces appearing on the board.

Fig. 4. What will the industry look like in five years' time? The chessboard revisited. © 2010 McKinsey & Company, Inc. Not for further reproduction or distribution.

Times were very different then and, like everyone else, McKinsey did not anticipate a crisis of the scale observed over the last 24 months. However, in the new normal, the redesigned chessboard in fact does not look so different from our proposal back in 2007. If anything, the crisis has accelerated some of the trends that were already in the process of reshaping it.

How do the three discontinuities discussed above affect the industry landscape?

The regulator steps in. As the regulator is expected to step in more significantly, retail end-to-end wealth advisers and retail distribution mega-malls are expected to emerge prominently. We envisage a few end-to-end solution factories that have low-cost proprietary channels. These players will offer low costs and scale solutions, will build their distribution engine on superior customer insights, and will also conquer the world of direct and online channels.

The distribution mega-malls, on the other hand, will address investors' concerns by turning most notably to new, advice-based fee models. As we will most likely see significant consolidation of IFAs and smaller advisory networks, these mega-malls will gain much more bargaining power in the shifting power game between distributors and producers. Their success will also rely on distinctive brands with strong reputations, much as leading companies in the US already enjoy.

The end of 'fake' alpha. We will continue to see the emergence of a handful of $1trn firms, especially large-scale beta factories. They are likely to absorb significant passive/ETF inflows, and the result for investors will be cheaper and more innovative beta products. While these large-scale beta factories will gain ground, true alpha entrepreneurs will remain. Some will be boutique players; others large players with superior investment and risk management capabilities – attributes that clients will be willing to pay for. However, the players that do not provide true alpha are likely to come under pressure and eventually disappear. A few specialised institutional trusted advisers will also emerge, including large asset managers, investment consultants and institutional sales units of combined investment banks and asset managers.

Barbarians at the gate. Regional and global champions will emerge on the chess-board, as well as a small number of boutiques with global reach. These players will distinguish themselves from the rest with their unique ability to understand local and global client needs and deliver on them. In addition, and as we outlined a few years ago, we still expect to see investment banks, private equity firms and hedge funds competing aggressively for space. Last but not least, wholesalers with strong brands and a specific focus on the retail arena are expected to find a sustainable place on the future chessboard.

Of course, it is impossible to predict exactly what the industry will look like, but there is value in understanding what types of players will be successful and why (see Figure 5).

Fig. 5. The revisited chessboard in the new normal. © 2010 McKinsey & Company, Inc. Not for further reproduction or distribution.

Keys to renewal

What must asset managers do now to prepare themselves for the challenges of the new normal? Now that they have emerged from the shock of the economic downturn, the longer-term challenge of managing in the new normal remains. This is definitely not the time for asset managers to put their heads in the sand.

Instead, asset managers should see the crisis as an opportunity to build on their strengths while acknowledging that the market has changed. To get a sense of this notion of renewal, it is useful to look beyond financial services to different industries.

Perhaps it is far-fetched, but the evolution of the Swiss watch industry may provide some valuable lessons on how to successfully convert industry shocks into a period of strength and growth. The traditional Swiss watch industry faced significant pressure in the 1970s, when Japanese quartz watches aggressively entered the market. After a period of refusal to change, the industry learned how to fight back, and now the 'high-end' watch industry has some parallels with the asset management industry. Taking a look at its structure, we observe a combination of boutique players, large-scale players with multiple brands, some international players, and 'beta' in the form of brands that trade on being both simple and Swiss. With this structure, the industry has been able to fight back against competitors over the past 30 years.

Another example – though, again, far afield – is McDonald's. Like the asset management industry, McDonald's faced a severe crisis in a context of very low client trust when it was discovered that BSE (commonly known as 'mad cow disease') could also infect and kill human beings. The issue first arose in 1996 and again in 2001. McDonald's responded to consumer distrust by reinforcing and standing by its products. It took the opportunity to (re)discover an obsession about quality at the core, and not only communicated but also demonstrated excellence in execution – most notably by having ensured the traceability of the ingredients it used, thereby establishing much-needed transparency as the foundation for rebuilding trust.

Applying the same logic, asset managers could think about measures to reinforce the value of the core business and extend its traditional space. What if this industry could say: "We promote the financial health, wealth, and literacy of our clients. We are committed to providing consumer information and elevating the awareness of investors at large and their ability to make wise investment choices?" What past shocks and crises teach is that, rather than remaining in denial, the asset management industry should take the crisis as an opportunity for renewal, to build on existing strengths while acknowledging the new state of the industry, and to find new spaces to cover.

Success in the new normal

The new normal is indeed a tougher place in which to operate. Profits are lower, and scrutiny from clients, regulators and shareholders will be more intense. The winners are outpacing rivals in terms of growth, profitability and market share. Success certainly remains possible, but not for everyone. Those that achieve it will have to capture the benefits of the long-term mega-trends that are driving the world economy.

Success will also come from a nuanced understanding of potential changes in the industry and their implications. Whether it is a regulatory shock, the demise of 'fake' alpha or global competition, it is important that firms prepare accordingly.

The agenda for winning asset management executives has two elements. First is excellence in execution: simply do what you do better than everybody else. This includes managing risk, containing costs, preserving a steady pace of asset growth, generating revenue and securing investment performance. Second is the search for new spaces to conquer. This could be in new regions or in adjacent businesses such as investment banking or private and wealth advisory.

The industry as a whole will succeed only if it collectively reinvents itself, rebuilds client trust and moves into new spaces. This could mean building a distribution engine to reach out to retail clients, a renewed value proposition for institutional clients, or a more varied investment universe combining with investment banks and private banks.

The industry has been through a rocky patch, but there are still many opportunities in the new normal for the nimble, the brave and the smart.

About the author

Adam Schneider is a Principal at Deloitte Consulting LLP, primarily serving clients in investment management, wealth management and capital markets. He has a B.Sc. from the Massachusetts Institute of Technology and an MBA from Columbia University.

Mr. Schneider has managed Deloitte's consulting programme for both the securities industry and for investment management. He assists firms in large-scale transformation, including strategy, programme management, operational engineering, finance, cost management and technology.
Contact: aschneider@deloitte.com.

6
After the storm: four innovations
changing investment management

ABSTRACT After a long period of generally excellent performance, the investment industry is now challenged by volatile markets, changing revenue models and substantial client issues. As a result of the 2007–2009 financial crisis, many investment management firms are facing revenue shortfalls, product performance issues and the need to adjust strategies to changing conditions. Two years after the beginning of the market crisis, firms are beginning to shift from reactive measures such as cutting costs to more innovative strategies focussed on long-term expansion. This chapter examines the implications of the market crisis for investment managers and outlines four specific innovative strategies firms are using to position themselves for growth.

6 After the storm: four innovations changing investment management

by Adam Schneider

Introduction

After a long period of generally excellent financial performance, the investment management industry is now challenged by volatile markets, decreasing revenue and substantial client retention issues. As a result of the 2007–2009 credit crisis, many firms are facing revenue declines, product performance issues and the need to adjust their strategies to changing conditions.

Two years after the beginning of the credit crisis, investment managers are beginning to shift from reactive measures such as cost cutting to more innovative strategies focussed on retaining clients and growing revenues. This chapter examines the implications of the market crisis for investment managers and specifically outlines a series of innovative strategies that firms can use to position themselves for growth.

After two years of struggling and with some light visible in the marketplace, can firms begin to go on the offensive?

The need for innovation

Our research has identified a series of market 'realities' that have been brought upon us by the credit crisis and subsequent events. As significant participants in the financial markets, the effects of the credit crisis on the investment management businesses have been profound. These 'market trends' include the following:

1 An overall trend of financial institutions moving from relatively high-risk/high-leverage businesses in search of higher financial returns towards a much less leveraged, potentially lower-return set of businesses.
2 A formerly fragmented financial services marketplace that has moved rapidly towards consolidation.
3 The ending of a 'growth mindset' where firms previously managing for expansion are now finding themselves forced to manage in a no- or low-growth environment.
4 Significant failures in investment products, both in terms of some of the investments purchased by investment managers for portfolios and for some of the investment products sold to clients.[1]

---

1 The terminology of the investment business is often confusing, in part because while investment management firms may be relatively small, they work with significant asset values and are generally very complex entities. Investment managers have a full range of business functions (including marketing, sales, research, portfolio management, information technology, operations, finance and compliance); they generally

The magnitude of change has had significant effect on the entire financial services industry. Investment manager responses have included actions such as:

- Reducing costs. Numerous investment management firms have publically announced they are undertaking cost-cutting activities.
- Improving risk management, especially in light of the failure of certain investment portfolios.
- Improving investment management processes, including product selection and compliance procedures.
- Simplifying and consolidating channels and distribution strategies.

Innovation going forward

While necessary, these actions are essentially reactive, generally have short-term benefits and may not position a firm for growth. In our ongoing work with investment managers, we have seen a number of firms who are attempting to capitalise on the market change to their advantage. Typically this involves a very innovative approach to an existing problem. The following examples discuss where investment managers are using an innovative approach to deal with the market trends discussed above.

Market Trend 1

Financial institutions such as banks and capital markets firms have been forced by recent events to raise capital and/or reduce assets, e.g. to lower their balance sheet leverage. This has had the effect of moving many financial services firms towards a possibly lower-return set of businesses. This resultant shrinkage of industry balance sheets has two major implications for investment managers:

- There are fewer total available funds in the marketplace to manage. Certain types of firms, such as hedge funds, have business models that are critically dependent on borrowing. The tightening of credit and move towards 'less leveraged lower-return' businesses has directly impacted such firms due to their lack of ability to finance assets.
- Due to increased conservatism in the market, remaining assets under management (AUM) may have moved to lower-margin products. In other words, clients who had a bad experience with 'high-risk/high-return' products are now more likely to seek 'lower-risk/lower-return' products. However, and unfortunately for investment managers, the fees for managing the higher-return products are generally higher than those for the lower-return products, directly impacting revenues and profitability. As an extreme example, in the institutional market, fees for man-

manage multiple investment strategies (such as growth equity, fixed income or cash); and these strategies are packaged into a variety of products that clients can purchase (such as separate investment accounts, mutual funds or hedge funds).

aging a given dollar value of equity assets may be five to ten times as high as fees for managing cash equivalents.

The net effect of these two types of impact at many investment firms is to structurally lower AUM and lower the revenue obtained from those assets remaining.

In our discussions with a number of investment managers, we have seen several innovative ideas and strategies in response to this trend. These include two core techniques: resegmenting the market to focus on areas which can be profitably served and improving client pricing using optimisation techniques.

Trend response: focus on segments which can be profitably served
In the years of market growth, many investment managers expanded into new market segments. In some cases, large numbers of clients were taken on without any detailed understanding of the cost to serve or profitability. Growth was the priority. However, not all clients are managed and treated equally.

Like many businesses, investment managers often have a small number of highly profitable relationships that subsidise an array of marginally profitable and unprofitable clients. To focus revenue-enhancing efforts where they can yield significant results, we believe it is essential to understand client profitability and the factors contributing to the overall situation.

Many different business decisions can drive variations in client profitability, including client tenure, product usage and mix, level of AUM, client adviser productivity, degree of price concessions, and service intensity. The variety of contributing factors makes it difficult to determine how profitable client relationships are today, let alone how profitable they could be if managed more effectively.

Innovative investment managers are beginning to use analytic techniques to understand client profitability patterns and target specific clients for improvement. They use a holistic, analytical approach to understand:
-   which clients are underperforming relative to their potential;
-   what actions in what areas – service levels, pricing, product mix – might enhance these clients' performance;
-   which clients are beyond repair and need to be terminated to free up resources to focus on higher-potential prospects.

A typical approach includes a five-step process of enhancing an investment manager's understanding of client profitability and its drivers. The five steps are discussed in detail in our other publications[2] but in summary include:

---

2   This is a topic which is actively researched. Please see the series of publications located at www.deloitte.com/us/pricing.

1 **Quantify client profitability.** The analysis of individual client profitability forms the foundation for improving performance, allowing firms to uncover the root causes of client profitability differences.

2 **Benchmark and identify underperformers.** Profit performance is driven by many factors, which makes effective benchmarking a challenge. Traditional analytical approaches can be combined with modelling techniques to pinpoint under- and over-profit target clients.

3 **Develop action plans.** Client-specific action plans targeting the root causes of underperformance can help bring selected clients up to their profit-generating potential.

4 **Monitor results.** Effective monitoring and tracking of results provides feedback and allows definition of goals and metrics into performance incentives.

5 **Expand focus beyond individual clients.** By examining aggregated client profitability information, a firm can gain insights about the profitability of client adviser, office, region and channels.

Trend response: improving client pricing using optimisation techniques
In our experience and research, the active management of pricing and client price concessions is often neglected by investment managers.

Pricing is a key component of all businesses, and in theory pricing for investment management services should be quite simple. However, in our experience, price concessions at investment managers often create significant revenue and profit leakage. Firms may have a general belief that all clients are profitable at the margin, and, as a result, over time and through individual negotiations, clients have received various forms of discounts, rebates and ad-hoc pricing structures. In many firms, price concessions have become the norm rather than the exception. Our experience shows that margin leakage of 15–30% on gross profits is not uncommon. The prevalence of price concessions tends to feed on itself, as the current trend of more price transparency leads more demanding clients to ask for more frequent and greater concessions. We believe managing the process of granting price concessions is crucial because it directly affects the bottom line while having a disproportionately high impact on margin. In addition, pricing decisions, often the result of a one-time situation, can impact longer-term recurring revenues over a period of years.

Research indicates that, although the rate of price concession generally correlates to AUM or total revenue per client, such concessions often vary greatly across clients, even those investing similar amounts in similar products. In fact, firms may have low-revenue clients receiving high concessions, and occasionally we have identified clients with negative margins. In many cases, price concessions are granted with an expectation of anticipated future opportunities (such as new assets), but afterwards they are seldom tracked to determine whether the expected future assets truly materialise.

As a result, there are often shortcomings in the management of price concessions that leave unrealised opportunities. Innovative firms are enhancing their price concession management to significantly drive profit improvement.

The first step to improving management of price concessions is to create transparency in the concessions already granted. Greater insight into the current situation can improve price management strategies. This insight can help drive tangible initiatives to improve the process. Innovative firms are undertaking actions such as:

– Establishing a comprehensive pricing database that supports reliable calculations of price concessions and provides a holistic view of clients.
– Deploying pricing tools to calculate gross prices for each product on an account level. This requires an in-depth understanding of the actual often highly complex price structures in use.
– Performing in-depth analysis by product or service, by AUM tier, by channel or by region to identify drivers of profitability. The goal is to evaluate outliers, inconsistencies, high margin leakage patterns and current price sensitivity.
– Understanding the core reasons why price concessions are granted in specific situations. This can enable appropriate management action or countermeasures to be launched. For example, a particular client segment may be requesting and obtaining unreasonably large concessions. This information is then used to quantify the potential benefit of pricing and profitability management initiatives.

The second step is to identify required pricing strategy improvements. We have found that guidelines for price concession management need to be formulated based on business strategies and objectives as well as on the insights gained through the above-mentioned analysis. Following these steps can provide a foundation for price execution and monitoring, and it is essential to express them in a clear-cut way.

The third step is to enhance the execution of price concessions. This generally requires a set of tangible initiatives focussed on the goal of significantly reducing margin leakage. Figure 1 below shows a scatter chart of client accounts indicating what percentage of 'rack rate' fees are actually realised, plotted against asset size. With data of this sort, a firm can define specific initiatives at the account or client level to increase profitability. These initiatives can be sized based on their effectiveness in supporting strategic objectives and can then be prioritised in terms of their impact on client satisfaction, profit improvement, effort and risk.

In Figure 1, taken from an actual study at an investment management firm, we have plotted fees received as a percentage of 'list' price versus client AUM. The firm had a policy for the maximum fee reduction it would offer depending on client negotiation, which is indicated by the dotted line. Clients with significant assets who are charged far below the fee policy are in the 'area of opportunity'.

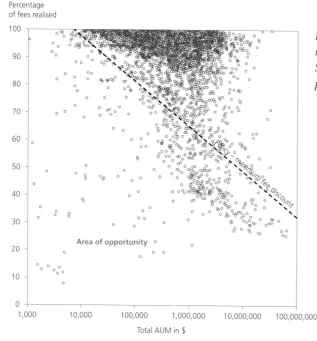

Fig. 1. Sample investment manager client fee analysis. Source: Deloitte analysis, private wealth client.

While each investment manager is different, there are a number of innovative high-value practices that have been demonstrated to be effective:
- Improve profitability strategy by:
  - defining profitability targets
  - defining objective criteria for concessions
  - providing sales negotiation training to client advisers.
- Define price concession process by:
  - eliminating unauthorised price concessions
  - resetting price concessions and limit duration
  - changing structure of price concessions
  - defining concession structures and limits
  - developing tracking system for negotiated terms.
- Improve client profitability by:
  - implementing profitability benchmarking and reporting
  - including specific margin leakage KPIs in sales incentive systems
  - implementing margin leakage reporting
  - calculating roll-out price concession profit impact.
- Obtain and assemble information on competitor pricing and concession strategy. Note that fees for some types of clients are public record and that there is a wide variety of anecdotal information available in the marketplace.

A fourth step is to use predictive modelling techniques to focus and organise the price concession process. Most investment managers enter client negotiations with little or no objective fact-based information upon which to base pricing decisions. Predictive modelling tools can help estimate a client's sensitivity to price and develop recommendations based on client, competitor and external market information. When implemented, this intelligence can be provided at the point of negotiation, maximising its value.

Fifth, innovative investment managers make a systematic effort to monitor price concessions over time. A monitoring system can identify disruptive developments, determine the effectiveness of measures taken, and reveal opportunities for improvement. An internal profitability and price concession benchmarking analysis exposes over- and underperformers and helps to achieve better results by encouraging implementation of more effective practices across the firm.

Based on hands-on client experience, we have seen investment managers use strategies like these to obtain significant profit improvement. Improving management of price concessions can be started with relatively small investments, can be piloted initially and implemented quickly, and are generally effective within a short period of time.

Market Trend 2

One result of recent market events has been significant consolidation across much of the financial industry. In a similar fashion in the investment industry we have seen the emergence of very-large-scale trillion-dollar AUM firms. This is a major change that directly affects firms throughout the industry. There are direct implications for most investment managers:

- Scale has grown in importance. The strategies of many investment management firms have been to organise as product- or sector-oriented boutiques and strive for outperforming in those areas. However, with the growth of giant competitors, smaller firms have lost market share and potentially lost relevance.
- Increased activity in mergers and acquisitions (M&A) may be warranted as a way to increase product breadth, distribution or scale generally. A discussion of M&A in the investment industry is beyond the scope of this chapter.
- The very largest firms can differentiate themselves and choose to compete on a different basis. For example, one firm may conclude its scale provides an ability to invest in market analysis tools to drive superior results. Another firm may seek to offer many different investment styles so that, as markets shift, they can induce clients to move assets across style, rather than seeing assets depart.

The effect is that firms must decide whether they want, or need, to grow. If scale is more important, what can investment management firms do to compete? Assuming investment performance is already a focus area, one innovative strategy is increasing the focus on client *service* satisfaction. Increasing the focus on client service should, other factors being equal, increase inflows, slow outflows, and generally make assets 'stickier'. However, this requires identifying what is important in servicing clients and optimising the service and delivery mechanisms to provide that.

We believe that, in the investment industry, the factors driving client service are generally segment specific. Specific recommendations for a set of defined investor segments are presented in Figure 2.

In general, the strategies focus on providing the following:

- Improved education so that clients can put their results in the context of historical returns.
- Additional communications and personal touch points (as may be economic) so that clients feel that they are getting the appropriate level of contact and support for their level of assets and situation.
- Developing a 'health check' process to confirm that clients are correctly allocated in light of their individual situation, current asset value and investment goals. The goal of the 'health check' is both to take a fresh look at the investment portfolio and to indicate to the client that the investment manager is taking special care given market conditions.
- One innovative strategy for clients that may want to change advisors is to offer a revised, alternate advisory path. The thinking goes that many clients change adviser by changing firms – and it would be far better to build a process to find a new adviser within the firm rather than lose the client altogether.

Investor segment	Typical service priorities	Typical investment priorities	Potential retention strategy in light of market events
Mass affluent **< $1m**	– Convenience – Advice – Ease of access	– Accumulation	– Educate and communicate – Alternate advisory path
Affluent **$1–5m**	– Relationship – Service quality – Advice	– Preservation – Next generation	– Educate and communicate – 'Health check' portfolio – Alternate advisory path
High net worth (HNW) **$5–25m**	– Personal relationship – Service quality	– Preservation and innovation – Philanthropic – Next generation	– Educate and communicate – 'Health check' portfolio – Increase touchpoints
Ultra HNWI **> $25m**	– Personal relationship	– Preservation and innovation – Philanthropic – Next generation	– Educate and communicate – Increase touchpoints
Institutions	– Service quality – Enquiry response – Accuracy/types of reporting	– Defined expectations – Performance consistent with expectations	– Communicate – Focus on sector rotation and longer term returns

Fig. 2. Improving client retention: strategies by investor segment. Source: Deloitte analysis

Innovative investment managers have also expanded their client contact and calling programmes to accomplish the above strategies. This includes creating the business reporting to confirm the programme is effective. What may have been ad hoc and not monitored becomes a formal programme with goals, methods, timelines and an assessment of effectiveness.

But trying harder is not enough. If improving service is indicated as a primary response to the market change, a second innovative response is to recognise that the level of service offered to a client segment can be defined, measured and controlled. While the majority of investment managers strive for excellent service, many use informal mechanisms for defining service levels and do not measure service as delivered.

In our research across many industries, we have found that leading service organisations explicitly link their business and client strategy to their service strategy. The research indicates that service leaders bring together five building blocks to drive service delivery success. These are as follows:

- **Service strategy definition.** We have found that defining the goals and objectives is essential and that creating and communicating this service philosophy is common across all service excellence strategies. As part of that process, leadership creates a clear vision for service excellence and drives it through the organisation. The importance of defining a firm's client service strategy cannot be overstated: firms with leading service cultures almost always explicitly state and manage to that strategic goal. The goal should be explicit, service focussed, and present throughout the organisation.

- **Employee/culture management.** We have found that, regardless of industry or strategy, service leaders infuse a service culture into their employees. This includes training, development, the routine use of performance guidelines, monitoring, feedback and leading by example.

- **Measurement and incentives.** Common parlance is that if something is not measured, then it did not happen. This requires defining standards for service and then tracking actual performance. Our research indicates that measuring client service is an area of focus for most service leaders. Measurement and incentives are very commonly used in such settings as call centres, so as a result, retail clients often serviced by a call centre may have such measures. However, in our experience these types of measurements are rarely performed for institutional servicing, a key omission.

- **Brand.** In our research, all leading service organisations associate their brand with service quality to create a strong perception of quality and increase expectations. This brand perception pervades, both externally and internally within the organisation.

- **Service delivery.** We have found that service leaders focus on ensuring positive service interaction, emphasising service recovery and a consistent client experience. This is often followed through a measurement mechanism such as client satisfaction surveys. Again, these techniques are commonly used for retail call centre operations and are much less common for institutional servicing.

Most investment managers have an aggregate measurement of success: the inflow or outflow of AUM. Given that most firms focus on maximising investment performance, the only other retention strategy available to many firms is to focus on service, ideally before they experience significant AUM outflows.

Market Trend 3

With the ending of the 'growth mindset', investment management firms are finding themselves managing in a no- or low-growth environment. The effect is that business models and organisational structures acceptable and affordable during the growth phase are likely to be less acceptable or perhaps unaffordable now. What are some of those practices?

– Allowing multiple investment organisations, possibly by strategy, to exist across the firm.
– Maintaining duplicative marketing/sales capabilities, generally by investment strategy or by subsidiary.
– Maintaining duplicative administrative functions, such as finance or human resources.
– Maintaining duplicative back office and technology functions.
– Not exploring 'next generation' opportunities for back office and technology functions such as new technologies that can leapfrog existing capabilities.

The lack of integration by investment managers in their business models is an interesting phenomenon of growth. Many firms have grown over the years through acquisition or combination, and often the functional duplication described above was deliberate, an outgrowth of the M&A process. It was common to promise individual firms or product areas significant autonomy.

The struggle is that business models that worked during a period of growth may no longer work going forward. Some firms are using this as an opportunity to pursue change. Much of this involves breaking down the structural silos that have formed and reorganising/combining them with a shared services model. Often there are substantial cost synergy benefits but with substantial expense to change and transition.

Shared services is not an applicable approach for all areas at all times. Firms must balance their individual needs – for example, adding new strategies, offering new products, entering new client segments, or changing geographic focus – with the inevitable issues inherent in building a centralised, cost-effective service.

We considered opportunities of this sort to be 'deferred merger integration' and urge investment managers to balance the commitments made during the M&A process against the potential cost, functional, and scale synergies potentially available through consolidation of services or capabilities.

A related tactic taken by some investment managers is to more aggressively think through their operating model as a basis for reorganising work. We have seen firms build and then implement a series of global operating principles. A typical principle might be 'there will be one functional capability such as performance calculation globally' or 'there will be one trade-clearing capability per geographic region', where the region in question is defined as the Americas, Europe or Asia.

These principles are aimed at fostering regional or global coordination, with a goal of optimising the processes, costs and capabilities.

Regional or global integration efforts are also not one-sided, and generally such efforts are balanced with the need to maintain local autonomy, especially in the areas of managing assets and in servicing clients. So a typical structure would involve, say, country-by-country investment management, country-by-country client service, and many functions organising into a regional or global hub. Trends observed in the market are summarised in Figure 3, but many firms use widely varying structures.

Investment managers are implementing governance at a global level to maximise economies of scale, apply consistent standards, encourage coordination and share scarce resources.

Market Trend 4

There have been significant failures of investment products, both in terms of some securities purchased for portfolios and for products sold to clients. However, there has been little in the way of a structural response.

Much has been made in the industry of the risks that have been uncovered during the credit crisis. In particular, a series of investment products failed in unprecedented amounts. Some examples include the following:

- Auction rate preferred securities sold as cash equivalents, where the risk of an auction failing was thought to be extremely small.
- Structured investment vehicles, where underlying long-term assets funded short-term cash such as investment returns, until the long-term assets lost value.
- Money market funds, where one major fund ended up 'breaking the buck' due to exposure to commercial paper that fell in value.
- Tranches of sub-prime mortgage CDOs, which fell dramatically in value when the underlying mortgage cash flows were lower than expected.

While the risks inherent within these investment products were generally understood as something that 'could happen', they were also generally considered to be very low probability by the broker/dealers and investment managers involved. More signifi-

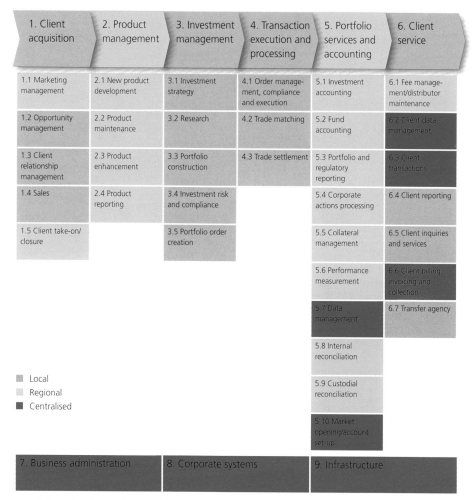

1. Client acquisition	2. Product management	3. Investment management	4. Transaction execution and processing	5. Portfolio services and accounting	6. Client service
1.1 Marketing management	2.1 New product development	3.1 Investment strategy	4.1 Order management, compliance and execution	5.1 Investment accounting	6.1 Fee management/distributor maintenance
1.2 Opportunity management	2.2 Product maintenance	3.2 Research	4.2 Trade matching	5.2 Fund accounting	6.2 Client data management
1.3 Client relationship management	2.3 Product enhancement	3.3 Portfolio construction	4.3 Trade settlement	5.3 Portfolio and regulatory reporting	6.3 Client transactions
1.4 Sales	2.4 Product reporting	3.4 Investment risk and compliance		5.4 Corporate actions processing	6.4 Client reporting
1.5 Client take-on/closure		3.5 Portfolio order creation		5.5 Collateral management	6.5 Client inquiries and services
				5.6 Performance measurement	6.6 Client billing, invoicing and collection
				5.7 Data management	6.7 Transfer agency
				5.8 Internal reconciliation	
				5.9 Custodial reconciliation	
				5.10 Market opening/account set-up	

▪ Local
▫ Regional
■ Centralised

7. Business administration	8. Corporate systems	9. Infrastructure

Fig. 3. Location trends for global investment management firms

cantly, the risks were considered so low that reserves or capital were rarely required to be held against them.

As the credit crisis unfolded, many firms stepped up to support their problematic products and funds. However, the market experienced significant uncertainty. It is clear that there are inconsistent standards for how a 'defective product' should or should not be supported.[3] To date, there has been little in the way of regulatory response to the issue.

The lack of 'product warranties' for investment products can be directly contrast-

---

3   As it turned out, most of the products that were ultimately supported were cash equivalent investment vehicles. While risks were often disclosed to investors, the analogy to government-insured bank deposits led many of the product sponsors to support them for client relations reasons.

ed to what happens when other types of products are purchased. One can go into an appliance store, buy a twenty-dollar toaster, and generally receive a money-back warranty that protects the purchaser if the product fails within a given time period. The company manufacturing the product reserves for that warranty cost, and in fact may obtain insurance for an excessive rate of failure.

This is a significant structural issue, in part because investment managers do not act like banks and do not think in terms of taking reserves against their products. However, some of the more forward-looking investment management firms are debating whether there is a way to potentially resolve this problem. We believe there are two sets of core questions:

– For investment products purchased, such as sub-prime CDOs: is there a way to improve the investment process so that the true components of risk are better understood? For example, in this case the core issue was the cash flow of the underlying mortgage collateral, especially in light of a decrease in real estate value. Is there a structural way going forward to incorporate lessons of this type in the investment process?

– For investment products issued, such as money funds: does the firm have a robust enough product management process so that underlying risks are identified, evaluated and if need be reserved against? Is there periodic monitoring on a frequent enough basis to alert a firm to a pending problem?

More generally: can product warranties be defined in a way that is structurally sound for the investor and the investment manager/issuer? As of this writing, this question remains open.

Conclusion

This chapter has summarised four market trends that have emerged from the 2007–2009 credit crisis and innovative responses seen in the marketplace. The investment industry is robust and is intelligently focussed on responding to what has happened. Key responses include the following:

1 The overall trend of deleveraging is being responded to by increasing focus on client service and client profitability.

2 The trend of a consolidating business environment is being responded to by an increasing focus on M&A and sensitivity to improving client service to maximise retention.

3 The ending of a 'growth mindset' is forcing changes in operating model such as regionalisation, globalisation or consolidation of functions into shared services capabilities.

About the author

Alistair Byrne is a principal in the investment practice at Investit, an investment management consultancy. He works with a broad range of investment management firms on investment process and product development projects, and market research. Mr. Byrne has particular expertise in pension fund investment and defined contribution pension plans.

He began his career in investment management at AEGON Asset Management UK, where he was investment strategist and head of equity research. He has also held academic positions at the University of Edinburgh and Strathclyde business schools and run his own financial services consultancy. Mr. Byrne has a Ph.D. in finance from the University of Strathclyde and is a CFA charterholder.
Contact: alistair.byrne@investit.com.

7
Designing products for reluctant investors: applications of behavioural finance

ABSTRACT This chapter considers how asset managers can use an understanding of client behaviour to build better products and drive growth in their business. The particular focus is the case of defined contribution (DC) pension plans, which represent a growing part of the asset pool in many countries. The chapter draws on a survey of investment professionals and in-depth interviews conducted in the UK in early 2007. We argue that most DC plan members can be characterised as 'reluctant investors', which means that they do not want to make investment choices and would prefer investment decisions to be made by experts on their behalf. Designing products for these reluctant investors typically means offering simple, transparent products, avoiding excessive choice and communicating clearly what the product is intended to do for the client rather than the intricacies of its manufacture. These are not approaches that come naturally to many providers in the asset management industry.

7 Designing products for reluctant investors: applications of behavioural finance

by Alistair Byrne

Introduction

Behavioural finance is often held out as offering an explanation why financial markets are inefficient and holding the prospect that an understanding of it can help active fund managers 'beat the market'. This chapter[1] argues that a more important use of behavioural finance is in understanding and meeting the needs and wants of your clients. The chapter focusses particularly on the case of defined contribution (DC) pension plans, which represent a growing part of the asset pool in many countries. It argues that most DC plan members can be characterised as 'reluctant investors' who do not want to make detailed investment choices and would prefer investment decisions to be made by experts on their behalf. Trends within pension plan provision mean these members have to operate without guidance from expert advisers and need to navigate the investment decisions on their own. Reluctant investors have limited interest in investment matters, are easily confused or put off by investment choice, and exhibit inertia that prevents them following through with decisions and actions. An understanding of the behaviour of DC pension plan members can allow an investment manager to offer better products to these clients and drive business growth. Typically, this means offering simple, transparent products, avoiding excessive choice and communicating clearly what the product is intended to do for the client rather than the intricacies of its manufacture.

The growing importance of DC

DC is becoming the most common type of pension plan in the UK private sector and in many other markets. In defined benefit (DB) plans, the employer bears the investment and longevity risk. In DC these risks are transferred to individual members, who must make complex decisions about which funds to invest their contributions in. It is unusual for employers to pay for face-to-face investment advice, and this lack of member-specific *advice,* as opposed to generic information and guidance, means most members end up in the default fund. Figures vary from plan to plan, but the 2007 NAPF annual survey found that, on average, 94% of members end up in the default fund (NAPF, 2007).

---

1   The chapter is based on the Pensions Institute report 'Dealing with the reluctant investor' by Alistair Byrne, Debbie Harrison and David Blake. See www.pensions-institute.org.

Most DC members can be described as 'reluctant' or 'disengaged' investors. By this we mean that these are individuals who, for a range of reasons, are not prepared to make an active investment choice and instead *passively accept* the default fund. The high proportion of plan members who passively accept default arrangements raises important questions for asset managers about the structure of the default fund and how to best serve the needs of these clients.

DC plans in the UK can be trust-based ('occupational DC'), in which case the employer establishes the plan under trust law and there is a board of trustees whose job it is to act in the members' best interests and negotiate on their behalf with service providers, including asset managers. The alternative is contract-based DC, and here the contractual arrangement is directly between the individual member and the provider, typically an insurance company. The key difference between these two structures, therefore, is that in contract-based DC there is no entity recognised in law or regulation that acts solely on the members' behalf. Contract-based plans do, however, fall under financial services regulation and Financial Services Authority (FSA) requirements for providers to 'treat clients fairly'. Our research found that the trend in the private sector is not only from DB to DC, but also from occupational DC to contract-based plans. Figure 1 shows an outline of the UK pension market. Figure 2 shows an estimate of the value of assets.

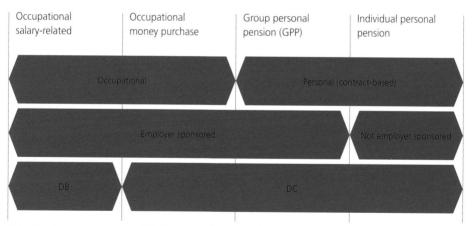

Occupational schemes can also be divided between self-administered and insurance managed. Most but not quite all DB schemes are self-administered.

Note: An occupational scheme is one with scheme trustees and governed by trust law. A personal pension (whether sponsored by an employer or not) has the legal form of a contract between an individual and a pension provider (usually an insurance company). Individual personal pensions are most common among the self-employed and others who are not entitled to join occupational schemes such as those in partnerships. Stakeholder pensions are a subset of personal pensions and can be either GPP or individual personal pension in form.

Fig. 1. Types of private pension provision. Source: UBS 2009, based on Pensions Commission report.

Type of scheme	£bn
Occupational DB (self-administered)	610
Occupational DC (self-administered)	205
Insurance administered schemes	175
Personal and stakeholder DC	260
Total pension assets	1,250
Other tax-advantaged savings vehicles	300

Fig. 2. Estimated total assets in UK pensions and tax-advantaged savings vehicles.
Source: UBS Pension Fund Indicators 2009.

The primary factors that determine the outcome of a DC pension plan during the accumulation phase are investment strategy – principally asset allocation – and the level of contributions. This chapter focusses on the former: the investment strategies offered by DC plans and, in particular, the default fund provided for members who do not want to make an active choice.

The remainder of the chapter is organised as follows. Section 2 explains our research method, while section 3 discusses governance in DC investment. Section 4 focusses on default funds, while section 5 looks at issues in investment choice and is followed by a brief conclusion.

Research method

In the fourth quarter of 2006, we undertook a thorough analysis of the DC investment strategies currently available to private sector employees in the UK. This research was supplemented by an online survey, which was completed by 54 experienced professionals from the DC pensions market. Respondents included individuals who work for fund management companies, pension plan providers and pensions consultancy firms, as well as pensions lawyers and professional trustees.

We also conducted interviews with over 60 pension and investment experts, either face to face or by phone. In many cases, these are the same individuals who participated in the survey, but the interviews allow for a more in-depth understanding of their views. Comments from individual respondents in this research are non-attributable, but we indicate the professional role of the interviewees. From these interviews we were able to build up a clear picture of the framework in which employers introduce DC, the advice they receive, current trends and innovations, and the nature of the problems that concern all parties involved in the design and delivery of plans for the reluctant investor.

Governance of DC investment?

Survey results

Of the pensions experts we surveyed, 69% say that the typical investment arrangements in UK DC pension plans do not meet most members' needs.

Respondents, on average, think that only 10–15% of DC plan members understand the investment risks they face. Over half put the figure at 10% or less.

In this section we ask the question, "what constitutes appropriate governance in the context of DC pension plan investment?" For members, understanding basic investment fundamentals and the confidence to make decisions are quite separate characteristics. Even where a member has a reasonable understanding of investment issues, putting this into action is a separate task. It is important not to underestimate the member's fear of making the wrong decision. This is a major factor that explains the concentration of members in the default fund, which further implies that additional information and communications, although very important, will not by themselves convert a reluctant investor into an active one. Our research suggests that what most members want is not more information, but rather to have an expert make the investment decision for them.

The main problem arising from this situation is that many investment 'experts' do not want to make decisions on behalf of DC members for fear of liability. As we discuss later in this chapter, this applies to various aspects of DC investment, including the selection of default funds, the decision on how much investment choice to offer to members, and the nature of information and advice provided to members. We have the perverse outcome that experts – who have the skill and knowledge to make investment choices on behalf of members – prefer not to make them because of fear of liability if the decision turns out to be wrong. The consequence is that decisions are made instead by the members – that is, those who, on average, have very limited investment knowledge. We argue below for changes to law and regulation so that employers, trustees and others who are in a position to support members of DC plans have less to fear from using their expertise provided they can show appropriate standards of care.

Differences in governance between trust-based and contract-based plans

Trust-based DC typically is used by larger employers and can be established with a high level of governance via the trustee board. In theory at least, therefore, a plan with a trustee board is better placed to ensure the member makes appropriate investment decisions. The trustees are responsible for meeting relevant investment regulations and investing funds in a manner consistent with the members' best interests. Their approach to this should be set out clearly in the statement of investment principles. In practice, however, the effectiveness of the trustee board can and does vary from plan to plan.

In some cases, trustees probably do not give DC the attention it deserves. Many trustees of occupational DC plans are also trustees of a DB plan, and the latter presents the most pressing problems at present due to underfunding and the prescriptive requirements of the Pensions Act 2004. Consultants report that DB issues dominate trustee meetings and that DC is frequently sidelined almost to the point where it becomes an issue listed under 'Any Other Business'.

Trustees sometimes neglect DC. They have their head buried in DB problems. **Consultant**

Trustee meetings for DC are inefficient. With DB the investment decisions affect the employer. With DC they affect the employee. **Consultant**

Some plans may benefit from having a separate group of trustees who oversee the DC plan from those responsible for the DB plan. This would suggest having a separate trust, which is the case in many, but not all, DC arrangements. That way, the DC plan may get more consistent attention. A DC sub-committee is another possible option.

As regards governance of contract-based plans, several advisers and consultants put forward the idea of establishing a board or executive which would undertake some of the responsibilities of trustees. This could oversee the selection and monitoring of investment managers and funds, and take a role in determining the information and guidance provided to members. The employer could invite employee representatives onto the committee and invite advisers and providers to report to the committee. However, such a committee would lack formal legal responsibility for the pension arrangements – which are contracts between the employees and the provider – and this might limit its effectiveness.

While employers want to help employees make sensible decisions, they don't want any legal responsibility for the outcome. The answer is to establish a pension committee for the contract plan, which can do everything that trustees did but without actually giving advice to members and having any legal responsibility. **IFA**

Trustees are not always best placed to supervise DC arrangements, but there should be a strong governance committee. Trustees often are reluctant to do much with what is members' money. I'm a big fan of intelligent governance, but I'm not convinced a board of trustees is the right way to deliver this. **Consultant**

As regards the role of investment consultants, some respondents suggested that trust-based DC gave the consultant the same commercial advantages as DB, in that they could advise but would not have to take responsibility for dealing with individual members.

Few people want to take responsibility for the end user in DC. Who wants to 'own' the compliance? The big consultants are the worst, and the life companies have an advantage there. **Asset manager**

The role of the employer

Many employees would like to turn to their employer for guidance on what to do with their DC pension investments. Employers, though, are often reluctant to help for fear of falling foul of financial services regulation or incurring other liabilities if the guidance they offer causes some disadvantage to members. There would seem to be merit in looking at what can be done to encourage employers to take a more active role.

I am in favour of making the law easier for employers to stick their neck out a bit in what they can say to employees without fear of being penalised by a regulator or an ombudsman. **Pensions lawyer**

The traditional way for the employer to offer support is to establish a trust-based plan with a board of trustees. However, as noted above, trust-based plans are in decline as employers move to the simpler contract-based arrangement. It is a very attractive proposition to employers weary of the trust-related administration, cost and liabilities.

Employers are switching to contract DC to put a distance between themselves and the plan outcome, so that all they have to do is collect and forward contributions – they don't want to be involved in the fund choice. **IFA**

We have virtually no new business enquiries for trust-based DC. We have lost trust-based clients to contract-based plans. The life companies' pitch is that they offer a more straightforward platform. **Asset manager**

While employers are moving from trust-based to contract-based plans to reduce their responsibilities, there are some indications that the regulators may wish to see employers take more direct responsibility for the oversight of contract-based plans. The section below highlights some important issues raised in The Pension Regulator's 2006 consultation paper on DC regulation.

The regulation of DC investment

In November 2006, The Pensions Regulator (TPR) published a consultation paper (TPR, 2006) setting out how it intends to regulate DC pensions. The paper notes four issues that TPR believes could contribute to poor investment practices:

- inadequate processes for the selection and ongoing review of performance of investment managers and funds
- provision of an inappropriate fund or range of funds
- inappropriate design of the default fund
- lack of member understanding.

In terms of fund choice, the paper notes that the investment range must allow members to make choices that suit their circumstances, but that providing too wide a range increases complexity and may increase the risk of administrative errors being made.

TPR says that it intends to offer guidance on good practice in the following areas:
- effective processes for selecting and reviewing investment managers
- effective processes for the review of investment funds
- how to offer a well designed fund or range of funds to suit member demographics
- examples of different approaches to the design of default funds
- examples of investment options, including diversification
- examples of clear and simple information that can be provided to members.

Perhaps the most important part of the consultation paper is the section covering the TPR's 'expectations', which can be viewed as a description of the standards that need to be met. The stated requirements are:
- there is a robust selection process for investment managers and funds, and regular performance reviews
- a suitable fund or range of well-managed funds is offered, especially in respect of the default fund
- steps are taken to help raise members' understanding of investment decisions, level or risk and potential impact on benefits.

The TPR's guidance on DC investment issues can play a key role in helping employers and trustees to design their DC arrangements in a manner that is helpful for members. If employers and trustees can show they have followed TPR's guidance, then that may have some impact on any discussion of liability for poor investment results. However, formal safe harbour provisions might be more beneficial.

Implicit and explicit advice
Many of the problems in DC investment could probably be solved by providing members with individual investment advice. However, this is quite rare due to the cost. Generic guidance has a role to play, but some of the professionals we interviewed noted that it was typically not sufficient to enable members to make confident investment decisions.

I believe that most people actually need far more than generic financial advice at points in their lifetime, for example on joining, transferring or retiring. **Consultant**

Employers and trustees are wary of giving advice, but members would like guidance from an expert. Furthermore, what the FSA defines as advice is a long way from the definition most employees would use. Many members will regard aspects of the design of their plan as implicit advice. This is particularly true of the default fund, which members can easily regard as being chosen as being suitable for them.

The selection and monitoring of the default fund or funds is absolutely critical to the success of the plan and to good governance. It doesn't matter that the regulations do not regard this process as 'advice' in the technical sense. Effectively it is advice, since most members take the default option on the assumption that it has been selected specifically for those who do not want to make investment decisions. **Trustee**

Safe harbour

One prospect for improving governance of DC plans is that each party to the plan – and this could include any combination of the employer, trustee, adviser, consultant, plan provider and asset manager – should be set clear regulatory responsibilities. In exchange for taking a greater fiduciary role, they should be protected through the introduction of safe harbour rules.

By safe harbour, we mean provisions that relieve the employer, trustees or other party from liability for the investment outcome, provided the decisions they take conform to the standards set out in the regulations. Details of safe harbour provisions used in the US are set out in the section beginning at the bottom of this page. It is not compulsory for employers and others to follow the safe harbour guidelines, but doing so provides important protections which many will be reluctant to forgo.

Our argument is that provision of a safe harbour could encourage employers, trustees and advisers – the relative experts on investment – to provide more support to members in investment decision making. Key areas of application include specifying and selecting default funds, choosing appropriate ranges of investment choice, and providing members with appropriate information and guidance.

Obviously, care needs to be taken in developing and specifying the safe harbour provisions. They are likely to drive behaviour, and if they are poorly thought out, that behaviour may be no better than the situation we have today. Nevertheless, we recommend the safe harbour approach as a possible way of ending the process of employers, trustees and advisers distancing themselves from investment decision making in DC plans.

US safe harbour provisions for DC default funds (QDIA)

The US Employee Retirement Income Security Act (ERISA) provides relief from liability for investment outcomes for sponsors ('fiduciaries') of DC pension plans, typically 401(k) plans, where members make their own investment choices from an appropriate range of funds on offer. This relief is known as a 'safe harbour'. Some plan sponsors have worried about potential liabilities arising from the performance of default funds on the basis of an interpretation that default funds are not 'chosen' by members. Many have responded by either refusing to have a default fund or choosing a low risk fund, such as cash, as the default to minimise the chances of short-term losses. These decisions can create a number of adverse consequences such as discouraging employees from joining (because they must make a fund choice), preventing use of automatic enrolment (which requires a default fund), and encouraging recklessly conservative investment strategies.

The Pensions Protection Act of 2006 contains several measures designed to support the use of automatic enrolment, one of which is an amendment to the ERISA safe harbour provisions. The new provisions create a safe harbour where:
- assets are invested in a Qualified Default Investment Alternative (QDIA);
- members have been given an opportunity to provide investment direction but have failed to do so;
- members have been given notice 30 days before the initial investment and again 30 days before the start of each plan year about how their assets will be invested in the QDIA;
- the plan offers a broad range of investment alternatives;
- members are able to switch out of the QDIA into the other funds.

The regulations also provide requirements for the QDIA:
- it must not impose any transfer penalties on switching to other funds
- it must be managed by a registered investment manager or investment company
- it must be diversified so as to minimise the risk of large losses
- it may not invest employee contributions directly in employer-issued securities
- it may be a lifecycle fund, a target-date fund, a balanced fund or a professionally managed account.

A key point about safe harbour provisions is that they are not compulsory for sponsors to follow. The sponsor is free to choose an alternative course of action. The provisions do, though, give sponsors a firm steer as to what approach the government regards as appropriate. If the provisions are well-designed, they provide a powerful indication of best practice.[2]

Default funds

In this section we examine what constitutes good default fund design. We also discuss lifestyle funds, given that lifestyle is a common approach for the default fund.

Survey results
Of the pensions experts we surveyed, 89% think that a DC plan should have a default fund.

2 For more details see http://www.dol.gov/ebsa/newsroom/fsdefaultoptionproposalrevision.html.

Respondents, on average, say that, where a plan has a default fund, typically 82% of members invest in it.

Of respondents, 57% think DC plans should offer a lifestyle fund as the default, while 39% think lifestyle should be available as an option members can choose.

The results of our survey, together with other surveys such as the NAPF 2006 Annual Survey (NAPF, 2007), show that typically more than 80% of plan members accept the default fund, many of them passively. Default funds, therefore, are essential for the reluctant investor, who is deterred from joining if membership involves making complex, often incomprehensible, investment choices. Default funds are obviously also required where automatic enrolment is being used.

It is tempting to suggest that a default should not be offered in order to force people to make a decision. However, thinking realistically, it is unlikely that we will, in the foreseeable future, get many people to engage with this decision, so I think a default is necessary and may produce better/less volatile results than would be true for people forced to make a choice. **Insurance company**

The NAPF 2006 survey reports that 83% of DC plans have a default fund. Despite this widespread use, our research revealed growing concern amongst some advisers about the potential liability of employers, trustees and advisers for any problems arising in the default fund.

The real purpose of the default is to encourage people to join. Without it, people will see that they have to make complicated choices and will not join. But, there is a trend away from defaults in occupational DC because the trustees are afraid they will be held accountable for the outcome. **Asset manager**

I am increasingly of the view that providers and employers can't escape liability for the outcome where there is a very large number of people in a default fund. Members who accepted the default will claim that they didn't actively choose it. **Insurance company**

Choosing the default fund

Many of the professionals we interviewed believe that members generally see the default fund as implicit advice. We investigated the selection process for the default fund and found that employers using contract DC usually delegate the choice to their adviser. The adviser in turn tends to recommend the default fund put forward by the selected provider. Historically this has been either a balanced managed or index-tracking fund, depending on the provider's areas of specialisation. This means that the default fund is not driven by buy-side needs, but by sell-side expediency.

With stakeholder plans the main driver is cost – so the default fund will be the life office's cheapest option. So, if you have an L&G stakeholder the default will be passive; a Scottish life company's default will be the active balanced managed fund. The [members'] 'choice' therefore, is illusory. Generally the consultant or IFA will select the provider, so the default is not a major consideration. **Asset manager**

The TPR consultation on DC governance notes the intention for the regulator to provide guidance on the process for selecting a default fund. This would seem likely to include issues such as considering the risk tolerance of members, the appropriate means of managing risk as members approach retirement, and the effective management of costs. As we argued above, it may make sense to go further and establish safe harbour provisions that protect the employer from liability for the outcome of investment in the default fund, provided that appropriate care has been taken in the selection decision.

Lifestyle funds as the default

Lifestyle (or lifecycle) funds switch members' pension fund assets from equities to bonds and cash as the planned retirement date approaches. A lifestyle overlay is a common component of default options, and it serves two important purposes. First, it ensures that members are invested predominantly in equities, or other growth assets, for most of the accumulation years. Secondly, it ensures that members gradually switch from risky to safer assets in the few years before retirement to avoid the potentially disastrous impact of a market crash at a time when earned income is expected to cease shortly.

The lifestyle approach is common in practice, with the NAPF (2007) survey reporting that it is used as the default in 63% of DC plans. However, there are disputes over:
- the length of the lifestyle switching period
- the exchange of assets involved in the switch
- whether lifestyling is even an effective strategy at all.

There is also a concern that where there is only one lifestyle default fund, this gives rise to an over-concentration of members in a single fund. As mentioned earlier, this poses potential problems for employers, in particular if members are dissatisfied with the outcome and complain that they were 'directed' into an inappropriate fund.

The variety of different lifestyle mechanisms that are in use across the DC market suggests that opinions vary about what is most effective. Different providers operate lifestyle mechanisms that start the switch into safer assets at any time from three to ten years (and in a few cases more) prior to the expected retirement date. Equally, the growth vehicle in use for the early years of membership varies across providers and can be a UK equity fund, a global equity fund or some form of balanced fund, with additional variations in terms of active or passive management. (Byrne et al., 2007.)

Lifestyle hasn't changed or developed for a decade. The thinking varies. Some argue that a three-year switch is optimal to allow for maximum growth, but in practice it does not work. This is largely because people don't know when they are going to retire and three years doesn't give enough flexibility – nor does five in many cases. The current trend is towards an earlier start for switching. One of our clients decided to err on the cautious side and recently changed from five to ten years because of the uncertainty over actual retirement dates. **Consultant**

The decision on the switching period is driven by two main considerations. The first relates to managing market risk: a longer switching period provides greater protection from losses, but on the other hand imposes a cost in terms of reduced expected return, given the longer period in low-risk/low-return assets. The other consideration relates to uncertainty in relation to the member's retirement date. A short switching period may mean that a member who is forced to retire a few years early is still heavily invested in equities – and hostage to market conditions – at that point.

Traditional lifestyle funds switch the member's investments from risky assets, such as equities, to safer assets such as bonds, as the planned retirement date approaches. Typically, this is achieved by switching the units of the funds the member is holding from, say, the equity fund to units in the bond and cash fund. An alternative method that simplifies unit holdings is the target-date fund.

Target-date funds work on a similar principle to conventional lifestyling, but the switching occurs within each dated fund. So, for example, a member expecting to retire in 2040 would buy the '2040 Fund'. This would have an internal lifestyling mechanism and would start to switch into safer assets in, say, 2030 so that by 2040 the fund is 75% in fixed income and 25% in cash. Target-date funds may be easier for members to understand: they simply choose the fund that coincides with their planned retirement date, and the manager does everything else. In this way they focus the member on the final outcome rather than on shorter-term performance. The Personal Accounts Delivery Authority charged with designing a new national DC scheme for the UK has suggested that target date funds will be appropriate for its target membership of low and middle earners without access to existing work-based pension plans.

Target-date funds may be appropriate for use as the default in a DC plan. As with many forms of funds, providers may take different views on what is an appropriate asset allocation to support the target date. This diversity is not bad in itself, but given diversity in the underlying asset allocations, employers, trustees and advisers need to make their selections very carefully with the member profile in mind.

Changing the default fund

In trust-based plans, trustees select the default fund and the investment range. An important issue arises when they decide the existing arrangements are no longer appropriate, for example due to sustained poor performance by the investment manager.

Where trustees decide to make a change, they need to think about how to deal with member's existing holdings in the fund that has been removed. Often the approach taken is to inform members of the change and invite them to switch. Trustees often seem reluctant to close fund options entirely and force members to switch. The result can be large numbers of members invested in legacy funds, with complications in administration, communication and ongoing monitoring.

Trustees are not bold enough. Where they do change an under-performing manager, many fail to ensure members automatically transfer. Instead they send a letter saying that there is now a new manager – and they leave it up to the member whether or not to switch. The result is that most members stay put and end up with under-performing legacy funds. **Consultant**

An alternative is to create a range of funds in the employer's name – for example the XYZ UK equity fund. This is sometimes known as a 'white-labelled' fund, where the asset manager provides the manufacturing on an unbranded basis. The trustees and/ or their adviser can then appoint one or more managers per fund and monitor them, replacing managers where necessary. This avoids the above problem because members don't have to make any decisions – they are automatically moved to the new managers.

This approach would appear to have benefits from a governance point of view and from an administrative perspective. It should be possible in contract – as well as trust-based arrangements. However, employers and trustees may be reluctant to adopt this approach for fear of liability, should their investment decisions turn our poorly. Again, there may be a need for safe harbour provisions that reassure the decision makers that they will not be held liable for the outcome, provided that they followed appropriate steps in taking the decision.

Investment choice

Survey results

Most of the pensions experts we surveyed think that DC plans should offer a relatively narrow range of funds for members to choose from. The respondents' views on the appropriate number of funds to offer can be contrasted with data from the NAPF 2006 Survey (NAPF, 2007) on the choice actually provided by DC plans (Figure 3).

Beyond the default, most DC plans offer a range of funds for active investors to choose from. The NAPF 2006 survey reports that 94% of DC plans provide members with investment choice. Twenty-three per cent of plans offer members 20 or more funds to choose from, and 10% of plans offer 40 fund choices or more.

Today most advisers and consultants recognise that wide choice can confuse members and that a small range of funds is preferable, but they do not always feel

Number of funds	Survey: % of respondents	NAPF data % of plans
1	0%	6%
2–5	17%	14%
6–10	57%	35%
11–20	9%	21%
20+	15%	23%
Don't know	2%	N/A

Fig. 3. The appropriate number of funds to offer according to respondents and the choice actually provided by DC plans. Sources: Pensions Institute report 'Dealing with the reluctant investor' (see Note 1) and NAPF 2006 Survey.

confident, from a liability perspective, in narrowing down the choice. Our interviews revealed that the selection of an appropriate range of fund choices in relation to membership profiles is hampered by the fear that the selection and elimination process could create a liability if it goes wrong. The concern is that members could later claim that they suffered because better funds were denied to them.

There have been a lot of articles recently on the inadvisability of providing choice. I have to say, having just joined my own firm's group personal pension plan, which had over 200 funds to choose from, I agree with this. **Pensions lawyer**

It is difficult for employers to pare down fund choice. Typically they will want their consultant to do it. Consultants are wary of cutting funds out of predetermined ranges – there is 'regret risk' that the ones they exclude will do well. **Asset manager**

We appear to have the unfortunate situation whereby experts believe that a small range of funds is appropriate but what is offered frequently is a much wider choice, even though this is confusing and unhelpful for most members.

Beyond the reluctant investor, there may be members who want and need a wider fund choice. If plans want to provide choice for this group, it is important they do so in a manner that does not impose costs and complexity on the vast majority of members with simpler requirements. One option would be to establish an appropriate filter system for the investment range. This would involve creating two or three layers of fund choices, so that members with basic requirements need only consider the simple choice offered in the first tier, and the wider range is only displayed to those who request it.

Risk-graded multi-asset funds

As we have discussed above, it is unlikely that a single default fund will meet the risk/ return preferences of 80%+ members of the plan. The issue may be that the default fund is the only 'packaged' option and moving from that to 'do-it-yourself' asset allocation using individual funds is too intimidating for most members. One alternative to this, which is growing in use, is to offer a small number of packaged options that members may choose from. For example, the plan could offer either three or five multi-asset strategies differentiated by the balance between risky and safer assets, with some form of lifestyle overlay to manage risk through time. Members can choose amongst them based on their perceived attitude to investment risk, and the funds can be described or categorised on that basis.

One way to characterise the funds is to give them names such as 'Adventurous', 'Balanced' or 'Cautious' (the 'ABC' approach). These names attempt to differentiate the funds for the reluctant investor. Underlying the classification can be a more objective measure of risk, for example where each fund has a target range for its value-at-risk or volatility parameters. An example is provided in Figure 4.

Asset class	Asset allocation		
	Cautious fund	Balanced fund	Adventurous fund
UK equities	30%	40%	50%
Overseas equities	30%	40%	50%
Fixed income	40%	20%	–

Fig. 4. Asset allocation of risk-graded managed strategies.
Source: Hypothetical example developed based on a review of fund options available in the UK pensions market.

Members can be provided with a risk profiling questionnaire to help them consider their attitude to risk. Some providers suggest that this type of approach has been helpful in reducing the percentage of members who end up in the default fund. The key is in making the fund choice more manageable for the non-expert, although it is fair to say that inertia remains strong and many members will, in any case, end up in the default fund.

Risk profiling of members can be advantageous. You're more likely to offer a suitable fund range and to get positive member feedback. But it's labour intensive and there are regulatory risks. **IFA**

While the ABC approach appears to have merits, employers, trustees and advisers need to make sure the provider's interpretation of risk profile matches their own view. It is unlikely that many members will be able to do so for themselves.

One issue raised by a number of our contacts was whether these types of funds should have descriptive names, such as 'Cautious' or names based on factual aspects such as the equity content (e.g. 'The 75 Fund', which has a 75% equity allocation). The argument for the latter is there is less risk of members being misled, for example by interpreting 'Cautious' in a way that is different from the provider's view. However, elsewhere we make the argument that members will be better served by communicating funds based on *what they are expected to achieve* rather than on the asset allocation and investment style.

Finally, it is worth noting that the ABC approach does not remove the need for a default fund: some members won't complete the risk profiling questionnaire, and some that do so still won't make an active choice of one of the three funds. It should, though, reduce the proportion of members going in to the default *on a passive basis* by providing a simpler menu for active choice.

Conclusion

Most of the pensions professionals we interviewed regard the majority of DC plan members as reluctant investors with limited investment knowledge and even less desire to engage with investment choices. Asset managers looking to grow their business in the DC market need to take account of this behavioural characteristic in their product design and marketing. Innovation for this market is not more and more complex products, but rather a few well-designed and effective products. Communication should focus on the details of the benefits the product delivers for the investor, rather than esoteric information on the manufacturing process. These are not approaches that come naturally to many providers in the asset management industry.

References

Byrne, A., D. Blake, A. Cairns and K. Dowd (2007), 'Default Funds in UK Defined Contribution Pension Plans', *Financial Analysts Journal*, July/August.

NAPF (2007), 'National Association of Pension Funds Annual Survey 2006', National Association of Pension Funds, London.

TPR (2006), 'How The Pensions Regulator will regulate defined contribution pension plans in relation to the risks to members', *The Pensions Regulator*, Brighton.

UBS (2009), 'Pension Fund Indicators 2009', *UBS*, London.

About the author

Pascal Wanner is SimCorp's account manager for the Swiss market. He was previously a member of the SimCorp strategic research team responsible for the strategic direction of the SimCorp Dimension integrated investment management system. He holds a bachelor's degree in economics with specialty in banking and finance and worked for KPMG Consulting before joining SimCorp Switzerland, where he held various sales and implementation positions. He rejoined SimCorp in Copenhagen after accepting a position as business system architect and project manager at Julius Bär to strengthen and improve SimCorp Dimension deployment there.

Contact: pascal.wanner@simcorp.com.

8
IT strategy in uncertain times:
taking it from alignment to enabling growth

ABSTRACT Market forecasts are improving, and companies are already reporting
positive results. But seeing the results of this recession, it becomes clear that the
basic business parameters of the banking industry – and in particular in the asset
management industry – are about to change drastically. It is apparent that there is no
going back to business as usual. Combined with the uncertain recovery of economies
worldwide, it is very difficult for any company to steer safely through this turmoil. Business cycle analysis suggests that the time to prepare for growth is now, even though
recovery is still volatile and downturns are expected. CEOs should currently be preparing their organisation for growth. New business strategies are required to survive
and ensure future success. A critical success criterion for today's asset management
organisation is to maintain an IT infrastructure that enables innovation and growth.
Having the right solution to support the value chain in an optimal matter is indispen-
sible. It is therefore of the utmost importance to align IT and similar investments with
the business strategy to ensure future support of the core processes. The target for
any organisation, however, should be the implementation of a systematic strategy
process – including information technology – that enables it not only to achieve the
required flexibility but to use IT and IT investments as a strategic tool in obtaining
long-term success.

8 IT strategy in uncertain times: taking it from alignment to enabling growth

by Pascal Wanner

Changes in production structures in the asset management industry

Everyone remembers the fatal developments in mid-September 2008 that created a financial turmoil never seen before. The collapse of Lehmann Brothers and its impact has shaken not only the banking industry but economies worldwide. Headlines in newspapers, magazines and journals in late 2008 and early 2009 predominately featured expressions such as 'economic crisis' and 'recession', and comparisons were made with the Great Depression after the First World War. Fearing the worst, central banks worked together with governments to release massive stimulus packages. Central banks expanded their money supplies massively to avoid the risk of deflation. In addition, governments agreed on large fiscal stimulus packages as well as direct investments to offset the reduction in private sector demand.

These actions showed effect, and in June 2009 a U.S. Federal Reserve Open Market Committee press release stated:

> [T]he pace of economic contraction is slowing. Conditions in financial markets have generally improved in recent months....Although economic activity is likely to remain weak for a time, the Committee continues to anticipate that policy actions to stabilize financial markets and institutions, fiscal and monetary stimulus, and market forces will contribute to a gradual resumption of sustainable economic growth in a context of price stability.[1]

The decline of economies in the different countries finally slowed down, and it is generally expected that the contraction will hit the trough. The worst is apparently over: GDP development forecasts are now positive, predicting between +0.1% and 1.5% for 2010.

Despite all the optimism of economists, however, it is feared that the positive developments are mainly driven by the effects of the stimulus packages, which will wear off in 2010. Thus GDP growth will most likely be uneven.[2] But predicting how and when the actual recovery will start is very difficult: economists all over the world have differing opinions and are discussing different shapes of the potential recovery. 'U' is the most popular shape, representing the claim that recovery will take some time. 'V'-

---

1   FOMC (2009), http://www.federalreserve.gov/newsevents/press/monetary/20090624a.htm.
2   IMF (2010), 'World Economic Outlook Update', http://www.imf.org/external/pubs/ft/weo/2010/update/01/index.htm, January.

shape proponents foresee a steady recovery after reaching the trough; 'W' adherents predict another dip before the actual recovery. There are even more shapes to chose from, with 'L' as the most pessimistic and 'N' for the optimists, who predict rocket-like recovery once the economy has hit the bottom.[3]

The impact and effects of the recession on the asset management industry have been long-lasting but are now basically over. The 'first hit' was catastrophic, as assets under management dropped by 30–40% and even more in some cases.[4] Businesses are still in full survival mode, trying to restructure their processes and find ways to reduce costs in order to remain profitable. These are difficult times for asset management companies to remain successful, so decisions of strategic importance are not taken lightly, especially since the ultimate consequences are still uncertain.

Governments, regulators and international groups (e.g. G8 and G20) agree that the financial turmoil revealed the need for coordination and harmonisation in accounting, regulation, and supervision on an international level. Proposals are being discussed with the intention to implement stronger regulation on capital requirements, to limit excessive risk-taking and excessive leveraging of balance sheets. The particular problem of specific banks which are 'too big to fail' is also fiercely discussed; however, the means to reduce or eliminate the problem are difficult to find. Even living wills are being discussed for banks, to at least limit the unease of unwinding failed financial institutions.

In addition to these regulatory initiatives, governments put particular pressure on offshore centres and light-tax countries, demanding more transparency and a greater exchange of information under threat of punitive measures.

These expected changes will impact the business parameters for tomorrow's asset management industry substantially. Also the shift in client requirements and expectations to asset management will pose additional pressure. Asset management companies will have to work hard to regain trust by delivering real value to clients. A new, stronger client focus is required to survive in this future business by:
- better articulating risk and reward;
- improving risk management, with particular focus on counterparty and liquidity risk;
- providing real customer-focussed products.[5]

It can be expected that clients, consultants and the investing public in general will scrutinise issues such as performance, management of risk, and counterparty exposure in much more detail than before. Only asset managers that can deliver the products and services that clients are asking for will survive.[6]

---

3   The Economist (2009), 'World economy – U, V or W for recovery.'
4   PricewaterhouseCoopers (2009), 'The day after tomorrow for asset management'.
5   PricewaterhouseCoopers (2009), 'The day after tomorrow – continuing the PricewaterhouseCoopers perspective series on the global financial crisis'.
6   Verdin, P. (2010).

These changes will require asset management organisations to focus more on their actual core competencies, to improve productivity and to be more efficient in managing client assets. Companies will have to compete in a tougher market in the low-paying asset classes with essentially lower returns.

These developments are putting a great deal of pressure on existing investment processes in particular, and some degree of industrialisation is necessary for companies to stay competitive. To survive in the future, organisations will have to deliver better services and products faster and cheaper than before, making a flexible and scalable IT infrastructure business-critical. Companies have been reluctant to make the necessary IT investments in the past. It becomes clear that these investments no longer can be postponed if companies are to remain competitive and enjoy long-term success.

The right combination of strategy and IT infrastructure will be the difference between winners and losers, and only this combination will enable asset management organisations to seize the opportunities that can be found in times of crisis.

Is it time to prepare for growth?

Looking at key economic indicators and making market trend projections is one piece of the puzzle for management teams to determine strategic direction. When laying plans for the future, it is of the utmost importance to have a longer-term perspective that puts the current recession in a different light. The concept of business cycles provides management teams with a more macroeconomic view that will help them plan future actions.

The term 'business cycles' or 'economic cycles' refers to economy-wide fluctuations in production or economic activity over several months or years. These fluctuations

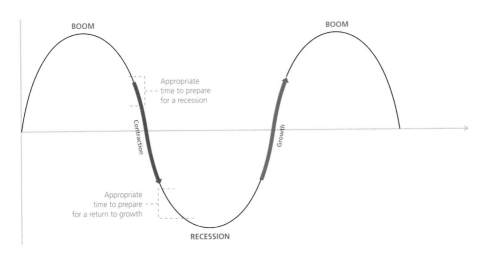

Fig. 1. Gartner business cycle

occur around a long-term growth trend and typically involve shifts over time between periods of relatively rapid economic growth (expansion or boom) and periods of relative stagnation or decline (contraction or recession), as depicted in Figure 1.[7]

In the United States, the National Bureau of Economic Research (NBER) is the final arbiter of the dates of the peaks and troughs of the business cycle. The NBER identifies recession or expansion based on a significant decline or increase in economic activity spread across the economy lasting more than a few months and normally visible in real GDP, real income, employment and industrial production.[8] In December 2007, after 73 months of expansion, the NBER announced that the US economy had reached its peak.[9] Starting from this moment, the US economy started to decline and has not reached the trough yet.

Two important observations can be derived from this statement. Firstly, the actual contraction in the US had already started before the Lehman debacle and, secondly, there will be a period of expansion again, independent of the severity of the contraction.

This enables management teams to carry out actions in the various phases of a business cycle. During the first phase of a contraction, controlling cost drivers is of the utmost importance, which is why companies normally react by using two very basic cost management tools: cutting labour costs and closing down business lines. The prevailing logic in this approach seems to be that less activity equals less cost. However, this short-term form of cost reduction fails to sustain lower costs beyond a 12-month period and – combined with increased competition, tightened regulatory requirements and a sustained pressure on margins – is even counterproductive and will not help organisations survive in the long term.[10]

As soon as the contraction slows down and the expectation of growth rises, organisations should begin preparing for the expansion. Although it is difficult to predict the future, it is essential to start planning before hitting the trough if organisations want to take advantage of the available opportunities. Economic indicators and studies[11] indicate that the worst of the downturn is over and, as mentioned above, that 2010 will see a return to growth. Thus it is important to begin planning for future success.

How to achieve growth?

The first actions after the turmoil had a clear focus on avoiding further damage by implementing improved risk management and cost-cutting measures to ensure survival. However, theory and experience have proven over the past decades that, after times of contraction, growth returns. The earlier that organisations can embrace the

7 O'Sullivan, A. and S.M. Sheffrin (2003).

8 NBER (2010), 'US Business Cycle Expansions and Contractions', http://www.nber.org/cycles.html.

9 NBER (2008), 'Determination of the December 2007 Peak in Economic Activity', http://www.nber.org/cycles/dec2008.html.

10 SimCorp StrategyLab (2009), 'Report on Global Investment Management Cost Survey 2009'.

11 Ernst & Young (2009), 'Opportunities in adversity: Accelerating the change'.

turnaround, the more successful they can be. According to Verdin, growth of an or
ganisation is not a strategy in itself, nor is it the consequence of pure market conditions, but solely a result of a successful business strategy.[12]

Organisational theory offers different business and market strategies with a
particular focus on growing market share in existing or new markets. One aspect
all these concepts have in common is their focus on the analysis of an organisation's own products and its position in the current market. One of the most well-
known concepts is the Ansoff Product-Market Growth Matrix (Figure 2). This matrix can be used as a strategic tool that suggests four basic strategies for growing
business by distinguishing existing and/or new products and existing and/or new
markets.[13]

Products		
	Present	New
Markets		
Present	Market penetration	Market development
New	Market development	Diversification

Fig.2. Ansoff's Product-Market Growth Matrix

The basic concept of this approach is that direction is not only dependent on market opportunities; a company's own basic capabilities have to be considered as well.
Thus a business strategy should not only be driven by customer needs: it should also
be driven by the firm's technical competence and its ability to respond to customer
needs, which must be factored into the definition of strategy and the selection of markets served and products offered. Only then can the firm distribute effort and resources among competing growth opportunities.[14]

The matrix also illustrates the fact that, depending on the direction chosen, the
element of risk increases, the further the strategy moves away from known quantities.
Product development and market extension strategies typically involve a greater risk
than market penetration strategy, although diversification strategy carries the greatest risk of all.[15]

Crucial in the evaluation is that the investments involved will differ considerably,
since market penetration and market or product development can usually be pursued
with the same technical, financial, and merchandising resources used for the original
product line. However, a diversification strategy requires new skills, new techniques

---

12   Verdin, P. (2010), 'Enable growth strategies with SimCorp Dimension',
      http://www.simcorp.com/video/Growth/default.htm.
13   Ansoff, I. (1957).
14   Frederick E. and J. Webster (1988).
15   Ansoff, I. (1957).

and new facilities, and as a result almost invariably leads to physical and organisational changes in the structure of the business that represent a distinct break with past business experience.[16]

Measuring success and the position of products in the market should not be too difficult for any asset manager; however, determining core competencies and identifying unique selling points is difficult. The expected pressure in the future from the client side, including changes in the underlying business parameters, will make the task at hand even more difficult. Only when organisations have identified their value chain and determined their support processes will they be able to (re)define their strategy and seize available opportunities.

An infrastructure that enables innovation in products and services by also providing the needed scalability in the core processes of a business is therefore a critical requirement in the asset management industry. The flexibility to launch new products, services or move into new markets when desired is essential. If it does not already have one, an organisation should build an IT architecture that provides the required flexibility to support short time-to-market to guarantee competitive advantage.

The impact of strategy on IT infrastructure

The value chain of an asset manager as illustrated in Figure 3 has substantial requirements to its IT infrastructure with respect to processing, functional coverage and data availability.

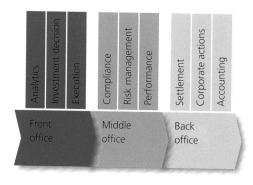

Fig. 3. The value chain of an asset manager

Depending on the individual business model, the infrastructure must support functionality not only from front office activities such as investment decision processing, trade execution, compliance control and risk management, but also middle office

---

16   Wikipedia (2010), 'Product-Market Growth Matrix', http://en.wikipedia.org/wiki/Product-Market_ Growth_Matrix.

activities such as post-trade operations, including compliance, risk measurement and return and attribution analysis. Information must be available on an intra-day basis to portfolio managers and for client reporting. Finally, dedicated tools are required to support all back office processes, e.g. corporate actions, income processing and tax services.[17]

Depending on the actual business strategy, some parts of the processes can be outsourced to third-party administrators (TPAs). The most commonly outsourced services are back office functions, whereas portfolio management, compliance and performance calculation often are considered as core competencies of the individual asset manager.

Requirements from these business models have resulted in two basic IT architectures to support the remaining functions and processes. A typical result of the outsourcing activities is an enterprise architecture with a number of systems in the front office and one or more TPAs handling all the back office operations.[18] This architecture is commonly referred to as best of breed architecture, where systems designed specifically to excel in just one or a few applications are used. However, this not only poses challenges such as increased training and support but also features more complex interfaces with other systems, duplicate data entry and redundant data storage.

Unlike best of breed architecture, integrated enterprise solutions (IESs) are based on a single database that contains integrated functionality for front, middle and back office, as shown in Figure 4.

This solution offers comprehensive business functionality based on the same underlying data in a consistent way, also for advanced front and middle office functions that are often not present in stand-alone packages. Additionally, integrated systems offer dedicated integration functionality to ensure flexible and easy integration with other systems and vendors.

Even today, the asset management industry is heavily dependent on a functional IT infrastructure to support their processes, their individual analytical tasks and – more importantly – their data and reporting requirements. Changing parts of the process or functional requirements will have a substantial impact on the infrastructure. Especially new client requests and new regulations will require even faster access to relevant portfolio and security data on intra-day basis. When margins are under pressure, the need to provide new and better services or products is absolutely crucial. This will, of course, require an even higher degree of flexibility in the process and functional support of any IT architecture. If the strategy proves to be successful, it is important that the infrastructure can handle the growth as well.

It should thus be clear to any CEO or board of directors deciding on a new strategy

---

17   Schröter, M. (2009).
18   Schröter, M. (2009).

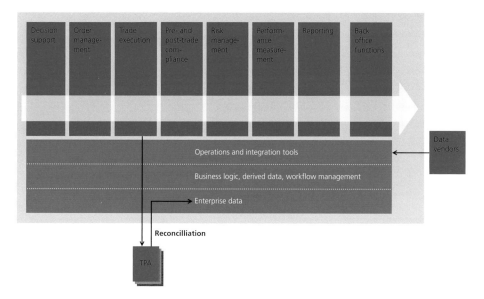

Fig.4. Integrated enterprise solution

that implementation will require investment in infrastructure, and that this might influence time to market. If the underlying architecture does not or does not sufficiently support planned strategic initiatives, it could endanger the success of the overall strategy. It is therefore absolutely crucial to be aware of the potential impact of any strategy on the architecture so that the required level of flexibility is known.

A high-level analysis based on the Ansoff market strategy matrix will provide some degree of understanding of how flexible the different IT architectures are and the risk an organisation may be exposed to when it chooses one of them. This approach will exclude the implied market risks as well as the various means of achieving the required targets.

Market penetration

Following the first market strategy suggested by Ansoff, the goal of a market penetration is to increase company sales of its current product offering in the current client market or segment. The organisation seeks to improve business performance either by increasing the volume of sales to current clients, receiving more assets to manage from current clients or finding new clients for the existing products.[19] This strategy requires that marketing activities be intensified to address new and current clients. Another key measure of market penetration is to change existing pricing models to

---

19   Ansoff, I. (1957).

offer the same products at more attractive pricing. This will, of course, only be successful for an asset manager when either volumes are increased (if the strategy is successful) or if production costs can be reduced, e.g. through an industrialised asset management approach.

In 2006, a major European asset manager decided to invest substantially in its reporting capabilities because of increased competition. The goal was to offer state-of-the-art reporting to current and new clients. This initiative did not only enable them to generate better and more frequent reports for their existing client base; it also improved their overall value proposition and lowered their production costs. These effects were the result of streamlined report packages, a standardised report generation process and the elimination of a great deal of manual work.

In the light of the latest developments, the ability to provide transparent and efficient risk management will become another opportunity to deliver added value to clients. Especially for clients who after the turmoil seek not only improved returns on investment, but clearly more controlled risk taking.

Product development

The second strategy approach is to increase market share by offering new products in an existing market segment. For any asset manager, an infrastructure that enables innovation and growth is a business-critical requirement. Especially the flexibility to launch new products as part of a strategic initiative can be a differentiator between success and failure.

In the past, the asset management industry has been able to produce new successful products to meet ever-changing client requirements. However, the recession clearly showed that neither organisations nor infrastructure could actually cope adequately with these complex products. This resulted in an increased demand for new investment products with a higher degree of protection or passive managed investment funds. It has become paramount for asset managers to maintain full control over the valuation of the products offered, over the execution process and over the risk management procedures. More than ever, organisations require IT solutions that support not only the creation and offering of these new products, but adequate functional coverage on the rest of the actual investment process. Only IT solutions of this nature provide asset managers with the flexibility necessary to meet client demands in a timely manner.

Market development

Contrary to the previously mentioned strategy, the main target of an organisation is to sell their current products to new market segments. This requires the organisation to either establish an own subsidiary or choose the way of cooperation or merger with or acquisition of other organisations. Such moves introduce quite substantial challenges, especially with the introduction of international accounting standards. Having to comply simultaneously with national, regional and international standards such as US GAAP or IFRS and to treat transactions or holdings in different ways makes considerable demands on an IT infrastructure. Entering new geographical markets and their regulatory environments, accounting standards and compliance requirements significantly increases the risks involved in a new business endeavour.[20]

Diversification

The riskiest strategy is to diversify the activities of the organisation by entering into completely new markets with new products. This approach obviously requires generally new skills, new techniques, and new infrastructures to be successful and thus also substantial investments. This strategy may be the last resort if an asset management organisation wants to stay in business: to actually change their current business model completely by adapting to the changes in market conditions. Especially the threat of increased capital requirements for asset managers may have a substantial impact, with some strategies that have been successful previously not being valid anymore.

The crisis has brought the value chain to the forefront in the awareness of all asset management companies. Focus on core competencies has become business critical. In this light, two major German investment managers decided to limit their business operations to actual investment management and to outsource their fund administration operation. Their main objective was to focus on core competencies and to use a dedicated provider to deliver the required services more cost efficiently. This initiative resulted in the creation of the largest German fund administrator, which is an independent organisation that can also provide its services to other market participants. The IT infrastructure played an important role in the overall decision process, with scalability and flexibility as critical business requirements.

Flexibility and scalability are key success criteria

All these strategies – even with small adjustments in a market penetration strategy, for example – require changes in a company's IT infrastructure. Depending on the flexibility and functional richness of the applications used, substantial investments may be necessary to enable the organisation to pursue its chosen strategy, which will greatly impact the time to market. Thus a critical success criterion for any organisation is an IT architecture that enables innovation and growth. This becomes para-

---

20 SimCorp (2010).

mount, considering the fact that asset management companies are not only pursuing one specific strategy but most often combinations of different market strategies to ensure future growth.

It may sound contradictory for asset managers who already have sophisticated and tailored infrastructures, but flexibility and scalability will be even more business-critical and necessary to adapt to fast-changing market conditions. Depending on the business model selected, some IT infrastructure types offer more flexibility and scalability than others. Figure 5 highlights the specific key advantages of each type of architecture based on the four different strategies.

	Integrated enterprise solution	Best of breed architecture
Market penetration	Data availability – all-in-one solution – standards covered Process efficiency – throughout the solution – high scalability	Data expertise – high sophistication Process specialisation – focus on single process – within application
Product development	Operational security – coverage throughout solution – dependent on functional availability	Agility – short time to market – not single provider dependent
Market development	Flexibility – modular functionality – limited implementation effort	Outsourcing – third-party administrator selection – interface requirements
Diversification	Value chain coverage – for vertical development – flexibility	Lean architecture – for re-sized operations – expert application

Fig. 5. Architecture fit for strategy development

Changes in the current production structures will result in organisations putting at the top of their agenda the ability to change business model to adapt to new demanding client requests and new regulations. This will put even more pressure on the asset management industry, and competition will certainly become tougher.[21] This will necessitate additional measures to boost efficiency in their processes, as well to shorten the time to market even more with the introduction of new products and services. In these efforts, however, it is important to not lose the ability to control market risk and continuously decrease operational risk.

For these reasons, organisations must prepare their processes, infrastructure and especially IT architecture to embrace the future. Essential to their success will be the ability to identify the IT architecture necessary to meet the challenges ahead.

---

21   PricewaterhouseCoopers (2009), 'The day after tomorrow for asset management'.

Aligning business strategy with IT strategy

As concluded in the previous section, business strategies cannot be determined without including information technology, which is why a new approach for strategy definition is necessary.

The start of a traditional strategy development process is a detailed analysis of the company and its active business environment. The goal is for the company to achieve insight into its own strengths and weaknesses and to understand better its own key competencies and value generators inside the organisation. Depending on the strategy definition, not only the company and its processes are included in the analysis, but also other business stakeholders as well as political and social influences. The outcome of this analysis enables organisations to determine potential business opportunities either based on their own strengths or a market position improved through regulatory changes, for example. The competitive advantages or market opportunities identified provide a reference point for the general vision and strategy definition. Strategy definition concepts that include market- and competition-specific analysis followed by systematic measurement and categorisation of business opportunities are necessary to ensure future success.

The next step is to define an action plan that describes the actual implementation of the strategy and maps objectives, activities and measures into a dedicated time and project plan. An important part of such a project plan is to evaluate the impact of the objectives on the organisation, on management and controlling systems, and on the IT infrastructure.

Including IT at such a late stage in the process of the generic strategy definition will never exploit IT innovation to its full extent, as illustrated in Figure 6.

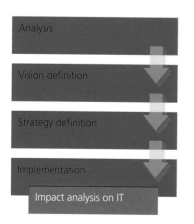

Fig.6. Generic strategy definition process

Instead, IT departments can only react to specific requirements from defined strategic targets that can neither be rejected nor redefined. More importantly, if potential implementation threats are identified very late in the overall strategy implementation project, this will have a dramatic impact on the overall risk, cost, and time to market. The last may even be the biggest risk, considering the fact that time to market can make the difference between success and failure.

The predominant view of executive and senior management has been that IT is an expense only and a commodity item that should be managed at a minimal cost. Investments and changes in the IT infrastructure have been driven solely by the business strategy and its derived business requirements. When IT is correctly aligned with the business strategy, investments can add significant value to the overall business strategy.[22]

To reach its full potential, IT strategy must become an integral part of the overall multi-year company planning to achieve competitive differentiation. Only by looking beyond immediate business requirements and by considering technology trends and the competitive landscape can IT investments play a proactive role in actually shaping business strategy. This statement is supported by a survey carried out by McKinsey that identified the most important factors in IT spending compared to bank performance. Factors such as operating scale or amount of IT spending did not necessarily translate into higher profitability. But banks that invested more in innovation and differentiation and had successfully aligned IT investment and business targets scored the best results.[23]

It is therefore recommended that IT analysis be included as an integral part of the overall strategy analysis, starting out with an internal SWOT analysis as shown in Figure 7.

Fig.7. Information technology analysis steps

The outcome should not only focus on the supported business processes and the individual software components, but should also provide an overview of how well

---

22   McKinsey (2007), 'McKinsey – The next frontier in IT strategy'.
23   McKinsey (2007), 'Better IT management for banks'.

the overall value chain of the organisation is actually covered. Thus particular focus should be given to user interaction (internal and external), process efficiency (e.g. avoid redundant data entry), scalability and ability to change.

The SWOT analysis will provide the organisation with clear indications on where they should invest to stay competitive in the market or which investments can result in competitive advantage. The identified strengths, weaknesses, opportunities and threats should be scrutinised on a detailed level and benchmarked with those of competitors. This should leave the organisation with an objective list of items which could help the company either improve or excel in different areas of the actual value-generating process.

The last step in this IT analysis process is to screen the technology trends, leading IT companies and competitors to new ideas on how investments could achieve the required result. An example of such trends could be providing the client with online access to reports on demand via mobile phone. One natural step, for example, would be to analyse diverse providers and their applets in detail to verify feasibility for possible usage in the banking industry.

The list of opportunities should not only contain IT-specific weaknesses or opportunities, but represent the company's overall business opportunities. With the incentive to lower internal operation costs for client trading, companies have introduced trading portals for clients which have not only boosted trading volumes but also increased service levels and reduced operation costs. There was a clear business goal behind this investment, but it nonetheless resulted in a competitive advantage when implemented.[24]

Following such an approach, however, requires a paradigm change in the qualification and quantification on IT investments in general. Organisations must understand that focussing exclusively on cost will limit their potential, and by simply passing on IT investments, companies will miss out on opportunities to gain a competitive advantage. As the previous example with electronic trading platforms for clients illustrates, IT investment can and should be used as a competitive weapon. A suggested approach for the management of IT investments is very close to the core business of the asset management industry. Organisations should manage their IT investments like financial investments, like a balanced portfolio. This IT portfolio approach[25] suggests a more active management of investments by categorising and balancing the overall investment across predefined categories.

A categorisation of the actual investments must reflect the risk of but also the return on these investments. A simplistic differentiation for organisations could be:
- 'Remain competitive': elemental investments in core business applications to stay in the market, to keep quality or to be able to provide the service;

---

24   McKinsey (2006), 'Divide and conquer: Rethinking IT strategy'.
25   McFarlan, F. W. (1981).

– 'Gain advantage': investments that will result in competitive advantages (improve services with new channels or with more flexibility, reduce prices for services, increase efficiency etc.).

This concept requires balanced investment in both categories. Organisations with a focus on remaining competitive may only be able to achieve some reduction in operational cost or ensure service and quality levels with dedicated investments, but this will not create a competitive advantage. To really create strategic advantage, it is paramount for organisations to balance their investment across the different categories.[26] Only by looking beyond the current infrastructure and business processes can the organisation identify the opportunities where IT investments could provide a competitive advantage.

Conclusion

Market forecasts are improving and companies are already reporting positive results, but the recovery is still volatile and downturns in the near future must be expected. Anticipation of market developments and derived business planning has become very difficult. In addition to these market conditions, the banking sector remains under the scrutiny of regulators and governments demanding new rules and increased monitoring. Clients who have experienced dramatic losses in this recession are now demanding real added value and a strong focus on their individual requirements. This change in business conditions will impact the current business models heavily and organisations will have to prepare themselves if they wish to survive.

Current understanding of business cycles clearly indicates to executive management of organisations that it is now time to prepare for growth. It is crucial for the long-term success of companies that their structures and processes are re-defined so that they are able to execute and implement changes rapidly.

Paramount to any strategy chosen in targeting growth is that real and perceived value is delivered to clients. Independent of the strategy chosen, information technology is the critical success factor. It is essential to the organisation that core processes are fully supported whilst maintaining the required flexibility to change and the ability to scale if the strategy proves successful. All these factors will determine the future success of an asset manager.

Most asset management organisations have understood the importance of IT in their business environment and have successfully begun align IT and business strategy. This can be seen as a first step in the direction of managing IT and treating investment in IT not as a simple cost, but using it as a growth driver.

---

26   McKinsey (2006), 'Divide and conquer: Rethinking IT strategy'.

If organisations are not only to achieve the necessary flexibility but also to use IT and IT investment as a strategic weapon, they must implement a new approach to strategy definition and IT management. IT must become an integrated part of the overall business strategy definition, with special focus on market trends and internal competencies. By including IT in the overall process, management can ensure not only the support of the strategic objectives targeted, but can also use investment in IT as the means to achieve or even exceed these objectives. This necessitates a change in the overall IT infrastructure management with respect to the identification and selection of investments that allow companies to remain competitive and possibly also achieve a competitive advantage. When a company's IT strategy is aligned with its business strategy, real added value can be achieved on a long-term basis, and the organisation can use IT investment as a tool to achieve growth.

References

Ansoff, I. (1957), 'Strategies for Diversification', *Harvard Business Review,* pp. 113–124.

Ernst & Young (2009), 'Opportunities in adversity: Accelerating the change'.

EZB. (2009), Press release, Retrieved from http://www.ecb.int/press/pressconf/2009/html/is091203.en.html, 3 December.

FOMC (2009), http://www.federalreserve.gov/newsevents/press/monetary/20090624a.htm.

Frederick E. and J. Webster (1988), 'The Rediscovery of the Marketing Concept', *Business Horizons,* pp. 29–39.

IMF (2010), *'World Economic Outlook Update',* retrieved from IMF, World Economic Update, http://www.imf.org/external/pubs/ft/weo/2010/update/01/index.html, 26 January.

McFarlan, F. W. (1981), 'Portfolio approach to information systems', *Harvard Business Review,* pp. 142–150.

McKinsey (2006), 'Divide and conquer: Rethinking IT strategy', *The McKinsey Quarterly.*

McKinsey (2007), 'Better IT management for banks', *The McKinsey Quarterly.*

McKinsey (2007), 'The next frontier in IT strategy: A McKinsey survey', *The McKinsey Quarterly.*

NBER (2008), 'Determination of the December 2007 Peak in Economic Activity', retrieved from http://www.nber.org/cycles/dec2008.html, 28 November.

NBER (2010), 'US Business Cycle Expansions and Contractions', retrieved from http://www.nber.org/cycles.html, 15 January.

O'Sullivan, A. and S.M. Sheffrin (2003), 'Economics: Principles in action', Pearson.

PricewaterhouseCoopers (2009), 'The day after tomorrow for asset management'.

PricewatherhouseCoopers (2009), 'The day after tomorrow: Continuing the PricewaterhouseCoopers perspective series on the global financial crisis'.

Schröter, M. (2009), 'Extended enterprise data management', SimCorp A/S.

SimCorp (2010), 'Growth acceleration strategies', *Enable growth strategies with Sim-
Corp Dimension,* pp. 16–17.

SimCorp StrategyLab (2009), 'Report on Global Investment Management Cost Survey 2009'.

The Economist (2009), 'World economy: U, V or W for recovery'.

Verdin, P. (2010), 'Reinventing value for growth in global asset management', *Enable
growth strategies with SimCorp Dimension,* pp. 10–11, SimCorp A/S.

Verdin, P. (2009), 'Time to return to growth', *Journal of Applied IT and Investment
Management,* pp. 21–26, SimCorp A/S.

Wikipedia (2010), 'Product-Market Growth Matrix', Retrieved on 8 February 2010
from Wikipedia, the free encyclopedia: http://en.wikipedia.org/wiki/Product-
Market_Growth_Matrix.

About the author

 *Jacob Elsborg* is Head of Technology for ATP's investment department and holds a master's degree in economics and mathematics from the Copenhagen Business School and an MBA from the Henley Management College in the UK. Most of his professional life he has worked in the financial industry, starting his career as an IT economist for Danmarks Nationalbank, the central bank of Denmark, from 1995 until 2000. For the last ten years he has worked for ATP, a statutory pension fund covering 4.6 million members – virtually the entire adult population of Denmark. As Head of Technology, Jacob Elsborg is responsible for the development of the ATP investment department's operational platform. Contact: jae@atp.dk.

9
Operational platform and growth: a strategic challenge

ABSTRACT Over the past ten to fifteen years, the asset management industry has increasingly focussed on the development and utilisation of technology as a key driver for gaining competitive advantage. The expression 'operational platform' has been used over and over again, but the concept has not yet been properly defined. As a result, asset managers capable of defining what activities take place on the operational platform and how these activities are processed are rare. Likewise, how to properly analyse and integrate an operational platform as part of business strategy analysis is a question that has yet to be answered satisfactorily (as a consequence of the lack of proper definition). Due to this lack of strategic alignment between the operational platform and the business, there is, first, insufficient recognition of the fact that the development of this platform should be an ongoing and strategically managed process and, second, a lack of management focus on the operational platform. This situation will most likely cause platform instability, which again leads to increased expenses from the resultant necessary problem solving and extra working hours. This leads to the main postulate in this chapter: an appropriate and well-defined strategic approach to an operational platform is economically beneficial and can change IT expenses from costs into a strategic investment. It is explained why implementing an operational platform strategy is a necessary tool in the strategic management performed by an asset manager. Various tools for performing strategic management that can support growth are suggested, and the author also seeks to explain why it is beneficial to separate the strategic areas of an operational platform strategy from the organisation's IT strategy.

9 Operational platform and growth: a strategic challenge

by Jacob Elsborg

The consequences of lacking an operational platform strategy

The global financial crisis has been tough, and experts have varying views of future prospects. Some of the more optimistic analysts believe that the markets will return to 2007 levels in 2011 or 2012. The only possible conclusion to be drawn from comparing the various analyses is that the markets are not yet stable and that the higher level of volatility seen in the markets over the past couple of years will continue.

In this chapter, it is questioned how well asset managers in general are prepared for growth or at least a positive change in the financial markets. Searching the literature, none of the contributions have (to this author's knowledge) proposed ways to change the operational platform strategy to reflect changes in the business strategy caused by the financial crises. This indicates that asset managers may be preparing for growth and/or change, but none of them have considered changing the operational platform accordingly to support new business goals. This lack of alignment between an operational platform strategy and the business strategy is seen far too often. In fact, a proper operational platform strategy is extremely rare.

The following definition of an operational platform (Elsborg, 2008) is applied in this chapter:

An operational platform in the asset management industry is where the management of an organisation's data and information takes place, together with the execution of decisions.

The situation of a market set for change and growth opportunities puts a great deal of pressure upon asset managers. What are they to expect and do in a market like this? Unfortunately, there is no room for what would no doubt be an exciting discussion of the strategic initiatives taken by asset managers during the global financial crisis and how they have prepared for the future. What is interesting, as stated above, is that looking for evidence of changes to operational strategies, operational platform strategy or IT strategy (IT strategy is included here because many asset managers have no operational strategy) as an answer to changes in business strategy caused by the financial crisis, there are very limited results to be found in the available literature on the subject (close to none).

The conclusion that can be drawn from this is that any alignment of operational strategy with business strategy (investment strategy) is rare and that the operational platform is not usually a part of the response to changes in the market.

This situation illustrates a common problem in the industry. Many asset managers do not differentiate between an IT strategy and an operational platform strategy. Far too often, making no differentiation between these strategies causes the operational set-up and the development of this set-up to be based upon technical considerations stated in the IT strategy (if there is one). By contrast, an operational platform strategy – as defined in this chapter – is formulated by the business unit using the platform, which ensures that the management of an operational platform becomes an integrated part of the business. An operational platform strategy includes processes and the functional set-up of investment management operations. The difference between the operational platform strategy and operational strategy is that the former includes the functional set-up.

Once the operational platform strategy is defined, the underlying technological processes such as network, communications and hardware are managed within the framework of the IT strategy, which must of course be aligned with the operational platform strategy. The author of this chapter acknowledges that management of IT strategy is of equal strategic importance (and often more complex).

The approach of strategic management of the operational platform, however, can be more or less sophisticated, e.g. the basic model can be developed further according to the results of the analysis; the analytical approach is extendable; and the strategies and drivers of the platform are equally extendable. It is all a question of how complex a business the operational platform must support.

The value of defining and strategically managing the company's operational platform, however, exceeds the cost, with the following main benefits:

–   Management buys into the development of the operational platform through working with alignment of the operational strategy with the business strategy.
–   Development of the operational platform is not driven by a day-to-day approach, but by defined long-term business goals.
–   The platform development processes become more precise and timely due to the integration on a strategic level with the business strategy, which leads to a decrease in cost.
–   A more stable platform results from the long-term perspective development and it is thus less of a 'putting-out-the-fire' platform.
–   A better understanding develops between the users and developers of the operational platform due to the strategic alignment.
–   On a strategic level, IT and operational management are separated, leaving the purely technical strategy and decisions to the technical staff and the operational strategy and decisions to the business unit.

The conclusion is obviously that the choice and design of an operational platform is not an isolated technical decision, but a strategic management tool that either supports the development of the business or creates obstacles if not well-managed. The operational platform can be seen as a way to gain competitive advantage from cost-efficient design, reliability, flexibility and scalability. In short, the main goal for strategic management of the operational platform is to create alignment of the operational development with the development of the business so that it supports the strategies of the business and thus enables growth.

Case: order management

To illustrate the concept of defining an operational platform strategy, the following example shows how the order management process in its simplest form is strategically based (Figure 1).

Order management in its simplest form consists of the following elements requiring action/decisions:

a   instrument trading
b   legal contracts/financial security
c   pre-trade compliance
d   order generation
e   order execution
f   trading system
g   interface to other systems
h   data repository
i   connectivity
j   IT security

An investment strategy defines what instruments are to be handled within the framework of order management and how the legal aspects of order management are handled. The objectives and strategy of pre-trade compliance, order generation and order execution are handled within the framework of an investment strategy, whereas the processes and integration executing the orders are defined in an operational platform strategy.

An operational platform strategy should specify which instruments (instrument classes are defined later in the chapter) are to be handled electronically, and the choice of system choice must be aligned with the investment strategy. The integration processes and functional set-up (pre-trade compliance, execution, data storage, etc.) are handled within the operational strategy and again aligned with the objectives of the investment strategy.

An IT strategy should cover physical tasks such as communication, both the internal interface between trading system and treasury system (if the systems are separate) and the handling of the external communication, e.g. whether all external communication is through a broker. The IT security set-up and processes are also included in the IT strategy.

Case: order management			
	Strategic framework		
Elements requiring action/decision	Investment strategy	Operational platform strategy	IT strategy
Instruments traded	X		
Legal contracts/financial security	X		
Pre-trade compliance	X	X	
Order generation	X	X	
Order execution		X	
Trading system	X	X	
Interface with other systems		X	X
Data repository		X	X
Connectivity		X	X
IT security			X

Fig. 1. Strategic order management framework

It is obvious that if there is no operational platform strategy, the strategic framework of both the investment strategy and the IT strategy must be widened to cover what is defined in an operational platform strategy. As a consequence, both strategies will be less focussed, and the management owning the strategy will manage areas that are not part of their core business. In this case, the investment strategy ought to be defined by the investment professionals focussing on markets, instruments and business opportunities. Having to define operational processes and platform strategies covering all the aspects of operations will indeed make the strategy broad and unfocussed.

The same thing happens with an IT strategy that has to cover aspects that are not an integrated part of a general IT strategy: it will lack focus.

Thus the operational platform strategy is a necessity if one wants to focus both the investment strategy and IT strategy. An operational platform strategy will also support the managerial focus on the operational side of the business.

Far too often, the areas that ought to be defined as part of the operational platform are left in a strategic vacuum covered by no strategy at all. In such a situation, the operational platform is relegated to day-by-day development with no real management.

The strategic framework

A business strategy is the foundation of any successful organisation. A strategic framework depends upon many factors: company type (e.g. pension fund or hedge fund), size of company, corporate culture and investment universe. The discussion above focussed on the problems that arise when a firm has no operational platform strategy.

The definition of a business strategy derives from the usual steps: analysis followed by definition of vision/mission, objectives, strategy and tactics (VMOST) (Sondhi,

1999), which again leads to the definition of an investment strategy (it has been seen that the strategy and tactics definitions of the business strategy are the definition of the investment strategy). This is the main strategy for the entire organisation and, depending upon the size of the company, may also be a high-level strategy.

For the most part, implementation of an investment strategy as the strategy/tactics of the company strategy is not an appropriate way to define the strategic framework, except for companies that have asset management as their only activity; otherwise this kind of strategic mixing often leaves a gap between investment strategy and operational strategy and an unclear strategic direction. Thus a proper strategic framework ensures that an investment strategy is defined, and this strategy supports the overall business strategy.

It is upon this basis the operational platform strategy is defined. The implementation of the operational platform strategy thus becomes an integrated part of the implementation of the business strategy. Some asset managers define an operational strategy as the strategy that incorporates the tactics and processes that support the investment strategy. The operational platform strategy expands the operational strategy by including the overall functional set-up as a part of this strategy. Sometimes the functional set-up is defined within the framework of the IT strategy, but, far too often, the functional definition is left in a no man's land (not a part of any strategy).

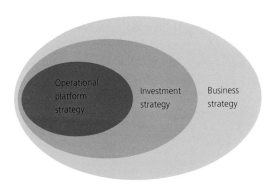

Fig. 2. Strategic alignment

It is outside the scope of this chapter to define a business or investment strategy, which means it is impossible to define a specific operational platform strategy. However, it is possible to define basic operational drivers without having the precise strategic scope of the business, the investment or the operational platform strategy. Creating a successful operational platform strategy requires accurate market assessment and subsequently identification of actions required to achieve the goals of the investment strategy.

Model framework of an operational platform

To implement a strategic approach to managing an operational platform, a functional model must be defined and in place. This model is the main starting point in conducting analyses and setting up a strategy for an operational platform.

Defining the activities of an asset manager within the concept of a value chain (Sondhi, 1999) forms the basis of the functional model (Figure 3).

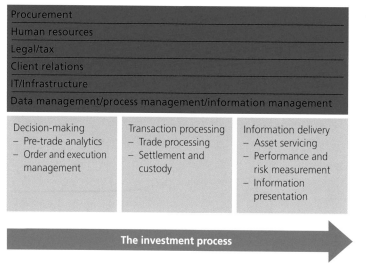

Fig. 3. Value chain

The value chain consists of three primary activities, which are the investment processes:

1 decision-making
2 transaction processing
3 information delivery.

Using this definition of the activities of an asset manager with respect to an operational platform, a model in its simplest form can be used to show where the management of an organisation's data and information takes place, together with the execution of decisions (Figure 4).

In order to define a strategic approach to managing an operational platform, the primary activities in the value chain have to be defined separately. The next part of this chapter is an analysis of the primary activities of an operating platform. Figure 5 gives a brief presentation of a functional model framework (Heyes, 2007; Elsborg, 2008) for the defined activities of an operational platform.

Within the framework shown in Figure 5, a differentiation based upon the characteristics of the instruments is suggested. The asset classes are:

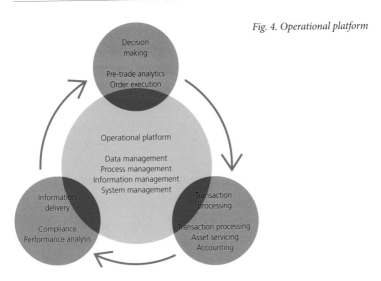

Fig. 4. Operational platform

1 **Cash.** Cash instruments are equities, fixed income and FX cash instruments.
2 **Exchange-traded derivatives (ETDs).** ETD instruments are listed futures and options on all underlying instruments.
3 **OTC (named 'Vanilla' OTC).** OTC products are instruments with standardised procedures.
4 **Illiquid and private assets.** Illiquid and private assets are complex OTC derivatives and private or physical assets.

The assets within each group have the same characteristics in terms of their defined main functions, and they are thus useful when analysing the operational platform. It is not the intent of this chapter to discuss in detail the characteristics of each asset class or how to use the various instruments in terms of portfolio management; however, one must be aware of the differentiation when defining a strategic model of an operational platform.

The basics of an operational platform analysis

The basic analysis of the operational platform is based on the objectives and strategic direction of an operational platform, which is again based on the overall business strategy. The basic analysis is therefore defined as the strategic analysis of the operational platform, and the analysis is performed as a standard basic analysis of a strategy (Henley Management College, 2002). The critical success factors (CSFs) and the main operational drivers of the platform can be determined from this process, along with the key performance indicators (KPIs) (Henley Management College, 2002). Figure 6 illustrates the flow of the analysis.

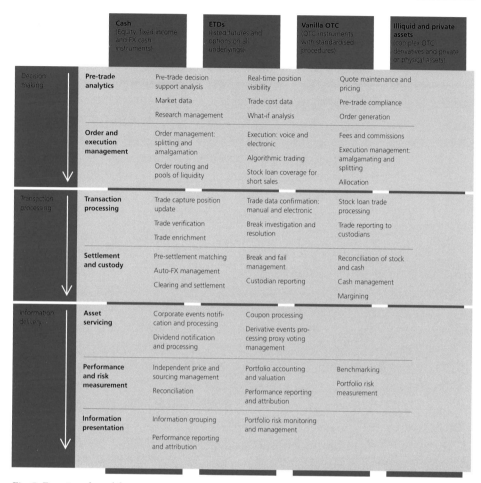

Fig. 5. Functional model

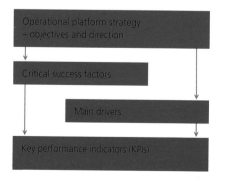

Fig. 6. Strategic analysis of operational platform

The analytical steps for the model presented in Figure 6 are:
1 operational platform strategy
   – objectives
   – strategic direction
2 definition of critical success factors (CSFs)
3 main operational drivers
4 key performance indicators (KPIs).

Strategic analysis forms the basis for information and process analysis. For this reason, analysts must be careful when defining CSFs, main operational drivers and KPIs: some of them have dual uses (used in both information and process analysis), but many of them have only a single use.

Operational platform strategy: objectives and direction
To conduct a proper information and process analysis, its strategy/objectives must be defined. As stated above, this strategy is based upon the business strategy.

It is vital that the objectives of the operational platform cover the three main functions defined above.

The strategic direction of the operational platform should be defined by developing an operational platform strategy. A useful framework for defining the strategic direction of the operational platform is Michael Porter's competitive strategies (Porter, 1985; see Figure 7).

	Advantage	
	Low-cost	Differentiation
Competitive scope		
Broad	Broad low-cost	Broad differentiation
Narrow	Focussed low-cost	Focussed differentiation

Fig. 7. Michael Porter's competitive strategy (Porter 1985)

The alignment of the strategic direction of an operational platform with the business strategy is crucial because this direction has a direct impact on all levels of an operational platform strategy.

Several drivers (which are not the same drivers as the operational drivers) are reflected in an operational platform strategy; they depend on the business strategy on which the operational platform strategy is based. Three main drivers that should be considered when developing an operational platform strategy are:
– flexibility
– scalability
– technology.

These drivers are highly dependent on the strategic direction defined for an operational platform.

As identified within the competitive scope above, costs can be considered as a separate driver or simply as a function of the drivers defined above.

Having defined a functional model and strategic direction/drivers for a platform, a strategy for an operational platform can then easily be defined. Afterwards, a strategic fit between the existing operational platform and the strategy should be determined in order to decide on the future development of the operational platform.

Before starting the information and operational analysis, the main operational drivers, CSFs and KPIs should be defined. All three definitions are then used in the information and operational analysis.

CSFs

There are many different approaches to defining CSFs. According to the approach developed by Sondhi (1999), the CSFs determine the success of an application for the organisation. CSFs can be product-oriented (e.g. higher product quality or innovative design), development process-oriented (e.g. a more efficient and effective development process), or standards-oriented (e.g. the product complies with standards), or they may have societal goals (e.g. a product that can be used by people with special needs).

In other words, the CSFs are the critical activities a business must undertake to be successful (Sondhi, 1999). Identification of these factors has its origins in the strategy and the strategic direction.

Main operational drivers

The main operational drivers can be defined as the factors that cause changes to the platform. Again, it is crucial that the identification has its origins in the strategy and the strategic direction. Various operational drivers are defined in the literature, and they are extremely dependent on the business, of course. What follows is a list of some of the most common operational drivers in the industry.

Number of decision-makers (e.g. portfolio managers)
The number of decision-makers is defined in the business strategy and is typically based upon the number of markets the asset manager chooses to be in and the variety of instruments used. This is an important number because the infrastructure of the platform is dependent on where and how many clients it has to serve.

Number of geographical representations
This mainly concerns the infrastructure of the operational platform because it has great impact on the infrastructure if you are running a 24-hour business spread across the globe compared with only one location.

Instruments traded on the platform

The complexity of the operational platform depends on the number of instruments traded on the platform. No instruments are the same, so the degree of complexity rises almost proportionally with the number of instruments handled on the platform.

Number of transactions

The number of transactions is as specific as the other numbers mentioned above. The possibility for bulk processing of trades exists, so it is vital to be aware of how the various transactions are to be processed.

Other operational drivers (Solvency II, number of clients, reporting etc.) can also be defined, depending on the strategic business goals of the asset manager. The five operational drivers defined above are simply examples that are often used.

KPIs

The KPIs help organisations achieve the goals for their operational platform through the definition and measurement of progress (Sondhi, 1999). The key indicators are measurable indicators that will reflect the critical success factors. The KPIs selected must reflect the goals of the operational platform; they must be key to its success, and they must be measurable. KPIs are usually long-term considerations for the platform.

The analysis

A basic analysis can be defined based on the KPIs defined above. The analysis comprises two steps based on two questions:
- What information is required at what level? (Kanter, 1987)
- Is the operational platform capable of performing the task? (Wild, 2002)

To answer these questions, the basic analytical model is structured in three parts (Figure 8).

Fig. 8. Main function analysis model: basic framework

The strategic scope of the operational platform

Information analysis

Process analysis

As illustrated above, the basis for the model is the strategic direction definition of the operational platform that was presented above. The analysis consists of an information and operation analysis performed on this basis. The analysis is outlined below.

Basic analytical framework: information analysis

The main purpose of information analysis is to define what information is required at what level (Kanter, 1987). This process must be performed for each of the main functions defined in the functional model (Figure 5). Also, the second target is to conduct a gap analysis to define the informational need (Henley Management College, 2002).

The information requirement very much depends on the business strategy. If the business aims for growth targeting new markets or products, it is vital that the operational platform includes the generation of the new information requirements.

The analysis is based on the KPIs defined in the strategy analysis outlined above. The structure of the analysis is described in Figure 9.

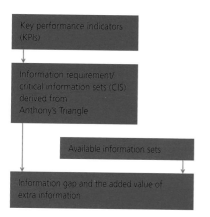

Fig. 9. Basic information analysis

KPIs

The KPIs derive from the strategic analysis mentioned above, and they are used to determine the information requirements. These requirements are expressed as critical information sets (CISs) based on the KPIs. (A model for analysis is Anthony's Triangle [Kanter, 1987].)

Information requirement/CISs

In attempting to categorise how and where information is applied, it is useful to define a taxonomy of terms. The starting point was to define the KPIs, and the next step is to 'build' a framework using Anthony's Triangle, which diagrams operational activities, management control and strategic planning. These three levels of management activity in the model are defined by Ropert Anthony in his 1965 book 'Planning and Control Systems: A Framework for Analysis'. Richard Hackathorn (2002) and Turban et al. (2004) summarise the three levels as follows:

Level	Hackathorn	Turban
Strategic planning	– Definition of goals, policies – Determination of organisational objectives	Defining long-range goals and policies for resource allocation
Management and tactical	– Acquisition of resources, tactics etc. – Establishment and monitoring of budgets	The acquisition and efficient use of resources in the accomplishment of organisational goals
Operational planning and control	Effective and efficient use of existing facilities and resources to carry out activities within budget constraints	The efficient and effective execution of specific goals

Fig. 10. Anthony's three management levels

Fig. 11. Anthony's Triangle. The framework is often shown as a management pyramid, in which a few are engaged at the strategic level while many more are involved at the tactical and operational levels (Hackathorn 2002).

The problem-solving and decision-making domain extends right across an organisation at all management levels. Anthony's Triangle provides a framework that allows something that is highly complex to be broken down into easier-to-understand parts (Hackathorn 2002).

In Figure 12, the framework is applied in basic terms to information use and other aspects using Anthony's model in this framework, based on a broad and general definition of terms. These definitions can vary from company to company.

	Levels (Anthony's taxonomy)		
Information characteristics	**Strategic**	**Tactical**	**Operational**
Information users	Management (CIO, CRO, COO)	Portfolio managers, middle managers	Operational staff
Nature of decisions	Investment-strategic decisions	Investment decisions	Analytical and process decisions
Scope	Broad	Intermediate	Narrow
Term focus/ Time horizon	Future-oriented (1 year +)	Within the current plan (3 to 12 months)	Day-to-day, usually with immediate ramifications

Fig. 12. Anthony's Triangle: basic terms of information use

Other writers and authors have also taken Anthony's taxonomy and used it as a basis for characterising information at different management levels.

The next step is simply to define the critical information sets (CISs) that can be derived directly from Anthony's information needs for each level.

Available information sets

The available information sets need neither method nor model to be determined. The term is simply used to define what information is available and provided by the operational platform (Henley Management College, 2002).

Information gap

To conclude the analysis, the information gap is defined as the residual between the CITs, which are the information sets the users of the operational platform need, and the available information sets provided by the operational platform (Henley Management College, 2002).

Taking a look in the rearview mirror at some of the financial crises from the past, it is obvious that not all asset managers had all the right information available on their operational platform, or the information was at least not available in a form useful to the decision-takers. If a firm wishes to grow or is targeting new markets or products, information analysis is crucial to success, because it is a way to ensure that the right information is generated and made public on the operational platform.

Basic analytical framework: process analysis

The basic process analysis of the operational platform has the same foundation as the information analysis: it is also based on the strategic analysis of the operational platform as defined above.

The analysis defined below is a simple process analysis, and it would only determine the basic parameters for the operations. To bring the analysis to a higher level would depend on the actual operational platform, so the choice of analysis is dependent upon that as well.

The main approach differs from the one used in the information analysis, because the process analysis is made in parallel with the strategy analysis. For this reason, a gap analysis of the KPIs is performed.

Figure 13 illustrates the flow of the analysis, which must be performed for all the main functions outlined in the functional framework defined above.

The operational flow is defined on the basis of Slacks' framework (2002) and Wild's system structure (2002). These frameworks were chosen because of the simplicity they represent. In general, asset management operations are extremely simple compared

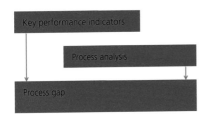

Fig. 13. Process gap analysis

with those of manufacturing companies because the former involve no actual physical transactions (no inbound or outbound logistics).

The analysis has two main layers (Wild 2002):

1   Process mapping
2   Capacity analysis.

These two analytical methods/models will be defined in the section below, and then the conclusion that can be derived from them will be defined and reviewed.

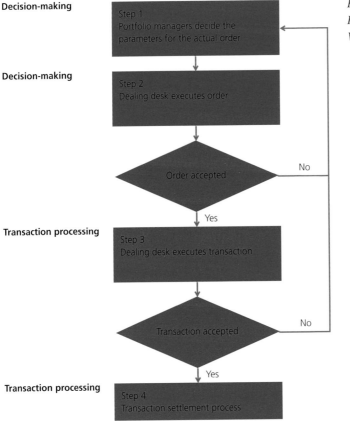

Fig. 14. Process mapping.
Framework source:
Wild 2002.

Process mapping

Process mapping is defining each process that takes place on the operational platform. The processes must be mapped to analyse how capacity against fluctuation in demand is handled. Multiple mapping designs exist (Wild 2002) and it is not important in this connection which mapping design is chosen.

The aim of this part is to define what and how conclusions can be drawn based upon the mapping of the processes.

The mapping process is defined for each service on the platform. Figure 14 shows the high-level process mapping of an order or transaction process. It is a well-known fact that the complexity is in the detail, so the analyst must be aware of the level of detail included in the mapping. The level depends on what the intended use of the analysis is.

Some conclusions that can be drawn from this analysis after having mapped all flows are how sufficient the flows are and whether the degree of straight-through-processing is acceptable. With respect to changes in the business, another aspect of the analysis is whether the process can include the new business the asset manager intends to take in. This has to be held up against the objectives of the operational platform.

Capacity analysis/management

The capacity analysis/management is about handling the flow of information, orders, transactions and data. Wild (2002) has defined this as follows: "The determination of capacity requires not only the estimation of steady-state or average demand levels but also decisions on how best to deal with demand level fluctuations."

The scope of the capacity analysis is to define where there are bottlenecks and how they are managed. A simple approach is the 'decision tree' used in the selection of capacity management strategies. The tree is taken from an original by B. Melville at the University of Waikato in New Zealand (Wild 2002; see Figure 15). The capacity analysis has to be done for each service defined upon the operational platform. The flow of the analysis is as follows (Wild 2002):

- Are the objectives and KPIs for the service defined with a primary goal of resource utilisation or as a customer service?
  - If the primary goal is customer service, i.e. that the service can be used as needed, then the service has to be maintained with excess capacity. One example is transaction processing: the platform must be able to execute the transactions made by the portfolio manager (2a).
  - If the primary goal is resource utilisation, another question arises: Are the output stocks feasible?
    - If yes, a stock has to be built up to absorb demand fluctuation (2bi).
    - If no, there are two ways to handle the fluctuation in demand:
      - with a fixed upper capacity: there is a maximum level of how much the users can utilise the service (2b).
      - by providing an efficient adjustment of the capacity (1).

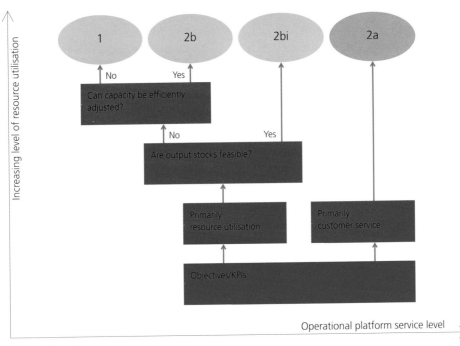

Fig. 15. Capacity tree

Employing this approach with all the services on the operational platform, the steady state of each can be determined and bottlenecks can be identified and dealt with.

Conclusion

Defining and implementing a strategic approach is not an easy task, which is why many asset managers instead choose using a technical IT strategy or some general statements as guidelines instead.

Taking a strategic approach to managing the company's operational platform is fairly time-consuming, not only with regard to defining the first strategy, but also with regard to aligning the business strategy and operational strategy with the gap analysis and maintaining the functional model of an operational platform.

The value of defining and strategically managing the company's operational platform, however, exceeds the cost, and if the operational platform is left in a strategic vacuum, it is not an integrated part of the business and thus not an active asset when changes occur.

To support growth, management has to buy into the development of the operational platform by defining and implementing an operational platform strategy that is aligned with its business strategy. The separation on a strategic level between IT and operational management (in two separate but aligned strategies) provides both the business and its IT management with clear and focussed strategies, leaving the business strategy decisions to the business management and the pure technical strategy/ decisions to technical staff.

Having defined the long- and short-term goals within the operational platform strategy and the alignment with the business strategy ensures that development of the platform changes from being a day-to-day approach into one with long-term defined goals, and this ensures sufficient support of the business growth strategies. This is a cost-efficient development approach rather than a constant-fix-the-burning-platform one, and this focusses both time and development resources on development that supports the firm's business goals. Aside from these advantages, a well-defined development process will also increase the stability of the operational platform.

Depending on the size of the business, a strategic approach to management of the operational platform is beneficial in terms of development, stability and cost, and will support a firm's business goals in a timely manner.

References

Elsborg (2008), 'The Operational Platform – A Way to Gain Competitive Advantage', dissertation, Henley Management College.

Hackathorn, R. D. (2002), 'The BI Watch: What Do We Do with What We Know?', *DM Review*.

Henley (2001), 'Managing Performance', Henley Management College.

Henley (2002), 'Managing Information', Henley Management College.

Heyes, Richard (2007), 'Example operating principle', UBS Prime Brokerage Services.

Kanter, J. and J Miserendino (1987), 'Systems architectures link business goals and IS strategies', *Data Management Magazine*, November.

Porter, Michael E. (1985), 'Competitive Advantage: Creating and Sustaining Superior Performance', Free Press.

Slack, N.D.C. (2002), 'Operations Strategy', London: Financial Times/Prentice Hall.

Sondhi, Rakesh (1999), 'Total Strategy', Airworthy Publications International Limited.

Turban, E., Aronson, J. E., & Liang, T.-P. (2004). 'Decision Support Systems and Intelligent Systems' (7th edition ed.): Prentice-Hall.

Wild, Ray (2002), 'Operations Management', Continuum.

Part III: Growth and value creation in asset management: a strategic perspective

About the authors

Mathias Schmit **holds a Ph.D. in finance from the Solvay Brussels School of Economics and Management (Brussels), where he is a part-time professor** and member of the Emile Bernheim Research Centre. He has worked in banking and public affairs-related activities since 1995. Currently, he is conducting research and consulting activities in banking and risk management. Dr. Schmit is also a regular speaker at major conferences around Europe on banking issues, with a special focus on financial analysis, risk management and strategic risks. Contact: m.schmit@sagora.eu or mschmit@ulb.ac.be.

Lin-Sya Chao **graduated from the Solvay Brussels School of Economics and Management with a major in finance. Having a special interest in strategic** issues underlying the financial crisis, she completed a master's thesis on the topic 'Strategic Risk Management: The Next Challenge for Financial Institutions', under the supervision of Professor Mathias Schmit. Contact: lchao@ulb.ac.be.

10
Managing growth and strategic risk

ABSTRACT The current financial crisis has caused multi-billion dollar losses and broken a long period of strong and steady growth in the investment management industry. Despite the importance of strategic risks, current management practices tend to cope with them poorly, particularly when facing strategic risks linked to growth. Strategic risks are those exposures that materially affect the capacity of a company to survive. By reviewing the literature and exploring how the world's top 50 banks recognise strategic risks in their annual reports, this chapter highlights the fact that these risks are not adequately perceived by the financial world and draws lessons from the current situation. Furthermore, this chapter suggests a clear definition of strategic risk and shows that uncontrolled growth is a major potential source of strategic risk and increases the vulnerability of an organisation. Finally, this paper discusses a number of key factors that need to be taken into account to manage growth risk effectively in order to secure sustainable value growth.

10 Managing growth and strategic risk

by Mathias Schmit and Lin-Sya Chao

Introduction

The financial crisis has caused multi-billion dollar losses and put an end to a long period of strong and steady growth in the investment management industry. More importantly, the crisis has revealed the weaknesses and unsustainability of the growth achieved by several financial institutions.

Year	Northern Rock	Kaupthing	Fortis	Merrill Lynch
2005	"The Northern Rock strategy encompasses efficiency, *growth* and value for both customers and shareholders … By growing lending and improving the mix of higher margin products, Northern Rock aims to *grow earnings* and improve returns to shareholders, at the same time as providing innovative and consumer friendly products to our customers." [1]	"In recent years, Kaupthing Bank has been *one of the fastest growing financial groups in Europe.* The Bank's expansion has been achieved through *sound organic growth and a number of strategic acquisitions.*" [2]	"There are three strategic axes to the new strategy we launched at the beginning of 2005 … Drive organic growth through sharpened customer focus … Increase focus outside Benelux [and] seize non-organic growth opportunities." [3]	"Our goal is simple … establish a foundation from which we can continue to invest for growth in revenues and profits while producing strong, consistent financial performance; attract and retain top talent; and, above all, add more value to every client relationship." [4]
2006		"Year of Organic Growth. Kaupthing Bank reported net earnings of ISK 85.3 billion (€972m) in 2006, an increase of 73% from the previous year. Earnings per share amounted to ISK 127.1, increasing by 69% from 2005. Return on shareholders' equity was 42.4% in 2006, which is well above the Bank's long-term target of 15%." [5]	"Our success in the past two years has given us the confidence to reconfirm and accelerate our strategy of growing this company into a leading European provider of high-quality financial services." [6]	"Our rapidly expanding franchise outside of the U.S. generated revenue growth of 42% in 2006, increasing non-U.S. operating revenues to 37% of total, the highest proportion in our history. Since 2004, we have announced more than 30 acquisitions, alliances and other strategic investments to accelerate our growth across a broad range of businesses and geographies." [7]

Fig.1. Extracts from annual reports of several banks pursuing a strategy focussed on growth.
Source: Banks' annual reports.

1   Northern Rock, 2005 and 2006 Annual Report, p. 1.
2   Kaupthing Bank, 2005 Annual Report, p. 2.
3   Fortis Holding, 2005 Management Report, p. 2.
4   Merrill Lynch, 2005 Annual Report, p. 2.
5   Kaupthing Bank, 2006 Annual Report, p. 5.
6   Fortis Holding, 2006 Annual Review, p. 1.
7   Merrill Lynch, 2006 Annual Report, p. 3.

Well-known examples include Merrill Lynch's market share push in CDOs, Northern Rock's liquidity crisis, Fortis' hazardous acquisition of ABN Amro, and the disastrous rapid international expansion of Icelandic banks. As apparent from Figure 1, which shows extracts from their annual reports, these financial institutions pursued a strategy focussed on growth. These financial institutions made the common mistake of neglecting the strategic risk associated with their growth strategy, and this can be one of the most serious causes of value destruction.

In this turbulent context, the aim of the present chapter is to discuss how sustainable growth in the financial industry can be achieved through effective management of the strategic risks. By reviewing the literature and exploring how the world's top 50 banks recognise strategic risks in their annual reports, this chapter highlights that these risks are not adequately perceived by the financial world and draws lessons from the current situation. Furthermore, this chapter suggests a clear definition of strategic risk and points out that uncontrolled growth is a major potential source of strategic risk and increases the vulnerability of an organisation. Finally, this chapter discusses a number of key factors that need to be taken into account to manage growth risk effectively in order to secure sustainable value growth.

Literature overview

Definition

Currently, the literature on strategic risk is extremely limited compared to the literature on other types of risk. Moreover, we find a wide variety of approaches, with a multitude of definitions and interpretations of strategic risk.

Jorion was one of the first authors to provide a definition of strategic risk as the "result of fundamental shifts in the economy or political environment",[8] thus implying that strategic risk arises from *external sources* and is not under the control of the firm. Similarly, the definitions given by Slywotzky ("the array of external events and trends that can devastate a company's growth trajectory and shareholder value"[9]) and Allen ("external risks to the viability of the business arising from unexpected adverse changes in the business environment with respect to the economy [business cycle]; the political landscape; law and regulation; technology; social mores; and the actions of competitors"[10]) take into account only external sources of risks. Although most other researchers follow a similar approach, a few also consider internal sources of strategic risk.

8   Jorion, P (2001), *Value at Risk*, McGraw-Hill, p.3.
9   Slywotzky, A. and J. Drzik (2005), 'Countering the Biggest Risk of All', *Harvard Business Review*, April.
10   Allen, B. (2007), 'Strategic risk: The best-laid plans…', *Risk – London*, 20(7), p. 142.

STRATrisk,[11] for example, suggests that strategic risks are "those 'big picture' risks which can destroy shareholder value and even threaten the very survival of organizations"[12] and distinguishes a number of *internal sources* of strategic risk ("Strategy, Structure, Systems, Skills, Staff, Style, Shared Values") from the *external sources* ("Political, Economic, Social, Technological, Environmental, Ethical, Legal"). Beasley et al. (2007) also uphold the view that strategic risk can originate from internal as well as external events. While not considering internal sources of strategic risk, Emblemsvåg and Kjolstad (2002), for their part, make the link between external and internal factors in strategic risk management. They argue that while many strategic risks may arise from the organisation's environment and hence be external, how these external risks are managed is determined by the organisation's internal characteristics and competencies.

Several researchers highlight the relationship between *strategic risk and the firm's strategy, strategic decisions and/or strategy implementation.* For instance, Raff provides a definition based on strategic decisions: "All strategic decisions induce and impose constraints on the types of risk banks traditionally monitored and managed.... Strategic decisions also impose a new type of risk...which also needs to be analyzed, monitored, and controlled."[13] The definition proposed by Emblemsvag and Kjolstad, "the risks that arise in pursuit of business objectives",[14] also suggests a link with the organisation's strategy. Gilad (2003) introduces the term 'strategic risk' to describe factors that can erode a company's ability to implement its business plan and that appear when the strategy does not fit the market reality anymore. Asher and Gale also uphold this view: "We define strategy as preparation or investing for success, and for our purposes define strategic risk as the risk that these preparations will fail, or – perhaps more often – that insufficient preparation will be made for optimal decisions in future. We therefore see these risks as a by-product of strategy."[15] In agreement with Asher and Gale, Mango defines strategic risk as "unintentional risks as by-products of strategy planning or execution".[16]

Definitions often indicate the potentially *devastating nature of strategic risk*, as in the definitions of Slywotzky and STRATrisk,[17] both of which present strategic risk

---

11 The STRATrisk research project is a collaborative venture between a professional institution, two universities (Bath and Bristol) and industry, aimed at, firstly, gaining an understanding of how strategic risk is identified and managed in UK construction companies and, secondly, providing a toolkit for company boards to better understand and manage those strategic risks and opportunities.

12 *STRATrisk* (2005), interim report, available at www.stratrisk.co.uk.

13 Raff, D. (2001), 'Risk Management in an Age of Change', working paper, Reginald H. Jones Center – The Wharton School (University of Pennsylvania), p. 2.

14 Emblemsvåg, J. and L.E. Kjolstad (2002), 'Strategic risk analysis – a field version', *Management Decision*, 40(9): 846.

15 Asher, A., and A. Gale (2007), 'Strategic Risk Management: Mapping the commanding heights and hazards', *The Institute of Actuaries of Australia*, p. 2.

16 Mango, D. (2007), 'An Introduction to Insurer Strategic Risk – Topic 1: Risk Management of an Insurance Enterprise', *Enterprise Risk Analysis, Guy Carpenter & Company, LLC*, p. 145.

17 See footnotes 4 and 5.

Source of strategic risk		Emblemsvåg and Kjølstad (2002)	Sadgrove (2005)	Drew et al. (2005)	Gilad (2004)	Allen (2007)	Van den Brink (2007)	Slywotzky (2005)	STRATrisk (2005)	Allen and Beer (2005)	Total
Macro-environment	Political		•		•	•	•		•	•	6
	Economical					•	•		•	•	4
	Social				•	•	•		•	•	5
	Technological		•	•	•	•	•	•	•	•	8
	Environmental								•	•	2
	Ethical								•	•	2
	Legal/regulatory				•	•			•	•	4
Market environment	Suppliers			•			•	•		•	4
	Customers		•	•			•	•		•	5
	Competition		•	•	•	•	•	•		•	7
	Substitutes			•			•	•		•	4
	New entrants			•	•		•	•		•	5
Internal environment	Strategy/projects							•	•	•	3
	Style								•	•	2
	Structure								•	•	2
	Systems								•	•	2
	Staff			•			•		•	•	4
	Skills								•	•	2
	Shared values								•		1
	Brand							•			1
Others	Stagnation							•			1
	Critical resources			•							1
	Other stakeholders						•				1
	SWOT	•								•	2

Fig. 2. Sources of strategic risk identified in existing literature

as the *risk to the sustainability and viability* of the company. Similarly, in the above-mentioned definition, Allen (2007) emphasises the potentially devastating nature of strategic risks ("external risks to the viability of the business arising from unexpected adverse changes in the business environment"[18]). Likewise, Drew et al. define strategic risks as those risks that "threaten a firm's long-term competitive success and survival: risk to its market position, critical resources, and ability to innovate and grow."[19]

As shown later in this chapter, the lack of a unique and recognised definition of strategic risk plays a key role in its misunderstanding by financial institutions, and hence in its inappropriate management.

---

18   Allen, B. (2007), 'Strategic risk: The best-laid plans…', *Risk – London,* 20 (7), p. 142.
19   Drew, S., P. Kelley and T. Kendrick (2006), 'CLASS: Five elements of corporate governance to manage strategic risk', *Business Horizons,* 49(2), p. 128.

Sources of strategic risk

In addition to defining strategic risk, several authors have classified the sources of strategic risks (see Figure 2). Using classic strategic tools, as suggested by STRATrisk (2005) and Allen and Beer (2006), four strategic risk categories can be distinguished: the macro-economic environment (using a PESTEL), the micro-environment (using Porter's five forces), the internal environment (using McKinsey 7S framework) and 'Others' – which include strategic risks not included in previous categories, as well as the SWOT matrix suggested by Emblemsvag and Kjolstad (2002) and Allen and Beer (2006).

Figure 2 shows that strategic risks are mainly considered as arising from the external (macro- and micro-) environment and hence not under the control of the firm. In the macro-environment, strategic risks related to technology are the most widely recognised type of strategic risks, followed by risks related to the political, social, economic and legal/regulatory environment. As regards the micro-environment, the most frequently mentioned strategic risks are those resulting from competition, followed by the risks arising from customers and new entrants. Again, strategic risks are seldom considered as arising from the internal environment; only STRATrisk (2005) and Allen and Beer (2006) include internal sources of strategic risks.

This literature overview suggests that strategic risk can arise from a wide variety of sources, making it even more difficult to apprehend and to manage.

A suggested definition of strategic risk

For the purposes of this chapter, and working on the basis of our review of the available literature (despite its scarcity and the disparity between the approaches of different authors), we have defined strategic risk as follows:

Strategic risk is the risk to the sustainability and viability of an organisation as a result of inadequate strategic decisions or improper implementation of strategic decisions by the organisation's management body, or lack of responsiveness of the management body in relation to the internal and/or the external environment.[20]

This definition is based on three dimensions: the level, the sources and the magnitude of the impact of strategic risk.

Firstly, following the approach of Raff (2001), we believe that strategic risk arises from inadequate strategic decisions or lack of responsiveness to developments, strategic decisions being decisions taken at a high level in the organisation, i.e. at the board of directors and/or top management level. For example, the decision to pursue growth

---

20   We use the same definition of 'management body' as in the CEBS (Committee of European Banking Supervisors) Guidelines on the Application of the Supervisory Review Process under Pillar 2 (CP03 revised), p. 6: "The term 'management body', which represents the top management level of an institution, is used in this document to embrace different structures, such as unitary and dual boards."

objectives or to enter into a merger or an important acquisition is a decision taken at the level of the management body and hence might induce strategic risk. As in the case of Mango (2007), our definition states that the implementation of strategic decisions can create strategic risks, but in our view this is so only if strategy implementation is decided/conducted at the level of the management body. In order to avoid any confusion and overlap, we believe that risks arising from strategy implementation not conducted by the management body should be categorised as operational risks.[21]

Secondly, we believe that the sources of strategic risk are both internal and external, as suggested by STRATrisk (2005), Allen and Beer (2006) and Beasley et al. (2007). This point is especially important when we consider that internal sources of strategic risk, though often neglected, can be an important cause of value destruction, as shown later in this chapter. Figures 3 and 4 summarise the different kinds of factors – in both the internal and external environments – that can induce important strategic risks.

Lastly, in agreement with most definitions found in the available literature, we state that strategic risk can have a devastating impact on a company's value and vi-

Event type	Definition	Example
Strategy/project	Losses due to inappropriate decision or lack of decision concerning plans to reach identified goals	Overreliance on a category of customers, decision to outsource a crucial activity, mismanagement of financial aspects of a growth strategy
Critical resources: capability and availability	Losses due to inappropriate decision or lack of decision concerning the allocation and management of the firm's scarce and critical resources: human, financial and technical resources.	Insufficient training to compensate for skills gap, inadequate recruitment process causing skills gap
Structure	Losses due to inappropriate decision or lack of decision concerning the way the firm is organised regarding the hierarchy, communication channels, cooperation, decision-making process, etc.	Lack of coordination between multiple hierarchical layers, inefficient communication channels causing loss of information
Systems and processes (incl. models)	Losses due to inappropriate decision or lack of decision concerning internal rules, processes and systems such as remuneration schemes, models (for pricing, valuation, risk management, etc.) and IT systems	Choice of an inadequate model to measure market risk, use of non-precise project valuation model
Style	Losses due to inappropriate decision or lack of decision concerning management and leadership style	Authoritarian leadership preventing participation
Shared values	Losses due to inappropriate decision or lack of decision concerning values, work ethics and corporate culture	Lack of clear and strong shared values

Fig. 3. Sources of strategic risk arising from the internal environment

---

21 Operational risk is defined in Basel II as "the risk of loss resulting from inadequate or failed internal processes, people and systems, or external events. This definition includes legal risk, but excludes strategic and reputational risk."

Event type	Definition	Example
Political	Losses due to inappropriate decisions or lack of responsiveness to changes in the political environment: subsidies, government policy, public investment, trade restrictions, tariffs, tax policy etc.	Governmental decisions not to rescue a major bank
Economic	Losses due to inappropriate decisions or lack of responsiveness to changes in the economic environment: economic growth or recession, inflation etc.	Inadequate response to the economic recession
Social	Losses due to inappropriate decisions or lack of responsiveness to changes in the social environment: ageing population, population growth rate, cultural trend etc.	No initiative to attract and retain the ageing population
Technological	Losses due to inappropriate decisions or lack of responsiveness to changes in the technological environment: R&D investment, technological shift, automation etc.	Investment in the wrong new technology
Environmental and ethical	Losses due to inappropriate decisions or lack of responsiveness to changes in the environmental and ethical environment: climate change, fair trade etc.	Missed opportunity to offer green investment products
Legal and regulatory	Losses due to inappropriate decisions or lack of responsiveness to changes in the legal environment: discrimination law, competition law, employment law, consumer law, antitrust law etc.	Lack of responsiveness to a new regulation facilitating the entrance of non-traditional competitors (ex. MiFID)
Competitors	Losses due to inappropriate decisions or lack of responsiveness to changes in the competitive environment: new competitor, substitute, rising competitor, switching cost etc.	Retailers beginning to offer financial services
Customers	Losses due to inappropriate decisions or lack of responsiveness to changes in consumer behaviour: buyers' incentives, price sensitivity, brand awareness etc.	Not realising that customers are changing behaviour
Suppliers	Losses due to inappropriate decisions or lack of responsiveness to changes in suppliers: forward integration, switching cost, suppliers concentration etc.	Bankruptcy of one of the main suppliers

Fig. 4. Sources of strategic risk arising from the external environment

ability. This destructive characteristic was confirmed in a survey conducted in 2006 by The Conference Board (*The Role of U.S. Corporate Boards in Enterprise Risk Management*), which found that 53 per cent of board members believe strategic risk poses the greatest threat to the company, while only 15.7 per cent identify financial risk as a key concern. Similarly, Funston's (2004) study of the 100 companies with the largest stock-price losses from 1995 to 2004 concluded that 66 per cent of the companies suffered strategic risk while 37 per cent were harmed by financial risk.

Having defined strategic risk, we now turn to examine how strategic risk is defined and managed in the financial industry.

The world's top 50 banks and strategic risk

Methodology

The analysis of strategic risk definition and management was conducted among the world's top 50 banks (source: FT Global 500, ranked by market value)[22] on the basis of their annual reports and public information.

Strategic risk definition

A preliminary analysis shows that only 56% of banks (28 out of 50) recognise strategic risk. Moreover, of these 28 banks, a mere 15 clearly define strategic risk, while the others just list it among their risk factors or mention it without further explanation (Figure 5).

Banks recognising strategic risk		Banks clearly defining strategic risk
Wells Fargo	Unicredito Italiano	Bank of America
Bank of America	Standard Chartered	BNP Paribas
Royal Bank Canada	China CITIC Bank	Commonwealth Bank of Australia
Westpac Banking	Mizuho Financial	Credit Suisse
BNP Paribas	Nordea Bank	Intesa Sanpaolo
Commonwealth Bank of Australia	Hang Seng Bank	Toronto Dominion Bank
Credit Suisse	Banco Brasil	UBS
Intesa Sanpaolo	Shanghai Pudong Dev Bank	Deutsche Bank
Toronto Dominion Bank	Barclays	Unicredito Italiano
Bradesco	Lloyds Banking Group	Nordea Bank
UBS	Resona Holdings	Banco Brasil
National Australia Bank	Bank of Montreal	Barclays
Bank of Nova Scotia	CIBC	Lloyds Banking Group
Deutsche Bank	Northern Trust	Bank of Montreal
		CIBC

Fig. 5. Banks recognising and clearly defining strategic risk among world's top 50 banks

A closer examination of the definitions used by these 15 banks enables us to draw up the following comparative Figure 6. The dimensions selected are based on the literature overview and include the level at which strategic risk is considered, the recognised sources of strategic risk, and the perceived extent of the impact of strategic risk on the organisation.

Confirming the findings of the literature overview, our analysis shows that the majority of banks analysed (13 out of 15) place strategic risk at the level of strategy definition. Only seven of these 13 banks also set strategic risk at the strategy implementation level. This reflects the prevailing confusion concerning the level at which to deal with strategic risk.

With regard to the sources of strategic risk, Figure 6 shows that of the 15 banks that clearly define strategic risk, a majority (12) view strategic risk as something arising from the external environment. Only five of the world's top 50 banks recognise in-

---

22   For a complete list of the world's top 50 banks analysed in this study, see the appendix, page 200.

Company	Level		Source		Impact	
	Strategy definition	Strategy implementation	External	Internal	Impact on value	Impact on profits
Bank of America	•	•	•			
BNP Pariba	•				•	
Commonwealth Bank of Australia	•		•		•	
Credit Suisse	•	•	•	•		
Intesa Sanpaolo	•				•	
Toronto Dominion Bank	•	•	•		•	
UBS	•		•			
Deutsche Bank			•			•
Unicredito Italiano	•		•			
Nordea Bank			•			•
Banco Brasil	•		•		•	•
Barclays	•	•	•	•		•
Lloyds Banking Group	•	•	•	•	•	•
Bank of Montreal	•	•	•	•	•	•
CIBC	•	•		•		•
Total	**13**	**7**	**12**	**5**	**7**	**7**

Fig. 6. Analysis of definitions of strategic risk among world's top 50 banks

ternal sources of strategic risk. This very low proportion is in line with the literature, although internal sources of strategic risk can be a severe cause of value destruction, as described later in this chapter.

Interestingly, most banks (five out of seven) that include strategy implementation in their definition of strategic risk also consider internal sources of strategic risk. Furthermore, half of the banks (four out of eight) that recognise external sources of strategic risk consider only strategy definition – and not strategy implementation – in their definition of strategic risk. These observations might be explained by the fact that strategy definition is seen by these banks as being determined by the external environment, while strategy implementation is seen as an internal source of strategic risk.

Finally, the extent of the impact of strategic risk is rather unclear: seven banks believe that strategic risk can impact the company's value, while seven believe that it can impact the company's profits (with four of the latter group considering the impact on profits only).

Sources of strategic risk

In line with the literature overview, we found it interesting to identify the main sources of strategic risk recognised by the world's top 50 banks. Our findings are summarised in Figure 7 which – following the same template as for the literature overview – shows that the world's top 50 banks recognise a wide range of strategic risks.

Again confirming the findings of the literature overview, it is apparent that the surveyed banks mainly recognise external sources of strategic risk. In the macroenvironment, strategic risks associated with economic factors are the most frequently

Event of strategic risk		Bank of America	Commonwealth Bank of Australia	Credit Suisse	UBS	Deutsche Bank	Nordea Bank	Banco Brazil	Barclays	Lloyds	Bank of Montreal	CIBC	Total
Macro-environment	Political							•	•	•	•		4
	Economical	•	•		•		•	•	•	•	•		8
	Social		•						•	•	•		4
	Technological	•		•		•			•	•	•		6
	Environmental/ethical								•	•			2
	Legal/regulatory		•	•					•	•	•		5
Market environment	Suppliers												0
	Customers	•				•				•			3
	Competition/new entrants	•	•	•	•	•	•	•	•	•	•		10
	Substitutes	•								•			2
Internal environment	Strategy/projects			•						•		•	3
	Style												0
	Structure												0
	Systems									•			1
	Staff			•									1
	Skills												0
	Shared values												0
	Others										•		1

Fig. 7. Analysis of the sources of strategic risk recognised by the world's top 50 banks

mentioned category, followed by technological, legal/regulatory, political and social factors. In the micro-environment, competition is again the most frequently mentioned source of strategic risk.

Given that the number of banks recognising internal sources of strategic risk is even lower, we found even fewer banks providing examples or categories. The internal sources of strategic risk mentioned are mainly related to the organisation's strategy or major projects (mergers, acquisitions and growth), while strategic risks related to systems and staff were mentioned only once.

Only Lloyds provides a longer list of internal sources of strategic risks, and it is also the bank with the most comprehensive categorisation of such sources:

The Group's portfolio of businesses exposes it to a number of internal and external factors:
– Internal factors: resource capability and availability, customer treatment, service level agreements, products and funding and the risk appetite of other risk categories;

– *External factors: economic, technological, political, social and ethical, environ-mental, legal and regulatory, market expectations, reputation and competitive be-haviour.[23]*

Interestingly, Barclays and CIBC clearly mention that their growth strategy can in-duce strategic risk:

The Group devotes substantial management and planning resources to the develop-ment of strategic plans for organic growth and identification of possible acquisitions, supported by substantial expenditure to generate growth in customer business. If these strategic plans are not delivered as anticipated, the Group's earnings could grow more slowly or decline.[24]

Strategic risk arises from ineffective business strategies or the failure to effectively execute strategies. It includes, but is not limited to, potential financial loss due to the failure of acquisitions or organic growth initiatives.[25]

Impacts of uncontrolled growth on strategic risks

As shown in the previous section and the introduction, the banks surveyed mainly recognise external sources of strategic risk, including economic, technological, le-gal/regulatory, political and social factors. However, only five out of the 50 surveyed banks recognise internal sources of strategic risk, and only two banks (i.e. Barclay's and CIBC) mention growth impact as a source of possible strategic risk in their an-nual reports.

Furthermore, when we look at the main risks reported in the Banking Banana Skins surveys[26] between 1996 and 2010,[27] we find that concerns have changed over the period. Towards the end of the 1990s, the main perceived risks concerned poor management/strategy, competition, poor grasp of technology and poor product design. When we consider the past two years, the main perceived risks relate to more specific and external sources such as political interference, credit risk, over-regulation, credit spreads and macro-economic trends. In short, over the past de-cade, perceived sources of risk have shifted from strategic issues to factors originat-ing in the external environment.

These observations illustrate that strategic risk awareness suffers from blind spots. In fact, the sustainability of an institution can be threatened because risks concern-ing the availability of required resources are not adequately identified and assessed

---

23   Lloyds, Annual Report 2008, p. 48.
24   Barclays, Annual Report 2008, p. 74.
25   CIBC, Annual Report 2008, p. 82.
26   The surveys aim to describe the risks faced by the global banking industry as perceived by a wide range of bankers, banking regulators and close observers of the banking scene around the world.
27   Lascelles D. (2010), 'Banking Banana Skins 2010', CSFI, p.10.

in relation to strategic objectives, given the external factors that may occur. This can obviously happen when the financial system is under pressure. Growth and its management entail risk-management issues, in part because many executives see growth as something to be maximised and not to be restrained. However, experience shows that, from a management perspective, growth is not always a piece of good fortune.

Indeed, rapid growth can put considerable strain on a company's resources (financial and human), and unless management is aware of this effect and takes active steps to control it, rapid growth can lead to disasters, especially in the event of exogenous shocks such as sudden adverse business cycles. For example, it is a common tendency to over-rely on credit institutions when markets (particularly the wholesale market) are liquid. This was the case with the Icelandic banks that relied on the unlimited availability of strong currencies.

Looking at another example, hedge funds can be subject to massive losses. A key source of value – and, simultaneously, a source of risk – lies in leverage increasing *de facto* with the growth objectives. In normal market conditions, leverage – including short selling or repo transactions – provides extra liquidity to the financial market and allows expansions. A survey of global prime brokers by Fitch Ratings Ltd. found that leverage for some credit strategies could be as much as 20 times the assets under management. However, in times of turbulence, to meet leverage ratio, hedge funds are forced to liquidate assets and unwind positions at a rapid pace, thus generating massive losses for investors, combined with a possible contagion effect. The problem can be aggravated by the fact that hedge funds are taking illiquid positions, especially in instruments like CDOs and CDS. When they need cash to meet commitments like margin calls from creditors, hedge funds fall into a vicious circle, since they are unable to liquidate their assets and cannot find additional funding. Nowadays, to mitigate these potential risks, some hedge funds are starting to look for permanent funding such as IPOs, debt offerings and committed lending facilities. Examples include GLC Partners, Blue Bay Asset Management, Fortress and Britain's Man Group.

In order to reduce the frequency and impact of strategic risks, it is necessary to establish an effective risk assessment and management system based on a causality-driven approach as discussed in Ayadi et al. (2008). Although it is supposed to be well-defined by regulators and risk managers, risk delimitation remains a puzzle for a number of institutions, especially when it comes to strategy formulation and implementation. One of the main problems is the definition of boundaries between the different types of risk, leading to potential inefficiencies when assessing them.

There is a case, therefore, for developing an up-to-date risk taxonomy based on a causality methodology to distinguish between different types of risks and thus determine at which level of the company they should be tackled. The implementation of such a framework by financial institutions would help to prevent the use of unsuitable risk assessment and management methods that are based exclusively on the classification of events (effects) without taking into consideration either the causes or the possible misalignment between resources and growth objectives. This approach would have been most helpful in identifying and analysing the risks that led to the recent failure of major institutions. For example, funding or asset liquidity risk was mistakenly viewed as a primary source of risk dictated by the environment instead of being dealt with as one factor resulting from the strategic risk associated with the decisions taken at the highest level of the institution.

Uncontrolled growth leads institutions to follow a biased logic: the faster they grow, the more profitable they become from an accounting point of view, but the more vulnerable they become in terms of liquidity. Of course, leverage can be increased until investors refuse additional lending, particularly when market pressures are strong. However, as already pointed out by Higgins (1977), all of these problems can be prevented if the management body realises that growth above the company's sustainable growth rate creates financial challenges that must be anticipated and managed. The sustainable growth rate is the maximum rate at which a company may grow given the possible resources available under various scenarios. Management must anticipate any gap between actual growth and sustainable growth. To manage that disparity, the challenge is first to recognise it and, secondly, to implement a viable mitigation plan to manage it. Furthermore, it should be kept in mind that, when a company grows at a rate in excess of the sustainable growth rate, it is imperative for it to respond to the situation by adopting appropriate investment policies.

In this regard, given that the management body is ultimately responsible for the sustainability and viability of the financial institution, there is a need for an overall (strategic) assessment of resources at the management body level. Indeed, the management body should clearly define the institution's risk strategies and risk profile, which have to be translated into business objectives. Therefore, an adequate understanding, on the part of directors, of risk factors and the potential impacts faced by the institution is vital.

Once this high-level task has been carried out, it is essential to update the institution's risk prevention and management policies continuously on the basis of effective risk assessment methods in order to optimise the implementation strategy, especially in terms of availability of essential resources. In the event that a risk assessment system proves to be flawed when faced with an uncommon (not necessarily exceptional) environment, a financial institution should be able to take timely corrective action, such as increasing its essential resources or strengthening its risk management processes and control systems.

Of course, strategic risk management also has to rely on fair judgment from management bodies and experts within the framework of better governance structures, increased transparency and increased risk-control capabilities to meet the (standard) risk governance requirements. In addition to appropriate incentives for banks to establish institution-wide risk assessment systems, regulatory measures are required to ensure that the development of institutions can be effectively monitored and evaluated, and to impose limitations on business expansion when available resources prove to be insufficient in relation to the institution's overall risk profile.

Conclusion

The current market turmoil is the result of an exceptional boom in credit growth and leverage in the financial system, based on a long period of low interest rates and a high level of liquidity combined with the lack of a strategic risk-management framework. In addition to causing multi-billion dollar losses among financial institutions, the financial crisis has revealed the weaknesses and unsustainability of the long-term growth achieved by certain financial institutions. It has emphasised the importance of a resilient and stable strategic risk-management framework whose main aim should be to create the right incentives to improve the long-term viability of institutions that rely primarily on short-term funding.

As explained in this article, the sources of strategic risk are multiple. However, the key focus of this study is the strategic risk of financial institutions whose growth objectives and business models imply a high dependency on short-term wholesale market funding and high leverage. The sudden drying up of liquidity in markets has had serious consequences for these financial institutions. We suggest that financial institutions may have suffered from a tragic short-sightedness in the rapid-growth environment of the pre-2007 era.

Indeed, beyond 'growth targets' and 'growth achieved', the key challenge for long-term success is the ability to identify the relevant external and internal drivers of risks, including specifically those linked to the availability of the resources required in various stressed scenarios. To manage and thus sometimes to limit growth in order to meet sustainability objectives in the event of a stressed scenario is a difficult exercise for board members, executive managers and operating managers.

In our view, ensuring that strategic risks are managed at the highest level of the company is the main prerequisite for sustainable growth. We suggest that strategic risk management should rely on a methodical approach for coping with internal and external sources of uncertainty and should be a process at the core of decision-making. In fact, the primary aim of strategic risk management is to support the achievement of the mission and the objectives of the organisation while at the same time ensuring its long-term viability. The methodical approach aims to mobilise sufficient resources and time from the management body to ensure that significant strategic risks are effectively identified and appropriately managed. The response to strategic risks should consist of decisions taken by the management body on the basis of careful consideration of each situation, rather than result from a strong focus on economic capital allocation.

Finally, based on these conclusions, we strongly recommend calling on the relevant EU institutions and bodies to work towards developing sound and legally binding principles for strategic risk management and its governance. In our view, supervisors should provide high-level guidelines on the implementation, validation and assessment of strategic risk to ensure that it is adequately dealt with, instead of focussing inadequately on technically complex systems to assess capital levels, since such systems and their underlying approach do not ensure the availability of the required resources and may themselves generate additional risks, as is apparent from the current crisis.

References

Allan, N. and L. Beer (2006), 'Strategic Risk: It's all in your head', University of Bath working paper.

Allen, B. (2007), 'Strategic risk: The best-laid plans…', *Risk – London,* 20(7).

Asher, A. and A. Gale (2007), 'Strategic Risk Management: Mapping the commanding heights and hazards', The Institute of Actuaries of Australia.

Ayadi, R., M. Nieto, F. Musch and M. Schmit (2008), 'Basel II Implementation: In the Midst of Turbulence', Center for European Studies.

Beasley, M., M. Frigo and J. Litman (2007), 'Strategic Risk Management: Creating and Protecting Value', *Strategic Finance,* 88(11), p. 24.

Brancato, C., E. Hexter, K. Newman and M. Tonello (2006), 'The Role of U.S. Corporate Boards in Enterprise Risk Management', Conference Board with McKinsey and KPMG.

Drew, S., P. Kelley and T. Kendrick (2006). 'CLASS: Five elements of corporate governance to manage strategic risk', *Business Horizons,* 49(2):127–138.

Emblemsvåg, J. and L.E. Kjolstad (2002), 'Strategic risk analysis – a field version', *Management Decision,* 40(9): 842–852.

Funston, R. (2004) 'Avoiding the Value Killers', *Treasury and Risk Management,* April, p. 11.

Gilad, B. (2004). 'Early Warning: Using Competitive Intelligence to Anticipate Market Shifts, Control Risk, and Create Powerful Strategies', Amacom.

Higgins, Robert C. (1977), 'How much growth can a firm afford?', *Financial Management,* 6(2):7-16.

Jorion, P. (2001), 'Value at Risk', McGraw-Hill, p. 3.

Lascelles, D. (2010), 'Banking Banana Skins 2010', CSFI.

Mango, D. (2007), 'An Introduction to Insurer Strategic Risk – Topic 1: Risk Management of an Insurance Enterprise', Enterprise Risk Analysis, Guy Carpenter & Company, LLC, p. 144–172.

Merritt, R., I. Linnell and R. Grossman (2005), 'Hedge Funds: An Emerging Force in the Global Credit Markets', FitchRatings Special Report.

Raff, D. (2001), 'Risk Management in an Age of Change', working paper, Reginald H. Jones Center – The Wharton School (University of Pennsylvania), p. 2.

Sadgrove, K. (2005), 'The Complete Guide to Business Risk Management', Gower.

Slywotzky, A. and J. Drzik (2005), 'Countering the Biggest Risk of All', *Harvard Business Review,* April, p. 78–88.

STRATrisk Research on strategic risk in the construction industry, University of Bath, available at http://www.stratrisk.co.uk/.

Van den Brink (2007), 'Strategic Risk: can it be measured?', available at http://www.financeventures.nl.

Sector rank	Global rank 2009	Global rank 2008	Company	Country	Continent	Market value $m
1	4	6	Indl & Coml Bank of China	China	Asia	187,885.4
2	13	20	China Construction Bank	China	Asia	133,228.6
3	21	26	Bank of China	China	Asia	115,243.1
4	27	31	JP Morgan Chase	US	North America	99,885.4
5	29	15	HSBC	UK	Europe	97,408.9
6	54	64	Wells Fargo	US	North America	60,345.9
7	62	40	Banco Santander	Spain	Europe	56,198.9
8	64	67	Mitsubishi UFJ Financial	Japan	Asia	56,136.7
9	83	23	Bank of America	US	North America	43,657.4
10	88	142	Itau Unibanco	Brazil	South America	42,580.8
11	91	114	Royal Bank Canada	Canada	North America	41,129.2
12	94	105	Bank of Communications	China	Asia	40,409.7
13	100	204	Westpac Banking	Australia	Oceania	38,605.0
14	107	68	BNP Paribas	France	Europe	37,686.4
15	108	157	Commonwealth Bank of Australia	Australia	Oceania	36,649.6
16	110	118	Credit Suisse	Switzerland	Europe	36,110.3
17	113	69	Intesa Sanpaolo	Italy	Europe	34,360.0
18	122	103	China Merchants Bank	China	Asia	32,729.7
19	132	78	BBVA	Spain	Europe	30,404.7
20	137	186	Toronto Dominion Bank	Canada	North America	29,363.1
21	141	143	Bradesco	Brazil	South America	28,301.7
22	145	113	UBS	Switzerland	Europe	27,596.3
23	149	152	Sumitomo Mitsui Financial	Japan	Asia	27,242.7
24	153	179	National Australia Bank	Australia	Oceania	26,789.9
25	163	131	U.S. Bancorp	US	North America	25,642.6
26	170	182	Bank of Nova Scotia	Canada	North America	25,002.6
27	171	115	Deutsche Bank	Germany	Europe	24,976.9
28	176	149	Credit Agricole	France	Europe	24,569.8
29	185	70	Unicredito Italiano	Italy	Europe	23,683.3
30	186	214	ANZ Banking	Australia	Oceania	23,616.5
31	187	163	Standard Chartered	UK	Europe	23,565.6
32	190	260	China CITIC Bank	China	Asia	23,317.1
33	198	127	Societe Generale	France	Europe	22,745.6
34	210	199	Mizuho Financial	Japan	Asia	21,278.1
35	222	264	Al Rahji Banking	Saudi Arabia	Middle East	20,697.7
36	236	194	Nordea Bank	Sweden	Europe	19,986.7
37	240	97	Royal Bank of Scotland	UK	Europe	19,794.4
38	246	249	Hang Seng Bank	Hong Kong	Asia	19,254.1
39	252	259	Banco Brasil	Brazil	South America	18,797.1
40	269	422	Shanghai Pudong Dev Bank	China	Asia	18,159.9
41	277	119	Barclays	UK	Europe	17,783.6
42	292		Industrial Bank	China	Asia	16,814.0
43	297	153	Lloyds Banking Group	UK	Europe	16,563.9
44	327		Resona Holdings	Japan	Asia	15,119.4
45	349	411	Bank of Montreal	Canada	North America	14,178.8
46	350	419	China Minsheng Banking	China	Asia	13,992.8
47	355	373	CIBC	Canada	North America	13,897.1
48	358	53	Citigroup	US	North America	13,854.8
49	371		Northern Trust	US	North America	13,367.4
50	372	365	State Bank of India	India	Asia	13,346.4

Appendix: *World's top 50 banks*

Net income $m	Total assets $m	P/E ratio	Dividend yield (%)	Year end
16,196.2	1,425,722.0	10.8		31-12-2008
13,530.6	1,104,009.0	9.7	5.0	31-12-2008
9,404.3	1,015,785.0	9.1	5.7	31-12-2008
5,605.0	2,175,052.0	30.9	3.2	31-12-2008
5,728.0	2,527,465.0	12.0	12.6	31-12-2008
2,655.0	1,309,639.0	20.3	9.1	31-12-2008
11,671.4	1,380,206.0			31-12-2008
6,340.7	1,922,182.0	7.9	2.9	31-03-2008
4,008.0	1,817,943.0	12.2	8.2	31-12-2008
3,577.6	290,079.8	12.8	3.6	31-12-2008
3,711.3	589,775.3	10.5	5.6	31-10-2008
4,148.8	392,034.4	8.2	4.2	31-12-2008
2,765.8	315,033.1	9.0	7.7	30-09-2008
3,631.9	2,729,231.0	10.2	3.2	31-12-2008
3,433.8	349,452.8	9.3	7.9	30-06-2008
-7,097.2	1,010,317.0		0.3	31-12-2008
3,357.0	836,478.6	10.5		31-12-2008
2,227.3	191,499.0	11.5	2.3	31-12-2007
6,601.0	713,553.8	4.6	8.1	31-12-2008
3,123.0	458,887.3	8.7	5.6	31-10-2008
3,493.6	208,329.6	8.8	0.4	31-12-2008
-18,038.4	1,740,274.0			31-12-2008
4,596.8	1,115,064.0	58.4	0.3	31-03-2008
3,251.0	470,741.3	7.4	10.0	30-09-2008
2,946.0	265,912.0	9.0	11.6	31-12-2008
2,558.4	413,595.3	9.9	6.3	31-10-2008
-5,128.3	2,895,504.0		1.6	31-12-2008
1,346.5	2,173,890.0	16.3	5.4	31-12-2008
7,838.6	1,343,554.0	2.3	20.7	31-12-2007
2,378.8	337,592.6	9.0	8.9	30-09-2008
3,408.0	435,068.0	6.1	5.5	31-12-2008
1,216.0	147,755.3	11.2	2.1	31-12-2007
2,401.1	1,485,890.0	8.8	4.0	31-12-2008
3,099.7	1,537,921.0	7.5	5.2	31-03-2008
1,719.8	33,300.9	10.8	3.6	31-12-2007
3,512.2	623,380.3	3.7	5.3	31-12-2008
-34,449.9	3,514,578.0	89.7		31-12-2008
1,819.4	98,356.0	10.6	8.1	31-12-2008
4,035.8	238,982.1	4.7	7.1	31-12-2008
803.1	133,697.7	17.4	0.7	31-12-2007
6,412.6	3,004,331.0	2.4	8.8	31-12-2008
1,224.4	121,411.2			31-12-2007
1,198.5	638,090.7	4.8	18.4	31-12-2008
3,016.0	397,558.9	56.2	0.1	31-03-2008
1,611.6	338,983.2	8.5	8.7	31-10-2008
925.7	134,401.4	10.6	1.0	31-12-2007
-1,678.4	288,369.9		7.8	31-10-2008
-27,684.0	1,938,470.0		44.3	31-12-2008
794.8	82,053.6	16.9	1.9	31-12-2008
1,792.4	205,482.0	6.2	2.0	31-03-2008

About the author

Paul Verdin (Ph.D., Harvard) holds the Chair of Strategy and Organisation at Solvay Business School (ULB, Brussels) and is Professor of Strategy and International Management at KULeuven in Belgium. He is a former Distinguished Visiting Professor at INSEAD, where he has been on the faculty for over 15 years, and other international business schools, and has taught and consulted widely on strategic issues and processes in the financial sector (banking,

Dr. Verdin's extensively cited research focusses on the critical role of innovative company strategy and organisation in long-term value creation. His work has been covered in the professional and general business press across Europe and the US, including 'CFO Europe', the Economist Intelligence Unit, 'Treasury Management International', 'Accountancy', 'Optimize', 'Wirtschaftswoche', 'Handelsblatt', 'Manageris', 'Expansion Management Review', 'the Wall Street Journal Europe' and 'the Financial Times'. Contact: paul.verdin@ulb.ac.be or paul.verdin@econ.kuleuven.be

11
The strategic imperative of creating and capturing value

ABSTRACT In this final chapter we take a strategic look at the issue of growth and value creation in the asset management industry, mostly from an external non-specialist perspective. Based on ample evidence and experience from other sectors and studies, it is argued that long-term success is not primarily to be expected from simply riding the waves and fortunes of the industry or the economy; rather, it is proven to be the result of consistent and sustained strategy at the level of the firm or company concerned. *It's the company, stupid!* Then what is a good strategy? It is one that recognises and responds to the basic strategic imperative of any business operating in increasingly competitive circumstances: the imperative of creating and capturing value in a continual, consistent and mutually interactive way. While the times of easy capturing seem past us, the need for a keen understanding of what creates value for the client and the market is – more than ever – key. We elaborate on the basic elements of client value and propose an approach that should allow us to specify what our value proposition stands for and how it differentiates us from our competitors. This seems to be the moment of truth for the asset management industry: the moment for strategy – when the winners will be separated from the laggards. It leads us to our final point: that *growth* in and of itself, growth as an external or top-down target or objective, *is not a strategy,* and certainly not a good one (and dangerous as well, as argued in the chapter on growth risk also in this volume). It can only be *the result of a good strategy*: a strategy that respects and implements some of the basic principles laid out, as proven in so many other industries and circumstances. It also points to the huge potential – and the sobering realisation – that success is primarily the result of what companies do (and don't do). Success cannot be expected to be the outcome of a mere star-gazing exercise – hoping for external circumstances or macro-economic conditions to turn the tide. The latter is not even needed, and it probably won't happen too soon, either.

CONCLUSION

11 The strategic imperative of creating and capturing value

by Paul Verdin

Introduction: uncertain and challenging times

These are uncertain times. That is the understatement of the last few years, if not of the last decade. While this could also apply to the political, social, demographic and even the scientific, technological and climate front, what has happened on the financial and economic scene in the past couple of years is unprecedented in terms of magnitude and global coverage, even if the underlying mechanics and principles were not without parallel or historical basis and bias.[1]

The causes and the results of the financial crisis have by now been aptly and widely described.[2] The full consequences, however, have certainly not been well understood or played out – not for the financial market and the (dys)functioning financial system, nor certainly for the economy in general. We avoid here the term 'real' economy – as if the financial markets were rather imaginary or virtual, i.e. not real (if anything the experience of the last few years has blatantly illustrated how 'real' they actually are) or as if one could function without the other (no economy except the most rudimentary barter economy could exist without some kind of financial market or financial accounting).

The financial markets seem to have recovered significantly from their deepest contraction and have found a renewed type of stability. Risk appetite has returned in a shape and form that sometimes makes one wonder about the kind of amnesia that may be governing our current markets. Liquidity has been restored, although not quite across the entire spectrum of markets and instruments. Volatility is down again to almost pre-crisis levels, although this should not be confused with a possible decline in underlying risk – the different types and interactions of which we have just been reminded in the darkest days of recent market debacles.

In fact, it might be well argued that it was a substantial neglect of or at least underestimation of the correlation between different types of risk on the one hand and the confusion between actual *risk* (and how it may affect underlying value) and *volatility* (as measured by the latest market transaction prices) on the other that was at the root of many of our troubles.[3]

---

1   See some of the 'classics' on the subject, e.g. Galbraith (1954), Kindleberger (1978) and the work by the late Hyman Minsky.

2   Also in the first volume by Thomsen et al. (2009) in this SimCorp StrategyLab series.

3   We thus refer to the issue of partial risk models that take insufficient account of 'the big picture' or, in more technical terms, underestimate explicitly and especially implicitly the potential correlations between different risk classes or types of risk, especially in the case of rare but extreme events (the famous black swan or the long tail). We also refer to the role of 'mark to market' rules as they were applied and as they

In addition, we were reminded that 'markets' or 'financial systems' only function through people who are sometimes subject to very strange if (un)predictable swings in moods and behaviors, thereby giving a firm boost to the relatively recent field of 'behavioral finance': the study of how human behavior affects the (dys)functioning, particular opportunities and outcomes of financial markets and investing strategies, as well as their potential implications for new product development and design.[4]

Financial markets remain fragile, however, as they are still supported by the vast amounts of government support, actual or implicit. Very little, if any, structural reform has taken place so far, and the 'too big to fail' syndrome has propelled the previously rather academic concept of 'moral hazard' to the forefront of concerns for the immediate if not the distant future. In addition, the banking system is still not providing the amounts and especially the conditions for credit that borrowers would like to see, while both lenders and borrowers are still taking part in a massive deleveraging in large sectors of the economy.

The adjustments in the economy are still working their way out and may need a lot more time if history is anything to go by: perhaps years to come. Inadequate or untimely government 'exit strategies' remain a delicate and unpredictable threat, while concerns about the public sector deficits have thrown financial markets already back into heavy turmoil and questions remain about a 'private credit bubble' having been replaced by a 'public' one.

Is the 'real economy' recovery for real? The free fall has been halted, but is what we have seen more than just a bounce-back on its way to a 'double dip' (a W-type, assuming we recover after the second dip)? Or is it the beginning of sharp recovery (a 'V', most likely not for most economies given the available data) or a modest if sustained recovery (a full-fledged or asymmetric 'U', or 'amputated U or V' as some commentators call it)? Even an 'L' or protracted 'U' is not entirely out of the question in some places.

The resumption of growth in the 'emerging' economies is certainly impressive, up to the point that questions persist about its sustainability and it becoming the possible source of the next downturn, particularly in view of the overdue correction of global imbalances. Structural adjustments by nature or definition are difficult and painful, as fundamental shifts and changes are always hard to accomplish. They are hard to make real in the corporate world, and they are even harder to decide on and implement on a global scale, especially in the public sector.

"Predictions are hard to make, especially about the future", as I believe Keynes re-

---

were at least in part responsible both for provoking and exacerbating the crisis and for possibly creating the conditions for the emergence of the next one.

4 Behavioral finance is represented in this volume particularly in the contribution by Alistair Byrne (Investit, London) and his rather novel treatment of it from the point of view of product design as distinct from the more 'traditional' interpretation of it as a factor in explaining 'anomalies' and detecting opportunities for outperformance on the investment management side. For a recent overview of the academic literature on this subject see e.g. Byrne and Brooks (2008), or for a more popular and pragmatic treatment aimed at the individual investor, see e.g. Montier (2010).

minded us. We should not be spending much time or effort on predictions, for at least two reasons. First of all, the actual track record of economic forecasts and predictions is generally very poor. Several studies tracking the validity of forecasts against actual developments have confirmed this, and those studies include the possible 'self-fulfilling prophecy' bias potentially associated with any generally regarded and accepted forecasts, as planners, strategists, investors may base their decisions to some extent on the forecasts made, thereby helping them to become reality. Even so, most forecasts do not go further than extrapolating on the past (if not in trend, then in the structural model that is behind it) and they break down completely when confronted with the kinds of events that we have just witnessed. For this reason, we would argue to ignore the forecasts, but – given the high degree of uncertainty – keep a close eye on the actual data. Who was it who said, "In God we trust; everybody else, give us data" (not forecasts)?

Secondly and more importantly, from a business and corporate point of view, it is not the economy or the overall environment that will determine your success for the most part, but rather the other way around. *Companies are successful because of what companies do (and don't do)* in their own business, in their market, in their own organisation and strategy and not primarily because of what 'the economy' or even 'the market' or 'the sector' did or will do.

Likewise, 'the economy' is the result of what companies do – and not the other way around – a simple fact some economists (especially macro-economists of the 'old' school) sometimes seem to forget. Several studies over the last several years have illustrated or proven that point with a variety of approaches and data.[5] Similar results have been obtained on 'the way down' – i.e. what makes companies stumble or fail.[6] "Firms don't fail because of what the world does to them but because of what they do to themselves", as Jim Collins stated in the middle of the crisis.[7] Or exactly the opposite of what President Clinton used to say about his success in the elections: "It's the economy, stupid." But now and for us in the business world it is the *company*, stupid![8]

This is both good and bad news. It means we cannot just blame a poor performance on the economy or the sector – and we cannot or should not hope for the sector

---

5   See our own studies, for example, which are currently in the process of being updated with new and the most recent data, both for the US and major European countries: Hawawini, Subramanian and Verdin (2005, 2004, 2003).

6   Corporate Executive Board found that most companies' growth stalls at some point (and dramatically so) due to 12% uncontrollable external factors, with the remaining 88% due to their own strategic (70%) or organisational (18%) factors (2008); see also the Harvard Business Review (2008).

7   Collins, J. (2008), 'The Secret of Enduring Greatness', Fortune, May 5. This article provides an update to the author's best-selling books 'From Good to Great' and 'Built to Last', reporting on the key success factors of a large sample of outperforming companies over the long term.

8   Such was Peter Lynch's (1994) answer even from the point of view of an investor (one of the most successful of our times), considering the (ir)relevance of 'industry' or 'sector' much along the lines of the same argument: "If it's a choice between investing in a good company in a great industry or a great company in a lousy industry, I'll take the great company in the lousy industry any day. It's the company, stupid.".

or the economy to take us out of the doldrums. The good news is that much of our success lies in our own hands – certainly over the long haul. And this is what strategy and a strategic perspective are all about.

An increasingly competitive business

What does this all mean for the asset management business? As with many sectors, it certainly means that a quick return to (easy) growth is not in the cards, whatever some upbeat commentators and analysts are pretending.[9] Waiting for 'back to business as usual' will certainly not be our method. If anything it should be 'back to the basics of the business'. But what is the business about? And what is it that will make us successful going forward? How will we outperform in what might be a sloppy and probably also bumpy market environment?

Major regulatory changes are on the horizon or have already been enacted. A discussion and update is provided in Karel Lannoo's contribution to this volume (Chapter 4). There are calls for more transparency in the products, in the processes and in the organisation, and clearer guidelines on governance. Clients are becoming more demanding on liquidity and more sensitive to potential conflicts of interest within the organisations that asset managers often belong to.

And, last but not least, they are taking a closer look at fees, commissions and costs, especially as they are eating away a larger share of their return in a low-interest, low-return (and possibly also higher-tax, given the state of public finances) environment. In addition, as evidence is mounting throughout the crisis about the overall under-performance of the average active investment management business as compared to passive and low-cost or other focussed operators, the need for a clear re-assessment of strategy and strategic choices is apparent. Earlier in this volume (Chapter 3), Massimo Massa provides a chilling and sobering picture of what his and other academic experts' recent research shows us on this front.

One thing is clear as a result of all this: the business is certainly becoming more – rather than less – competitive and challenging. There has been and could be a trend towards further consolidation and a few large global players dominating the scene. However, there are equally important trends towards downsizing, particularly on the banking scene, and the shifts in preferences and power of the client as well as regulation could open clear opportunities for newcomers and focussed 'niche players' or outperforming 'boutiques'.

Other industries have been in such a situation before. For years, we could see the easy money flowing and the likely crisis coming. For a long time, nothing happened and everyone wondered why questions are raised about the sustainability – and then,

---

9   Examples have been quoted in our earlier article 'Reinventing value for growth in global asset management' included January 2010 in the publication 'Enable growth strategies with SimCorp Dimension' (SimCorp, 2010).

often in an unexpected fashion or due to an unexpected shock, major shifts take hold, and the business is shocked and taken apart. We may be on the verge of such a situation in asset management, or we may not (yet) be. At any event, now is the time to start asking (or repeat) the basic strategic questions. How will we be successful in the future? How will we do better than the business next door? How and where will we find the growth?

To illustrate the challenge facing the industry and as a push to start thinking about the possible answers – and formulating the right questions – we like to return to a simple framework we have developed over years of strategy-making in a variety of sectors and industries, not only in financial services.[10] What we are witnessing in the asset management business is not unlike the challenges many other businesses have been facing, especially those that used to be run on the basis of a rather limited competition, protected by regulatory conditions, stable technology, local market conditions, poor customer scrutiny and, as a result, the relatively strong power and mutual understanding of major players.

Such was the situation in the 'old' telecoms world and other not-so-old 'utilities' such as electricity, gas, water production or distribution, traditional pharma, and indeed in major areas of financial services and insurance industries. They found themselves earning a (more than) decent return without too much competition, able to capture a great deal of value (for shareholders or stakeholders such as management, employees or even the public sector) while only creating the minimum value for customers or the market. This situation is illustrated by the first position in Figure 1 (lower right-hand corner): in many ways the good old 'dream' of many businesses.

While the first position seems like a dream, enjoy it while it lasts, because dreams don't last forever. Sooner or later competition catches up, (de)regulation strikes, technology shifts or the market changes. We have observed this in many industries. It may occur much later or slower than expected, e.g. in different parts of financial services and asset management, or it may strike with a bang as in the 'Big Bang' of deregulation in the eighties and beginning of the nineties or, most recently, through the financial crashes.

Not that we could not see it coming if we were honest. There has undoubtedly been ample opportunity for the 'value-capturing' game in asset management, as bluntly stated by David Swensen, the celebrated manager of the Yale University Endowment:

The overwhelming number of investors fail because the fees charged by the investment management industry are egregious relative to the amount of value that is added. It is really quite stunning.[11]

---

10   An overview has also been presented in Verdin (2009).
11   Swensen, D. (2009), *Financial Times*, 26 Jan.

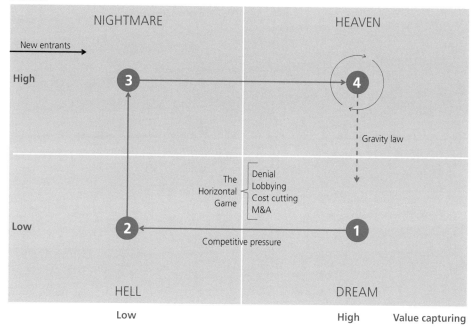

Fig. 1. The dynamics of the value creation-capturing framework. © Paul Verdin, 2009.

Worse still, long before the crisis struck, I remember some asset managers (from some of the banks that later were hammered by the crisis) confessing to me "we seem to be off the chart!!" by which they meant "we are earning good money by capturing value but actually we are not even creating any value for our customers", referring to the average underperformance of active asset managers compared to their benchmarks or the indices. That indeed would put them even below quadrant no. 1 in Figure 1 above, destroying value for clients – while still making handsome returns for managers and shareholders of the asset management companies involved. According to the former CEO of Credit Suisse Asset Management:

I have long believed customers are not getting a good deal from asset managers.[12]

The immediate reaction of market participants to increased competition or deregulation, however, often starts with denial, which turns into inertia or a slide back into old habits and tricks. It often moves further to outright attempts to restore the past and engage in defensive moves. "It won't happen to us," they say. "We are different." Or

---

12   Norman, D. (2010), *Financial Times*, 18 Jan.

perhaps repeating, "This time is different", "It won't happen so soon", "We will worry about it later" or "Professor, you don't understand. This does not apply to us: *we are a Swiss insurance company!*" (This was before the investment management side almost killed them.) Then again, there is the 'knowing-doing gap': "We'll change tomorrow; let's enjoy the ride while it lasts" and "Let's hope we can ride again when markets recover."

We can try and fight back, and hold onto privileged dominance through lobbying or other defensive tactics as embedded in 'strategic' alliances, (anti)competitive practices, and mergers and acquisitions inspired by 'buying competitors rather than beating them', 'capturing market share' or 'industry consolidation' (based on not-so-well-understood economies of scale, elusive synergies, or just a way to keep a too-high cost base in place).

Deliberate attempts to reduce transparency or sneak in price increases in the wake of mounting competition are very popular choices, as sometimes preached by desperate consultants or practiced by short-term opportunists, especially in today's high-pressure environment. I like to call this 'playing the horizontal game', i.e. trying to move back on the horizontal axis to position 1, just like one-off cost-cutting or re-structuring programmes, even if unavoidable in certain areas and conditions.

Sooner or later, however, we risk being pushed into the lower left-hand corner (position 2), this is not an enviable situation, as value added or value creation for clients is still under pressure and the possibility of capturing any of it is drastically reduced. This is typically the situation of commodity businesses or commodity traps. "We are stuck." How can we escape? It is hard, but not impossible: through the long, hard work of arduously climbing the mountain of innovation or value creation, moving up along the vertical axis.

This is exactly what CEOs were referring to when asked about their top strategic priorities in a 'survey of surveys', we carried out right before the crisis.[13] While acknowledging that increased competitive pressure was seen as the over-arching concern across a variety of industries, including the financial sector, top priorities were aiming at growth and innovation. It is interesting to note that both were seen to go hand in hand.

"Either you innovate or you are in commodity hell," declared Samuel Palmisano at IBM following Lou Gerstner's dramatic turnaround starting from the customer. According to Jeff Inmelt, CEO of GE: "Constant reinvention is the central necessity at GE....We're all just a moment away from commodity hell." These sentiments were echoed by many more, at least before the crisis. And while the crisis may have made this challenge all the more demanding, the fundamental requirements have not changed. "One of the biggest mistakes that can be made right now is to slash invest-

---

13   Our survey carried out in the summer of 2007 covering studies by Bain, BCG, IBM, McKinsey, PwC and
     the Economist Intelligence Unit, right before the crisis hit. Presented at EFQM 'Executive Roundtables'
     held in Athens in October 2007, Brussels in February 2008 and Paris in October 2008.

ments in innovation.…If you fail to fund the future, all you'll be left with is a really lean company trying to churn old ideas into new business," as aptly put by Anne Mulcahy, now chairman of Xerox.

The most recent McKinsey Global Survey confirms: "Executives expect that the most powerful effects on their companies will be increased innovation, greater consumer awareness and knowledge, and increased product and service customisation." [14]

Value creation *and* innovation

Value creation in competitive markets requires continuous innovation in order to provide ever more value to the client. There is no other way, however much our current effort and attention may be focussed on short-term fire-fighting or cost-cutting. In fact, *the more competitive your market gets, the less you should focus directly on your competition,* because the only way to beat that competition is to deliver better value to clients.

Even today there are really only two ways to consistently create value and innovate: either go for 'cost innovation', the continuous, relentless innovation in your business model, value or supply chain so that you can continuously offer ever-lower prices to clients, or go for 'value innovation', the continuous search to offer ever-better and -greater (and possibly different bundles of) value to customers, based on the drivers and attributes of value they perceive and appreciate most. Current recessionary times may provide a renewed impulse and opportunity to select this last option by forcing further improvements in value-for-money strategies.[15]

Climbing up the wall of innovation, however, still does not offer easy solace, as it makes us go through a nightmare (position 3 in Figure 1), even if we manage to please the client and add real or perceived value. Eventually, we need to be able to translate the higher value into higher margins: through higher prices, in the case of a value innovation strategy, or through higher volume driven by lower prices, in case of cost innovation strategies. Both strategies will lead to profitable and healthy growth. But growth is not the driver of the strategy; it is the result of it. Most – in fact, all – successful companies actually reach the point (position 4) of being able to add good value and capture enough of it in the process in a consistent and continual way.

We need to keep working at it, if only because of competitive pressure constantly trying to diminish or devalue our competitive advantage. Otherwise, we may start slipping, losing sight of the client, cutting innovation and eventually falling down into the lower right-hand quadrant. The law of gravity will take over. Blinded as we will be by our own success or our own strong position, we will be trying to hold onto value capturing while losing our value creation potential, jeopardising our long-term strategic health and thus sustainable growth.

---

14   McKinsey Quarterly, May 2010.
15   Williamson and Zeng (2009); Kim and Mauborgne (1997).

IBM, Microsoft and Intel, to name but a few, have gone through this cycle at least once before. Fighting anti-trust authorities is often part of the final stages, and time has come to face the next competitive cycle. The only way to avoid this ordeal is to focus again on innovating and facing up to competition rather than obstructing it.

In asset management as anywhere else, defensive 'value-capture strategies' have not quite fallen out of fashion, as illustrated by the following statement signalling a possible back-tracking from the 'open architecture' distribution model adopted at many banks before the crisis under increasing competition:

The current recession means many institutions are pushing their own products, in an attempt to keep all possible earnings from selling funds in-house.[16]

The question remains, however, whether such a move back is even sustainable in today's more competitive environment. Indeed, we hear many more wake-up calls than ever before, urging us to face up to the innovation and value creation challenge:

The asset management industry understands it needs to align itself better with investors' interests.[17]

We don't think enough with our clients and for our clients.[18]

Some observers are clearly pushing further, linking the need for a renewed focus on clients back to questioning the appropriate governance model:

Being created to think solely about the investor has been critical. We don't have to worry about family, shareholders, or partners. It is a wonderful business model.[19]

This argument was made by Vanguard, referring to their corporate governance model going hand in hand with a distinct client value proposition and business model (See also Figure 2 below).

In conclusion, a successful strategy should always be guided by creating perceived value for the client and the market, while of course also being able to capture at least some of that value through pricing (fees, commission, basis points, etc.) in a continuous and consistent way. An undue or unbalanced focus on either one of those two basic dimensions of strategy invariably leads to problems or even disaster, particularly over the medium-to-long term. This is exactly what strategy and growth should be concerned about.

---

16   Garland, R. (2009), *Financial Times*, 7 Sept.

17   Bolmstrand, N. (2009), *Financial Times*, 14 Sept.

18   Du Toit, H. (2009), *Financial Times*, 25 May.

19   McNabb, N. (2009), *Financial Times*, 4 May.

Beyond risk management and cost cutting, the next if not more important challenge for long-term success is to identify the relevant drivers or attributes of value for the groups of clients or segments we want to serve and new ways of delivering that value in a better, more efficient way than ever before. Growth can thus never be simply more of the same or a return to the past. In these trying times, it is a golden opportunity to examine these questions again and to go beyond the easy games of value capturing, merging and acquiring, or just riding the market booms which have benefited but also equally blinded many a provider in recent times.

Beyond cost-cutting and lean programmes

It is very likely that the preceding boom and asset price inflation have allowed excessive costs and non-value activities to flourish, covered by easy revenues from increasing volume of assets under management. The sharp drop in asset prices compounded with a decrease in net asset flows or even outflow of assets has exposed many asset managers' profitability. A focus on cost-cutting and lean programmes has therefore already proven quite popular, if not a condition for survival or short-term profitability for many.

You should be warned, however, that an overly eager focus on such programmes when not properly framed in the context of an overall strategy may not only turn out to be non-strategic (tactical or operational in pure survival mode) but may become even anti-strategic – if they divert attention from a proper focus on the required strategic focus of the company going forward. Unless you want to become the 'Ryanair' or 'Wal-Mart' of the industry, a focus on customer value and value creation should drive the strategy, not a mindless or strategically unfounded focus on cost reduction.

While a focus on costs has been understandable in today's lingering crisis environment, you cannot cost-cut your way out of the crisis and even less grow your way out of the crisis by cutting costs. Anne Mulcahy, former CEO of Xerox, put it quite nicely:

One of the biggest mistakes that can be made right now is to slash investments in innovation....If you fail to fund the future, all you'll be left with is a really lean company trying to churn old ideas into new business.[20]

More specifically, one should be careful to not smuggle in cost strategies – which are only sensible when accompanied by a consistent low-price strategy – where, in most cases, value strategies should be aimed at. Pure size, scale or leverage strategies are not a suitable answer either, as leveraging or scaling up a poor business or inadequate business model only lands you with a bigger bad business or a business model still performing poorly. In other words, as you cannot hope to grow your way out of an

20   Mulcahy, A. (2009), *Fortune*, May 4.

overhead that is too high, you cannot grow your way out of a bad business model or a poor strategy, either.

In addition, an ill-conceived growth strategy involves a risk of increasing your overall 'strategic risk' while not delivering any substantial benefit (as argued by Mathias Schmit and Lyn-Sia Chao in the preceding chapter, Chapter 10).[21] This should be a stern warning in view of the observation which emerged from the recent 'Global Investment Management Growth Survey 2010' by SimCorp StrategyLab that most asset managers are looking for growth (growth ranked as a top priority by 2/3 of those surveyed). Yet an equal number of respondents (2/3) do not have a particular framework as a concept for achieving such growth.[22]

A renewed focus on creating value for the customer

If a renewed focus on value creation for customers is the message, the question arises of what that really means. What constitutes 'value' to customers? As in other sectors and businesses, value is usually a multi-dimensional concept, a 'catch-all' that must be deconstructed and analysed in greater detail. The crisis has only made such analysis even more pressing:

Customers used to focus only on returns. Now they are asking questions about liquidity and transparency.[23]

Everyone is fundamentally re-thinking their approach to investing and manager selection.[24]

To illustrate a useful approach to this question, let us take a popular example: a car. What are you looking for when you are in the market for a new car: speed, status symbol, safety, comfort, fuel efficiency, versatility, ease of use, experience, or – who knows – perhaps even transportation (positive attributes to be maximised)? Or are you looking for low cost, environmental friendliness, least damaging to pedestrians or quietness (negative attributes to be avoided or minimised)? Of course, this list of 'attributes' runs much longer and should be further broken down into much greater detail, e.g. what do you mean by 'safety' (active or passive, for whom, under what conditions, etc.) or 'speed' (acceleration from zero or from a higher point, maximum speed, etc.)? What kind of comfort are you looking for (quietness, sound system, seat quality, dashboard, etc.)? Thus one can arrive at the long list of features and/or gadgets that end up decorating our cars, some 'standard' and others 'options'.

---

21   Schmit and Chao (2010).
22   Results from the 'Global Investment Management Growth Survey 2010' performed by SimCorp Strategy-
      Lab and The Nielsen Company, Spring 2010.
23   MacLeod, J. (2009), *Financial Times*, 7 Sept.
24   Walkerm, G. (2009), *Financial Times*, 7 Sept.

Clearly not all value attributes are equally important (for all customers). Some are much more prevalent than others. Some are so important they are to be considered 'basic' or 'must haves'. Others are more secondary and a means of differentiation from the competition. Note that competition takes place not always on the most important or crucial attributes, but often only on secondary ones. For example, safety for airlines may be seen as a top attribute for most customers but is generally well established and comparable across airlines, and (let's hope) most airlines do not actively compete on safety, in part because it is regulated but also because it is considered basic and essential by everyone.

Furthermore, not all attributes are equally valued by all customers. This leads us to an intuitive and useful definition of what may constitute a 'segment': a group of customers that value the same (selection of) attributes – and are willing to pay for it. Conceptually the 'willingness to pay' (a condition for 'value capturing') may be distinguished from the actual 'received' or 'perceived value' by the customer (the value created for the customer). In practice, however, value 'delivered' for which the customer will not pay is quite esoteric and in fact useless or a waste of resources from the company's (or even a society's) point of view.[25]

The strategic choice for any company therefore refers to (i) deciding which particular (bundle of) attributes to focus on and to offer profitably to its customer (segments) – by relating its offer to targeted customers' preferences of attributes – thus also deciding which attributes to ignore, and (ii) distinguishing its particular offer in any meaningful and sustainable way from that of any (existing or potential) competitor.

In order to do this profitably, of course, our offer should also refer to our particular strengths, assets, resources, competencies or capabilities, allowing us to deliver a superior offer to customers in a more profitable way than anyone else. Naturally, the basic tests for a good strategy remain valid: (i) how can we be better than the competition in any sustainable way and (ii) do we have what it takes?

Along these lines, Figure 2 provides a possible illustration of the Vanguard Value Curve (orange line) as compared to a representative competitor (brown line) on a number of selected attributes.[26]

This also implies that we constantly should strive to improve our value offer, as competition is bound to erode any advantage we may have on any (combination of) relevant attributes. Thus we should not only focus on delivering well the attributes 'as is' (as they are today) but also on the 'to be' (where we strive for and aim to improve going forward), setting out the direction of our strategic ambitions in very specific terms.

---

25   This does not diminish my earlier argument, developed through the 'value creation-capturing' framework, that in a competitive market any value captured can only be based on and driven by value created, or that we cannot hope to capture any value if we do not focus on creating any for the customer. In fact, it is precisely because we cannot measure or monitor the value 'created' for the customer directly and unequivocally that we must resort to 'willingness to pay' or actual price paid as a proxy or a measure, and therefore we often fall into the trap of only focussing on the price and the capturing – thereby ignoring the creating part.

26   See Koza (2002).

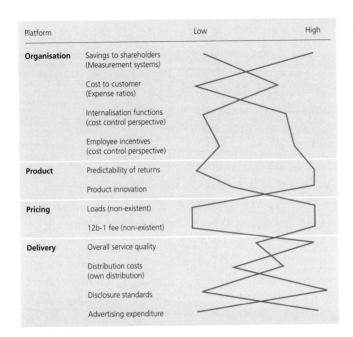

Fig. 2. The Vanguard Value Curve

This is illustrated in the accompanying chart (Figure 2) which shows, for illustrative purposes only, a list of (positive/negative) attributes, our 'current offer' to customers (as is), and our current (closest or most relevant) competitor offer, which all should be the result of a simple, but structured strategy process within your own company. In a more complete process, we should also include our 'to be' value curve, a validation with actual and potential customers, and of course the link to the required and available resources, competences or capabilities to be able to deliver the chosen attributes.

Various aspects of this approach have been covered in the illuminating and almost concurrent work by Gunther-McGrath & MacMillan and Kim & Mauborgne.[27] A focus on attributes leads to the conclusion that 'products are not products' – they are the (sometimes transient) carriers or conduits of attributes as the source of (perceived) value to the customer. Most, if not all, products thus are only valuable in so far as they are the source of delivering value attributes to the customer. And this reasoning may be extended to 'services' such as financial or investment or asset management services.[28]

More than ever, it is clear that strategy, then, is about choosing which value attributes to deliver and which to ignore or leave to the competition. We cannot be or do all things for all people. And then, of course, we have to deliver those attributes ex-

---

27   MacMillan and McGrath (1996); McGrath and MacMillan (2005); Kim and Mauborgne (1997); Kim and Mauborgne (2005).

28   The somewhat simplistic if not superficial distinction between 'goods' or 'products' and 'services' and a similar distinction between 'production' and 'service' sectors therefore evaporates again, as it had also been rightly questioned from complementary perspective such as that developed by Teboul (2006) in 'Service is Front Stage: Positioning services for value advantage' (INSEAD Business Press/Palgrave MacMillan, 2006).

tremely well, i.e. focus on operational excellence and superior execution in the context of a well-conceived and suitable business model.

An adequate and working IT platform and support function can either be an enabler for delivering any chosen attributes or, indeed, could be more at the forefront of the specific value proposition or attributes that (segments of) clients are looking for (e.g. transparency, speed and clarity of information, risk management information, etc.)

Where does price (charges, fees, commissions, etc.) come into the picture? Contrary to some popular representations, I believe that unless you are aiming to be the single-minded price leader in the industry, price is best *not* to be seen as an attribute (even if clearly a negative one usually[29]): rather it is the net result of all the attributes you are aiming to deliver, which is what lies behind the popular expression 'value for money' referred to above. 'Differentiation strategies' therefore require you to determine which (bundle of) attributes to target and what the value *proposition* is resulting from that target.

From value attributes to value proposition

A value proposition undeniably almost always contains price as a key component, as 'the other side of the equation' and is thus not in and of itself a value attribute.[30] Differentiation strategies almost always refer to the potential of a multitude of attributes to highlight and therefore can be considered as 'multi-dimensional' in most cases, in contrast to 'low-price' (read: low-cost) strategies, which are single-mindedly focussed on just one variable or dimension: price (for customer or consumer).

Whereas this approach is very much in line with the clear 'dichotomy' between cost and differentiation strategies as largely popularised by the work of Michael Porter[31] (it is *either* cost or differentiation *or* 'stuck in the middle'), it quickly becomes clear that the 'middle' may prove a very fertile ground for various kinds of differentiation or segmentation based on the choice of potentially new attributes to focus on. This reminds us of the third variant or 'focus' strategies as put forward by Porter – only in Porter's case this was dismissed somewhat as a possible 'niche' strategy, whereas we can see it as being applicable in a much wider context.[32]

In other words, 'price' is where 'the rubber hits the road' or the 'moment of truth' for checking whether the value bundle proposed at a given price holds up towards clients – as compared to relevant competition, obviously.

---

29 Price is the sacrifice made by the customer and therefore obviously in most cases a 'negative' value attribute. However, even if this seems obvious in most cases, it could be argued that in some (end) consumer markets, as well as in highly intangible services markets, price may sometimes act as a positive attribute insofar as it signals (otherwise unmeasurable) quality and/or price plays with a 'snob effect' or a 'show off' factor for high-end customers.

30 Except in the cases referred to above, in the previous footnote.

31 Porter (1985).

32 A similar argument has been developed in the current recessionary environment in the recent article by Williamson and Zeng (2009).

Further elaborating on what exactly constitutes 'price', however, the distinction between 'price' (or cost) and 'differentiation' strategies quickly becomes blurred, while we take into account such concepts as 'cost of ownership', 'lifetime user cost', service and maintenance costs, and, yes, even durability, reliability and serviceability, leading us to realise that even 'differentiation' strategies often come down to 'low-cost' propositions for the client, if one takes the broader and more long-term view of what constitutes 'price' or cost to the client.

In other words, quite a few 'differentiation strategies' then may prove to be more sophisticated 'low-cost' strategies, especially in professional or business-to-business markets in which the customer is a company, a business or an organisation that runs on budgets and accounts – with a long-term time horizon. Why would these customers ever pay more for 'differentiated' products or services? In fact, they would do so because they turn out to be cheaper in the long run, all things considered for their own business or that of their customers.

This approach thus forces us to take a more in-depth as well as a more integrated, holistic and strategic view of the value proposition for the customer and the basic strategies that go with it. They also lead the way towards taking a customer's perspective much more explicitly into account, with the implication that we believe that a 'value (innovation) strategy' is probably a better term than 'differentiation'. Likewise a 'low-price strategy' seems a better term than 'low-cost' – if only because a differentiation strategy ends up representing low cost to the rational or professional customer, at least over the long haul, whereas a 'value' strategy is clearly different from a low-price strategy.

Value attributes and the dynamics of competition

Value attributes and their relative importance naturally evolve over time – not only because of shifting customer preferences, but first and foremost due to the effects of competition (and the impact of regulation and/or the general progress in know-how, technology and economic possibilities). What were once 'differentiators' or even 'excitors' (e.g. turbo engine, airbags, ABS brakes or electronic traction controls) in terms of value attributes may soon be considered basic or neutral (for positive attributes), and what were once tolerable negatives (e.g. a diesel car that won't start in very cold weather) may turn into real 'dissatisfiers' or 'enragers'.[33]

As a result, competition will constantly try to devalue the (relative) value of your offer and thus eliminate or decimate any differentiation that is not based on a sustainable advantage or continuous improvement, as some observers have recently reminded us in the wake of the current crisis:

---

33   Referring to the different types of attributes as proposed by MacMillan and McGrath (1996).

Weaker institutions that cannot differentiate themselves on product, service, or any other critical factor will slowly disappear.[34]

This is further illustrated in Figure 3 below,[35] where the red arrow running from the positive north-eastern corner of the graph down to the middle and then down into negative attributes in the south-eastern corner of the graph represents the continuous pressure from competition constantly devaluing any potential temporary competitive advantage from a particular value attribute, while the blue arrow starting in the

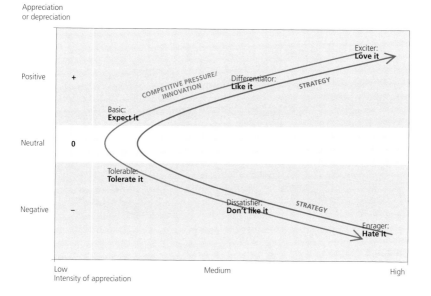

Fig. 3. Competitive pressure and innovation strategy in the Attributes Map. Adapted from Gunther McGrath-MacMillan (2005). © Paul Verdin 2010.

south-eastern corner pushing in the opposite direction represents the challenge of any dynamic competitive strategy constantly trying to reduce the impact of possible negative attributes or even turning them into outstanding positives.[36]

In other words, the value curves and their relative position as illustrated in Figure 2 tend to move, and the relevant list of attributes themselves may also change. Indeed, innovation does not only pertain to the strength of a particular (bundle of) attribute(s), but even more so to the continual development and discovery of new at-

---

34   BCG Global Asset Management Report 2009, 'Conquering the Crisis', July 2009.
35   My own adaptation of the attribute map developed by MacMillan and McGrath (1996).
36   The colours used are more in line with the 'red' ocean of competition on existing or known attributes discussed in Kim and Mauborgne (2005) versus the 'blue ocean' of new attributes that may allow you (at least temporarily) to avoid or outsmart the most competitive arena in your market.

tributes that customers may value. This means that, while listening to customers is always a useful and good thing to do, limiting yourself to the known and express needs of your current customers obviously can be quite a constraint as well. "If I had only listened to my customers….all they ever wanted was a faster horse!" is a well-known saying attributed to Henry Ford.

More confusing even is the fact that what customers say is not necessarily what they actually do, and what they say they want is not necessarily what they really need. More subtly still, they may prefer not to express their preferences, and this does not seem at all that far-fetched in such intangible and complicated areas as investment management, as Alistair Byrne illustrates brilliantly in his contribution to this volume.[37]

A strategic roadmap for growth

The approach outlined, while not rocket science or highly sophisticated, was intended to chart a roadmap for strategic growth and the milestones that must be laid out in order to get there. It hits at the basics of any successful strategy in increasing competitive markets. It requires in-depth analysis and close attention to changing needs and drivers of value to the customers: creation of value as a precondition for continuing to capture good value in the process. From the need for innovation and value creation, we must go deep into the elements of our specific value proposition, the business model necessary to make it work and the unique assets, systems, strengths and core competencies required to make them work – and to provide the basis for a sustainable advantage.

This work should be carried out by each company as a function of its own position, its assets and resources, and its ambitions. As much as in any other competitive market, this will require continuous improvement and refinement of the value proposition, which must be delivered in a consistently excellent manner, underscoring the importance of operational excellence and superior execution.

While not rocket science, it seems there is a great deal of room for improvement and opportunity: according to Massimo Massa's original contribution to this volume on the mutual fund industry, many funds lack even some of the most basic components to deliver the required basic value to clients – he even calls them 'cars without engines'. Before elaborating on the more sophisticated value attributes, there may be room to go back to some of the basics. Renewed calls for passive, index-based and low-cost investing are, of course, a logical consequence of the weaknesses of many a player in the sector.[38]

On the other hand, the doubtful recovery and economic prospects may precisely call for a more micro-based and company-focussed value investing, and the simulta-

---

37 Byrne (2010).
38 See e.g. Malkiel and Ellis (2010).

neous and unprecedented collapse of a wide range of markets, supposedly previously uncorrelated and a good basis for diversification, may have questioned even some of the most basic rules of asset allocation and may even have extended the potential need and reach of active investment management.

Let us conclude by reminding ourselves of some of the do's and don't for successful growth:

DOs	DON'Ts
Stay close to your core	Just extrapolate or multiply
Understand your core	Jump too far too fast
What are we good at? Really?	Go for size or growth per se
Leverage your strength	Spread yourself too thinly
Can we manage?	Make too many changes at once
Do we have the right resources?	Lose your identity
Know what you stand for	Lose sight of customer value
Continuously assess and improve the value created	Just 'capture' value

Fig. 4. Some dos and don'ts for successful growth.
© *Paul Verdin 2009*

Conclusion: Are you 'ready for growth'?

Good strategy leads to growth: if your strategy is successful, then it will lead to growth. For this reason, it is important to be ready or 'fit' for growth in terms of the scalability of your business model and supporting systems. An appropriate, flexible and scalable IT platform and supporting systems are then a must: a condition for growth. The critical role of IT in enabling and supporting growth is further analysed by Pascal Wanner (Chapter 8). Companies must thus ask themselves how 'ready they are for growth'. In our view, such growth should not be expected so much from an easy return to the favourable macro-economic and external circumstances, but more from a keen understanding and implementation of a successful strategy adapted to the increasing and changing requirements of delivering sustained and focussed customer value in an increasingly competitive market.

If we are successful in our existing activities, we may also be looking for ways to leverage or extend our success and explore new avenues in terms of products, customers (or segments) and geographic markets. However, such strategies can only be successful if they are based and built on a keen understanding of our existing core strengths and competencies. Expansion, diversification and internationalisation can only be successful if built upon a position of strength and success, not on weakness or underperformance in a search for a cover-up or an escape to 'the grass that is always greener' (on the *other* side).[39]

The more competitive your business becomes, the more you should realise that

---

39   As amply argued and supported in the path-breaking work by Zook and Allen (2001) and by Zook (2004).

sustained value creation and profitable growth will result from strategies that are aimed at creating and delivering superior value to clients – rather than entering a race to 'capture value' in existing markets or from pre-determined 'profit pools'.[40]

Long-term success, the essence of sustainable growth, will be as much of our own making as the result of spotting the right trends and riding the waves. "The real test is not whether a company has been smartest about predicting the timing of the recovery but whether it has been truly competitive in its preparation."[41] It will depend primarily on our taking our business into our own hands. And that requires a keen understanding of the present and the future, of the actual and potential needs of our customers and clients, of what it is that creates value for them as they see it, and of how we will be able to deliver that better, cheaper and faster than our competitors in a truly sustainable way.

References

Accenture Report (2003), 'Innovating for the upturn'.

BCG Global Asset Management Report 2009, 'Conquering the Crisis', July 2009.

Byrne, A (2010), 'Designing products for reluctant investors: applications of behavioural finance', Chapter 7 in 'Growth and value creation in asset management', SimCorp StrategyLab.

Byrne, A. and M. Brooks (2008), 'Behavioral Finance: Theories and Evidence', The Research Foundation of CFA Institute.

Gadiesh, O and J. Gilbert (1998), 'Profit Pools: A Fresh Look at Strategy', *Harvard Business Review*, May-June.

Galbraith, J.K.(1954), 'The Great Crash of 1929', Houghton-Miffon.

Hawawini, G., V. Subramanian and P. Verdin (2005), 'Is performance driven by industry – or firm-specific factors? A Reply to McNamara, Aime and Vaaler', *Strategic Management Journal*, vol. 26 (11):1083–1086.

Hawawini, G., V. Subramanian and P. Verdin (2004), 'The Home Country in the Age of Globalization: How Much Does It Matter for Firm Performance?', *Journal of World Business* (formerly Columbia Journal of World Business), Vol. 39 (2):121–135.

Hawawini, G., V. Subramanian and P. Verdin (2003), 'Is performance driven by industry – or firm-specific factors? A new look at the evidence', *Strategic Management Journal*, vol. 24 (1): 1–16.

Kindleberger (1978), 'Manias and Panics: A History of Financial Crises', Basic Books, New York.

---

40 While the notion and the definition, measurement and distribution of a 'profit pool' in any given industry or market is an extremely useful concept – ex post – as originally introduced by Gadiesh and Gilbert (1998), it should in our view not be taken as a predetermined or given factor that is external to the (successful) strategies and dynamics in that industry, as we have argued and illustrated elsewhere based on our large-scale empirical studies quoted above: Hawawini, Subramanian and Verdin (2003).

41 'Innovating for the upturn', Accenture Report, 2003.

Kim C. and R. Mauborgne (1997), 'Value Innovation – The Strategic Logic of High Growth', *Harvard Business Review*.

Kim, C. and R. Mauborgne (2005), 'Blue Ocean Strategy: How to Create Uncontested Market Space and Make the Competition Irrelevant', Harvard Business School Press, Boston.

Koza, M. (2002), 'Vanguard Inc. – Value Innovation in the Mutual Funds Business', INSEAD – CEDEP Case Study, 09/2002 – 4827, Teaching Note, p. 9.

Lynch, P. (1994), 'The Stock Market Hit Parade', article.

MacMillan, I. and R.G. McGrath (1996), 'Discover Your Product's Hidden Potential', *Harvard Business Review*.

McGrath, R.G. and I. MacMillan (2005), 'Market Busters: 40 Strategic Moves That Drive Exceptional Business Growth', Harvard Business School Press, Boston.

Malkiel, B. and R. Ellis (2010), 'The Elements of Investing', John Wiley, New Jersey.

McKinsey Quarterly (2010), 'Five forces reshaping the global economy: McKinsey Global Survey results', May.

Montier, B. (2010), 'The Little Book of Behavioral Investing', Wiley.

Pinedo, M. (2009), 'Operational control in asset management: processes and costs', SimCorp StrategyLab.

Porter, M. (1985), 'Competitive Advantage', Free Press, New York.

Schmit, M. and L. Chao (2010), 'Managing growth and strategic risk', Chapter 10 in 'Growth and value creation in asset management', SimCorp StrategyLab.

SimCorp StrategyLab (2010), 'Report on Global Investment Management Growth Survey 2010'.

Teboul, J. (2006), 'Service is Front Stage: Positioning services for value advantage', INSEAD Business Press/Palgrave MacMillan.

Thomsen, S., C. Rose and O. Risager (2009), 'Understanding the financial crisis: investment, risk and governance', SimCorp StrategyLab.

Verdin, P. (2010), 'Reinventing value for growth in global asset management' in 'Enable growth strategies with SimCorp Dimension', SimCorp.

Verdin, P. (2010), 'Growth and value creation in asset management', SimCorp StrategyLab.

Williamson, P. and M. Zeng (2009), 'Value-for-money strategies for recessionary times' , *Harvard Business Review,* March.

Zook, C. and J. Allen (2001), 'Profit from the Core', Harvard Business School Press, Boston.

Zook, C. (2004), 'Beyond the Core. Expand Your Market Without Abandoning Your Roots', Harvard Business School Press, Boston.